Dinosaur Country

Unearthing the Alberta Badlands

Renie Gross

Badlands Books

Wardlow Alberta

Canada

Copyright © Renie Gross 1998
Badlands Books
Wardlow, Alberta, Canada

All rights reserved. No part of this book may be reproduced or transmitted in any form or by any means, electronic or mechanical, including photocopying, recording or by any information storage and retrieval system without written permission from the publisher, except for the inclusion of brief quotations in a review.

Cover design and image scanning by J.A.(Sandy) Irvine, By Design Services, Calgary, Alberta

Cover photograph by John Walper

Text set in Sabon by Badlands Books.
Printed and bound in Canada by
Friesen Printers, Altona, Manitoba

Published by Badlands Books,
Box 12, Wardlow Alberta, T0J 3M0

The publisher acknowledges the financial support received for this publication from
The Alberta Historical Resources Foundation

Canadian Cataloguing in Publication Data

Gross, Renie, 1936-
    Dinosaur Country: Unearthing the Alberta Badlands

2nd rev. and enlarged ed.
Includes Index.
ISBN 0-9683385-0-X

    1. Dinosaurs--Red Deer River Valley (Alta.)
2. Paleontology--Cretaceous. 3. Paleontology--
Red Deer River Valley (Alta.) I.Title.

QE862.D5G76 1998   567.9'097123'3   C98-900207-1

Contents

	Preface	v
	Acknowledgments	ix
1.	Introducing Dinosaur Country	1
2.	Drumheller: A Town Fuelled by Fossils	12
3.	Royal Tyrrell Museum of Palaeontology: Showplace on the Red Deer	20
4.	The Age of Dinosaurs	30
5.	Alberta's Late Cretaceous Landscapes	42
6.	Dinosaurs Reborn	55
7.	Hadrosaurs: The Duck-Billed Dinosaurs	66
8.	Ceratopsians: The Horned Dinosaurs	79
9.	Pachycephalosaurs: The Thick-Domed Dinosaurs	89
10.	Ankylosaurs: The Armoured Dinosaurs	93
11.	Tyrannosaurs: The Big Flesh-Eaters	101
12.	Small Flesh Eaters and The Bird Connection	111
13.	Extinction	130

14.	Creation of the Badlands	140
15.	Badlands Treasure	152
16.	The Great Canadian Dinosaur Rush	167
17.	The Fossil Hunt Continues	187
18.	Dinosaur Graveyard: A World Heritage Site	198
19.	Present-Day Life in Dinosaur Provincial Park	212
	Alberta Dinosaurs on Display	226
	Sources	229
	Illustration Credits	232
	Index	236

Preface

The east windows of my house, which sits on a bench of grassland above the Red Deer River in southeastern Alberta, look out over the barren badlands wilderness of Dinosaur Provincial Park. Moulded by the elements into a seemingly infinite variety of landforms, the malleable raw materials of the badlands result from sediments laid down millions upon millions of years ago in dinosaur times. Erosion is ruthless in this portion of the river valley where it has slashed deep gouges into the surrounding prairie. Its effects, on a more restrained scale, may be seen again one hundred kilometres upstream around Drumheller. Here, multi-hued rock, only slightly veiled by vegetation, lines the valley walls. Intermittent badlands exposures appear along the river north of Drumheller to beyond Dry Island Buffalo Jump Provincial Park.

Although it is only recently that the valley of the Red Deer has gained recognition from a broader public, it has long been famous among members of the international scientific community as an incomparably rich fossil repository of the far distant past. Hundreds of skeletons of dinosaurs and their fellow creatures have been unearthed from their burial places in the sere strata of the badlands.

The appeal of the area for a fossil hunter is clear. At every turn the possibility of discovery is held out. Who knows what significant find lies just over the brow of the hill? For those others of us who know and love the badlands country, the attraction it exerts is somewhat more obscure. I am frequently asked how I can live in such a desolate place—much less prefer it above all others. Sometimes in reply, I speak of a sun-drenched day when the hills are bright with the showy yellows and pinks of blooming cactus and the pungent smell of young sage rises to mingle with the heady, cloying wolf willow and the sweet, wild prairie rose perfumes. Or, I describe the way the grasses, scorched to palest gold in autumn, blend with the warm ochres and siennas of the badlands; and how, when the first snows fall and the gnarled cottonwoods are bare and gray, the landscape takes on the sepia tones of an old monochrome print. Mule-eared deer browsing in the thorny thickets of the river terrace; the admirable sight of a herd of pronghorn racing across the prairie and skimming beneath the lowest strand of a barbed-wire fence with the merest hesitation in stride; the songbirds that arrive in early spring with the exuberant western meadowlark in the vanguard—each, and all, of these is a necessary part of the response the badlands country evokes in me. Yet, the essence of the place lies somewhere deeper. It resonates with time and change. It emerges with the bones of the long-dead dinosaurs from the chaos of landforms chiseled out of ancient rock by the relentless forces of erosion.

I remember the first time I saw the badlands. I was a little girl, one of a group of children bouncing along in a yellow school bus across a rough prairie trail on the way to an end-of-term outing. Bad lands. What wonderful words to tickle the imagination of a child steeped in the worlds of Grimm and Andersen. I remember the sense of excitement, mixed with apprehension, about the adventures that might await us. Images of dragons, ogres, trolls, and wizards floated tantalizingly at the edges of my mind.

It seemed the journey would never be over. Saturated by the haze of mid-morning heat engulfing the interior of the bus, throat and nose raspy with the dust of the dry prairie sifting in at the open windows, the edge of anticipation dulled by tedium, I thought we would ride forever until we bumped into the distant blue wall of the sky where it fastened onto the earth. The bus rolled on and on, over the rises and through the troughs of the limitless prairie. Then, abruptly, it stopped. Without any change of scene to alert us that our destination was near, we had arrived. There we were on the edge of a precipice looking down on a welter of peaks and pinnacles. Had I been asked, I would have been at a loss to describe the strange vista confronting me. Only as an adult am I able to put names to the wild confusion of shapes and forms. For as far as the eye could see, delicate spires, jutting knobs, rounded haystacks, giant hoodoo toadstools, knife-edged divides, grassy plateaus, steep-walled canyons, and the slotted gashes of coulees tumbled the land down to the deeply incised river valley below.

I was surprised. I had expectations about the nature of hills. One thing I was quite certain of was that one did not look down upon hills. Yet, here I was, doing just that. Puzzled by this apparent contradiction, I was relieved to learn that I had not been misled about dragons. They were definitely here, only they were called "dinosaurs." All day, I expected to meet a dinosaur head on, as we rounded the curves of hiking trails. But it wasn't until evening, as we were boarding the bus to go home, that I caught sight of one. As I glanced back across the hills, wrapped now in the soft purples of waning light, I saw the huge body of a dinosaur outlined in the dying rays of the sun. He was at rest, his heavy limbs folded under him. His long neck curved gracefully over his shoulder and his head was eased down upon his massive back. With a happy shiver, I jumped aboard the bus. Like the fairy tale princesses I read about, I had traveled through bad lands, the domain of this great and fearsome beast, and regained the safety of a familiar haven.

That little girl and her day in the badlands are long in the past. But perhaps the gist of the landscape's appeal is captured in this initial response to it. It is austere and somewhat harsh. Lacking the flattering effects of vegetation, its rocky forms are reduced to their fundamental nature, much like the unfleshed dinosaur skeletons they entomb. The landscape may not be beautiful in the conventional sense. What it offers, instead, is a depth of dramatic distinction which is mysterious and many-faceted. It is unexpected. It challenges the imagination with hints of other worlds and other times.

I came to live here after a long time spent in more gently picturesque parts of the world. Once again, I was captivated. Living on the very spot once populated by the dinosaurs seemed to intensify for me the sense of shifting time and place in the badlands. Disregarding a seventy-five-million-year lapse between their time and today, these fascinating beasts gradually floated up into my present.

At that time, almost nothing had been written for the non-professional reader about the Red Deer River badlands and the story in the rocks. I thought if I felt the lack of information, so must others. That perception was the origin of <u>Dinosaur Country.</u>

The time seemed right in 1997 to update the first edition but I was not long into the project before I realized that much more was involved than I had anticipated. I found myself writing an almost entirely new book. The structure remains basically the same as in the 1985 edition but more than one-half of the material contained was not in the original. This is partly because of the explosion of fresh data on dinosaurs and their world, and partly because I wanted to give the reader a little more of the history of the Red Deer valley, especially as it pertains to the central theme of the famous dinosaurs, their badlands graves and the humans who came in search of them. The information in this new edition strives to reflect the current lore about a distant time that continues to haunt the Red Deer River valley so many millions of years after its disappearance.

Acknowledgments

Thank you to all who helped in any way with the production of this book. Special thanks to those of you who read all or part of the manuscript and gave me the benefit of your particular expertise: Philip Currie; Ian Campbell; Marylynne Stumpf; David Eberth; Fred Hammer; Irene Vanderloh and Lorne Cole.

I have not forgotten that Lea Nicoll-Kramer, Hoyt Taylor and John Walper reviewed the original manuscript. Thank you to Lea for, once again, performing the task with this edition.

Thank you to my son Tony whose generous assistance with computer problems kept the project from coming to a standstill.

I appreciate the financial support the project received from the Alberta Historical Resources Foundation.

Finally, my love and gratitude to my grandchildren—Hannah, Nicole, Jake, Jack and Nathen—who, by including me on their 'bone hunts,' keep the magic of the badlands alive.

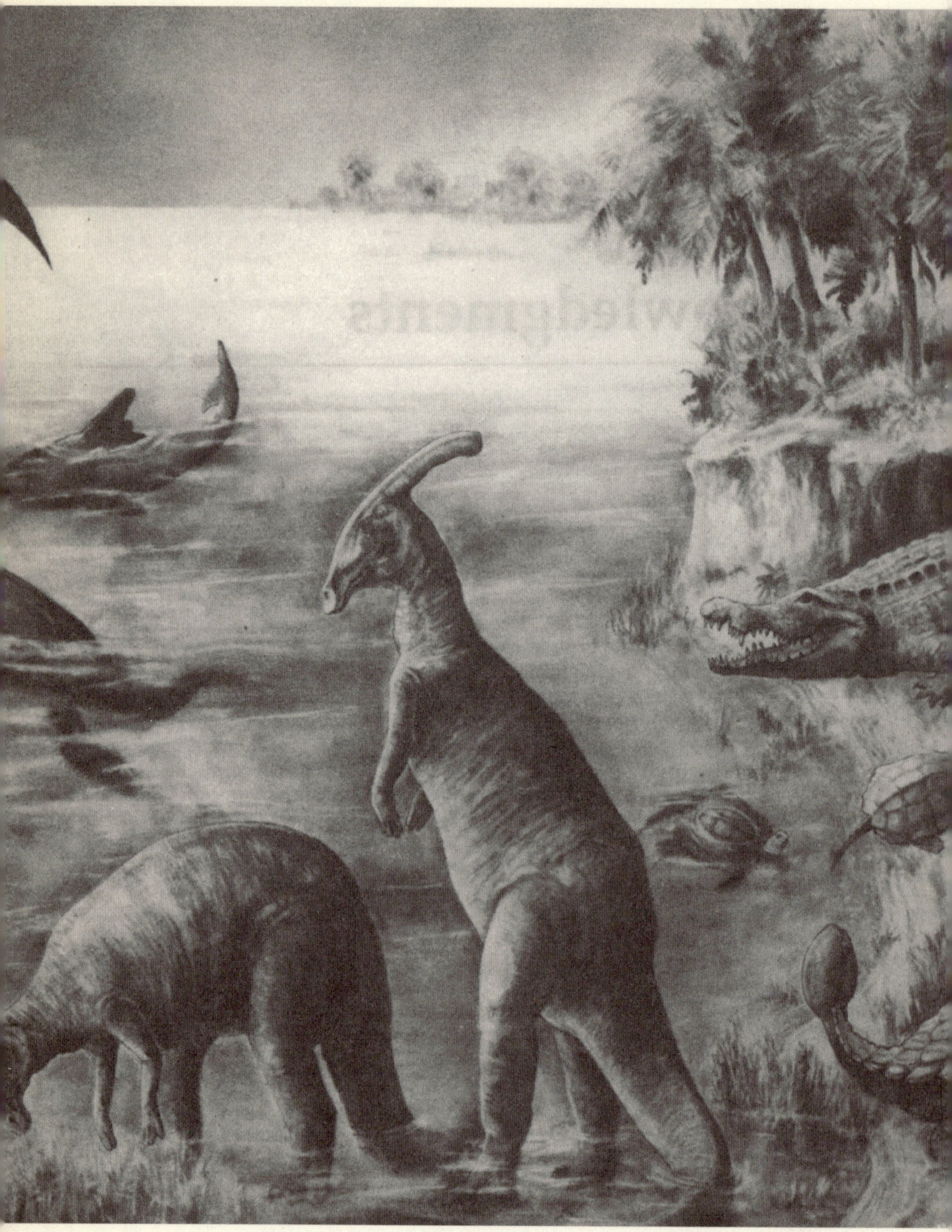

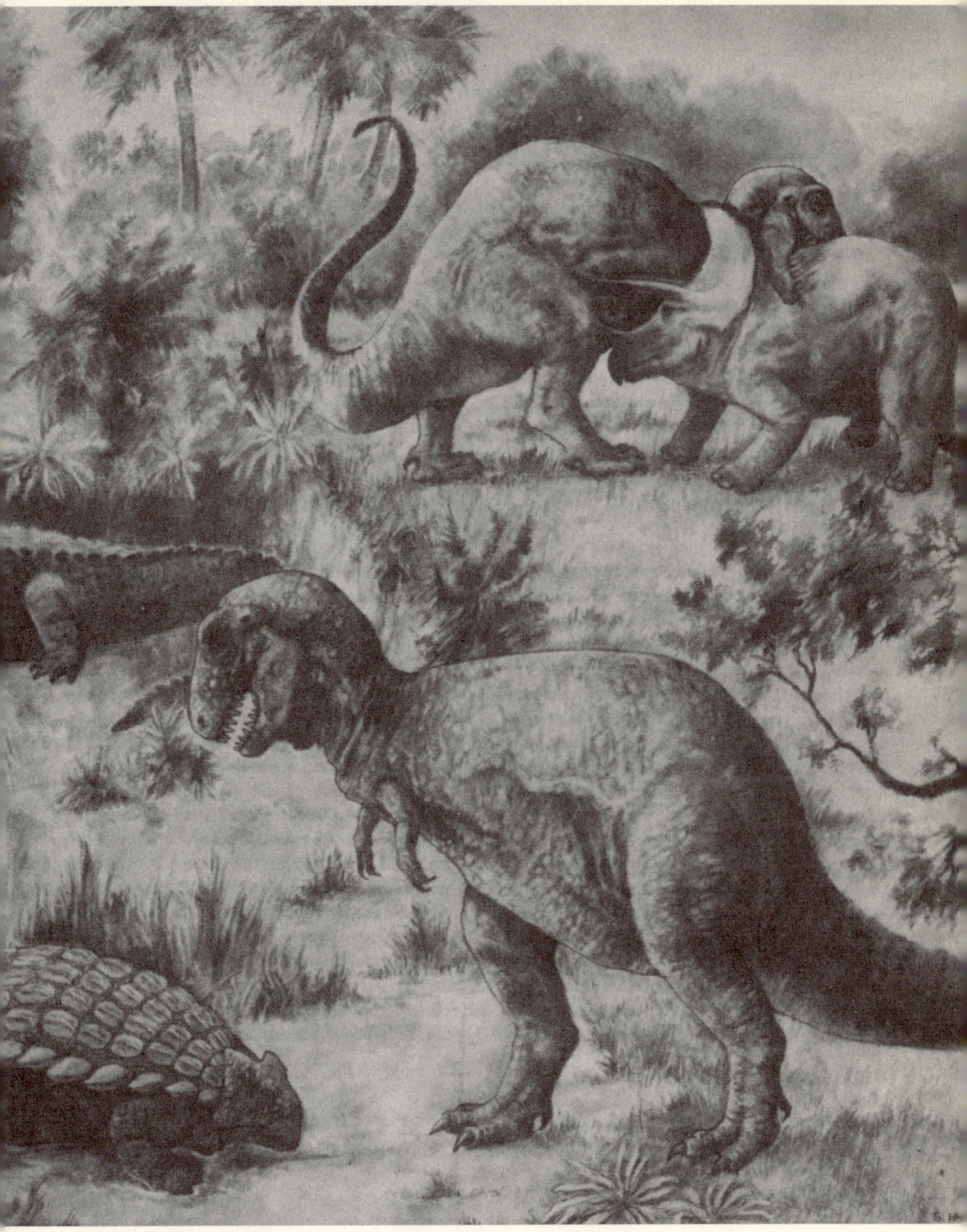

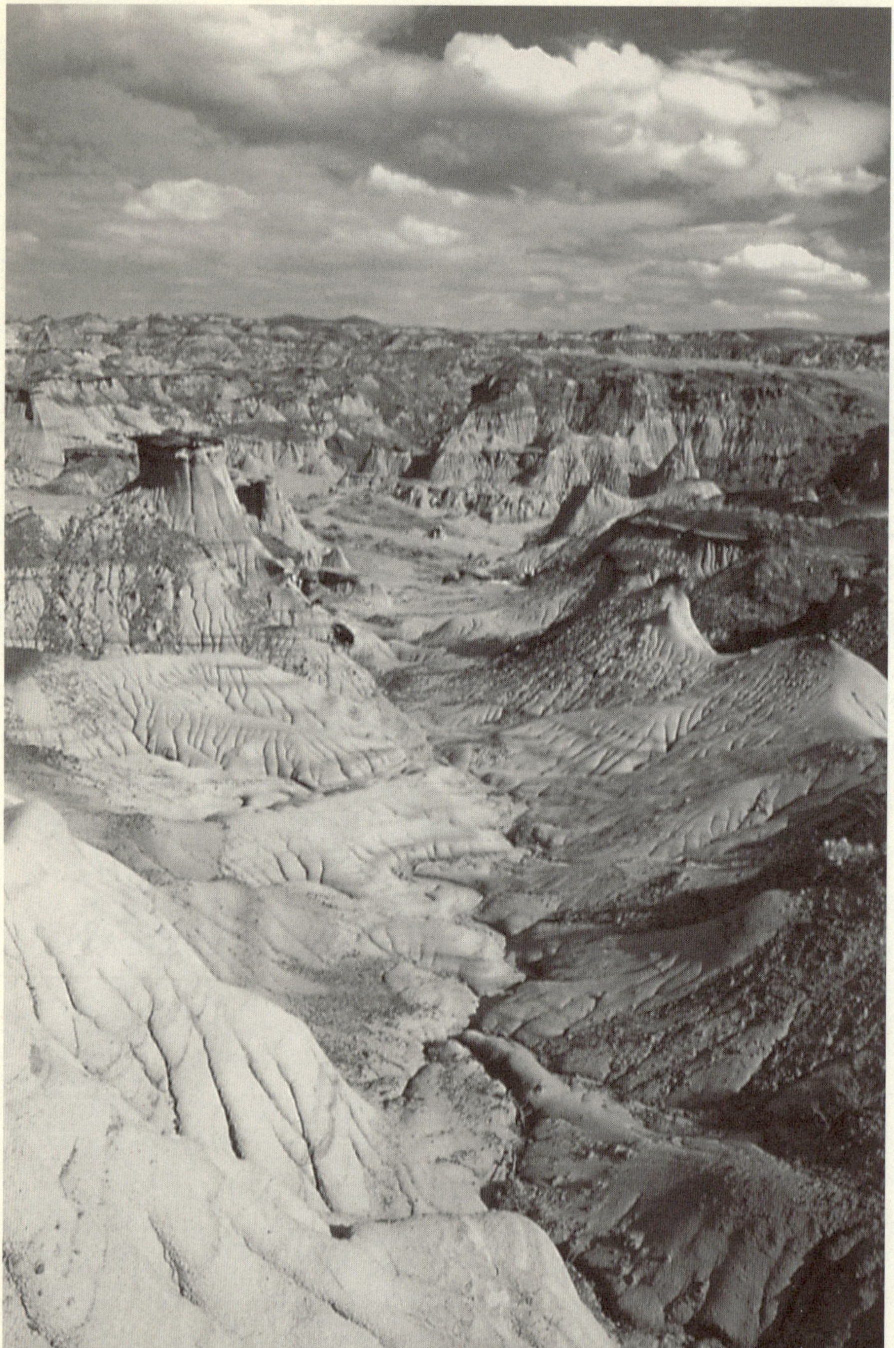

1

Introducing Dinosaur Country

Over most of our planet, evidence of the past is well concealed. Like the many cities of Troy, the landscape of each succeeding age superimposes itself upon the ones that went before. But sometimes Nature chooses to reveal traces of her past. She gives them out in bits and pieces, here and there around the globe. It may happen that older sediments are thrown into folds as a result of mountain building. Or, as is the case in the badlands of the Red Deer River, more recent deposits are stripped away to expose older ones that lie beneath.

Geologically speaking, the creation of the badlands is a relatively modern event. It began some 15 to 18 thousand years ago with the retreat of the most recent glaciation phase of the Ice Age. However, the rock formations uncovered by the turbulent action of the melting waters are many millions of years old. The youngest dinosaur-bearing exposures in the Red Deer River valley date from about 65 million years before our time, the oldest were laid down almost 77 million years ago. Considered together, they are like an enormous outdoor laboratory for the study of the evolutionary and geographical changes that took place during the 12-million-year period they represent. The fossils contained in the rock tell of the dinosaurs' last great hurrah, of a time when, measured by the numbers

Route of the Red Deer River through Dinosaur Country

Red Deer River Facts

Length of river from Banff National Park
to Alberta/Sask. Border .... 736 km

River Distances

City of Red Deer to Tolman Bridge .... 138 km
Tolman Bridge to Drumheller .... 59 km
Drumheller to Emerson Bridge at Hwy 36 .... 161 km
Emerson Bridge to Steveville Bridge .... 29 km
Steveville Bridge to Dinosaur Park .... 18 km
Dinosaur Park to Alberta/Sask. Border .... 136 km

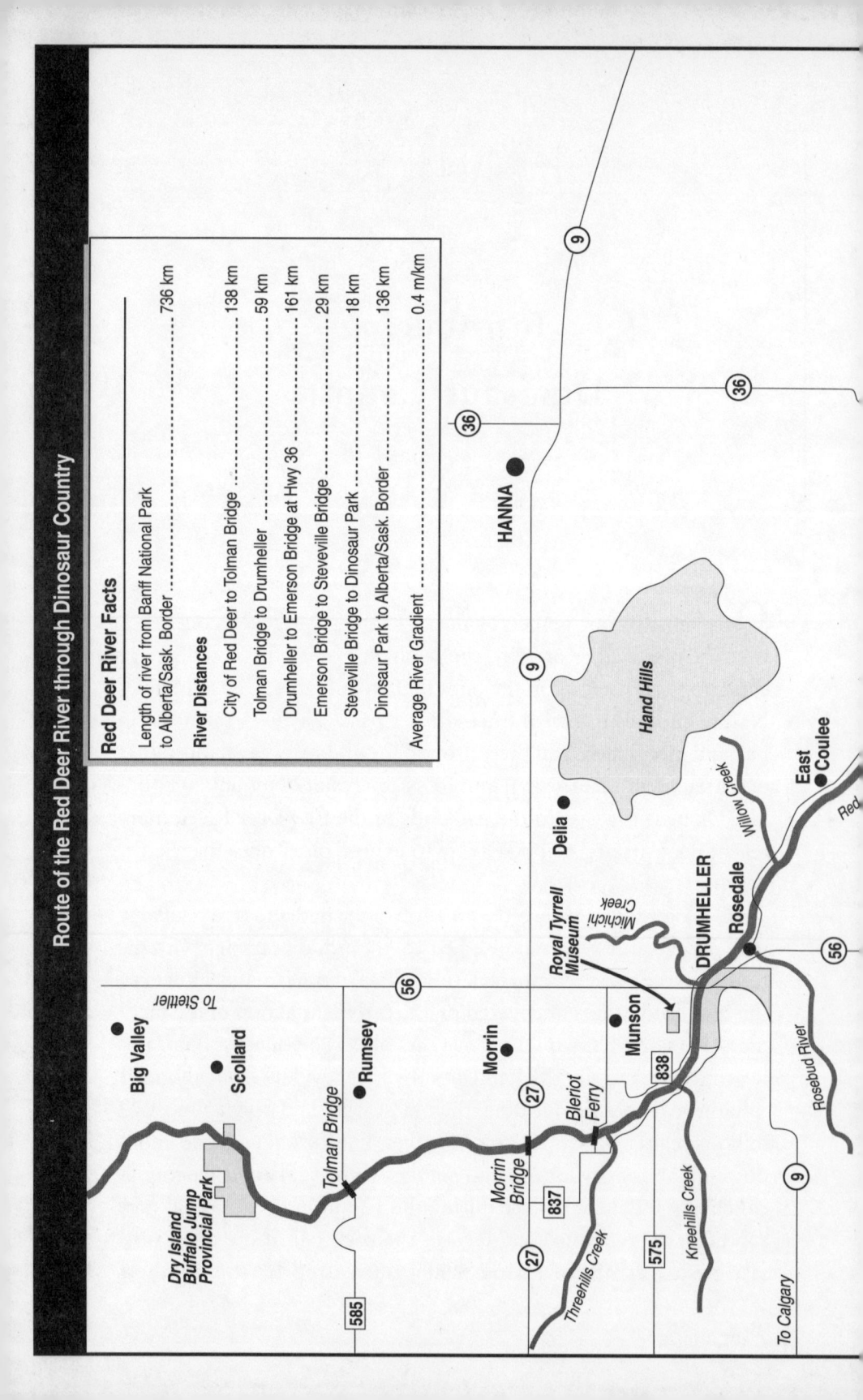

Average River Gradient .... 0.4 m/km

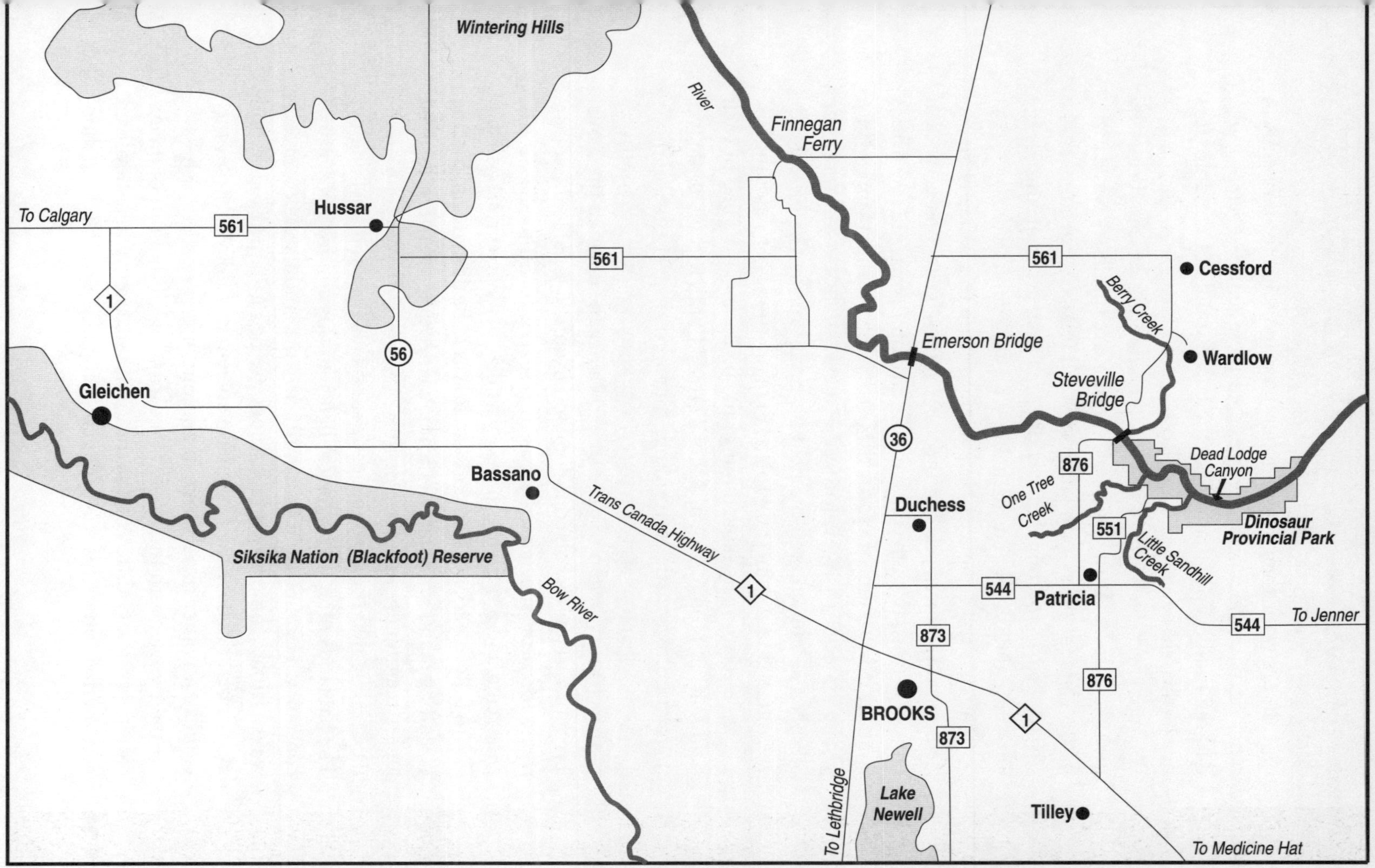

Wintering Hills
River
Finnegan Ferry
To Calgary
561
Hussar
561
561
Cessford
Berry Creek
1
Emerson Bridge
Wardlow
56
Steveville Bridge
Gleichen
36
Dead Lodge Canyon
876
Bassano
Trans Canada Highway
One Tree Creek
Duchess
Dinosaur Provincial Park
551
Little Sandhill Creek
Siksika Nation (Blackfoot) Reserve
Bow River
1
544
Patricia
544
To Jenner
873
876
BROOKS
1
873
Lake Newell
Tilley
To Lethbridge
To Medicine Hat

and diversity of their remains here and in contemporary sites in other parts of the world, they reached their zenith. Their waning, and the final eclipse that marks the end not only of the dinosaurs but of the Mesozoic Era, can also be read here.

Today, erosive forces carry on the sculpting process begun by melting glaciers. As the layers of soft rock are ruthlessly pared away by the elements, previously undiscovered fossils are brought to the surface yearly to contribute to the amassing store of knowledge about the dinosaurs and the living world they inhabited.

The first full-scale fossil excavations from this valley were carried out in the early years of the 20th century. The Great Canadian Dinosaur Rush brought the famous Barnum Brown of New York's American Museum of Natural History into competition with a group of equally well-known American bone hunters, the Sternbergs, who entered the field on behalf of the Geological Survey of Canada. From 1909 to 1916, many tonnes of dinosaur fossils were laboriously hauled out of the badlands at the end of each field season. Horse-drawn wagons crossed prairie trails to deliver their cargo to whistle-stop sidings for rail transport east.

As the skeletons were prepared for exhibition, the broad strokes of their history began to take shape. Under the aegis of the Royal Tyrrell Museum of Palaeontology in Drumheller, palaeontologists today focus on specialized areas of research to fill in the details, enhancing and modifying the story as new evidence presents itself.

To fully experience badlands country is to be drawn onto a plane of shifting realities. In spite of the knowledge that our planet evolved and is continually in a state of flux, it seems that we retain an innate feeling that the earth beneath our feet is firm and unchanging. The badlands offer a graphic challenge to this comforting sense of constancy. Here, erosion is steadily at work and its effects are always visible. Tomorrow's landscapes are being shaped today, and today's realities have their origins in ancient yesterdays. These other worlds and other times move in and out of one's consciousness.

Interwoven with the present landscape, itself the stuff of imagination, is the very different one the dinosaurs knew when they lived here. In their time, this was a flat coastal plain lapped by a shallow inland sea that covered much of the interior of North America. Rivers flowing from the west, where the ancestral Rocky Mountains were rising, deposited quantities of sediments and, having once accomplished that, cut through them to create meandering channels that fanned out into deltas and estuaries as they reached the unstable coastline of the sea. Where now there is golden grass, there was then a tangled growth of deep green fronds and ferns. Back from the swampy margin of the sea, there were groves of redwood rather than cottonwood. And where we see scrubby shrubs, there were earlier versions of flowering plants. A warm and humid climate nurtured this luxuriant growth. Could any environment be further from the one we experience here at the end of the 20th century? And yet the primeval past is all around, the events of its world encoded in the bands of subtly shaded sedimentary rock that compose the present-day landforms of the haunting and compelling landscape.

Sophisticated dating methods consign the exposures in the Red Deer River valley to three distinct time segments within the Late Cretaceous Period. Separated geographically, they are linked by the thread of the river flowing through them. The river rises in the Front Ranges of the Rocky Mountains in Banff National Park, its course contained almost entirely within Alberta's boundaries. No sooner does it cross the Saskatchewan border on its long voyage to Hudson Bay than its waters empty into the South Saskatchewan River.

The course of the river is through the Alberta basin, a trough containing layers of sedimentary rock that form a chronology of geological events, sometimes of a continental nature, sometimes marine. Much of the province's prosperity is due to reserves of oil and gas. Some of this is found in the deep-down pools of an ancient Devonian barrier reef. Some comes from nearer to the surface, from land and marine deposits laid down during dinosaur times, as the Western Interior Seaway washed in and out over tens of millions of years

For the first part of its run, the river has all the wild enthusiasm of a mountain stream. Gradually, it becomes calmer. Below the city of Red Deer, it makes one last dash through a canyon and then, entering a wide valley, it relinquishes its vigour to take on the lazy dignity of a prairie river. Were we, on a summer day, to put a raft in here and let it float downstream to Dinosaur Provincial Park, we would be carried on a leisurely two-hundred-and-thirty-kilometre journey back in time.

By river, the introduction to badlands terrain is gradual. Exposures dot the tree-covered banks of the Red Deer near Dry Island Buffalo Jump Provincial Park

The first exposures of badlands begin to appear at Content Bridge in the big valley above Dry Island Buffalo Jump Provincial Park. Moisture and soil conditions in this transition zone between parkland and prairie encourage vegetation. Much of the land bordering the river is graced by large stands of spruce and aspen; and warm green, grass-covered hills rise gently to the uplands. As the river flows south towards Tolman Bridge, outcroppings of badlands become more and more frequent. Fossil yields of dinosaurs are not as abundant here as they are further downstream but they are important because they represent an intriguing view of life 65 million years ago, just prior to the Cretaceous-Tertiary extinction. Tiny skeletal remains show that mammals diversified rapidly in these times just before they were to become stars on the Earth's stage.

Introducing Dinosaur Country

Little by little, the flow of the river slows and the chasm it moves through deepens. Erose forms become more emphatic. As the river cuts deeper into the prairie, the colour of the vegetation mutes. Pale greens and honey golds blend with the earth tones of the hills. Spruce gradually disappears from the landscape to be replaced by willows and plains cottonwood.

In the vicinity of Drumheller, from above Tolman Bridge for 77 km downstream to the Willow Creek inlet, the approach to the prairie summit is over 150 metres of broken terrain composed of bands of burnt sienna and ochre siltstones and silvery white sandstones. The deposits in this reach of the river are 71 million years old. They predate those further north by about 6 million years. Since 1910, there have been more than 150 skeletons excavated here. In addition, hints of the complex world dinosaurs inhabited are here in the many fossils of plants, fish, amphibians, mammals and reptiles other than dinosaurs.

For the next 115 km, the river is flanked by wide terraces. Where these have not been excessively disturbed by agriculture, they are

Early bonehunter Charles M. Sternberg photograhed the Drumheller badlands in 1917. This picture shows one of the largest exposures of the Horseshoe Canyon Formation.

dotted by cottonwood groves; further from the river banks, the approach to prairie elevation is over gently sloping grassy benchland. Sedimentary rocks made up of marine deposits, the bedrock of this stretch of the river, are friable and readily break down to form soil. Thus, vegetation is able to take hold and counteract the erosion that wreaks such havoc upon the slightly harder continental rocks that make up the badlands.

As the river meanders southeastward, its forward motion grinds down into slow gear. The channels become increasingly "hitherandthithering" and sand bars are larger and more frequent. Sluggishly, the river executes a wide bend and the badlands of Dinosaur Provincial Park sweep into view. The chief difference between the impact of these badlands and those at Drumheller is one of scale. The badlands around Drumheller are contained within a deep and narrow river wall with only a few extensions along old tributaries. In the park area, coulees extend back from the edge of the river's floodplain deep into the surrounding prairie.

The fossils unearthed in Dinosaur Provincial Park are described in superlatives: they are the oldest found in the Red Deer River valley, dating from 76.5 million years ago; and, they are far and away

When the Ice Age glaciers melted, the Red Deer River in Dinosaur Provincial Park was five times as wide as it is today. Swift flowing water sculpted jagged landforms from the soft prairie bedrock.

the most numerous and well-preserved. To date, there has been no other place found in the world with such an abundance of diverse dinosaur remains concentrated in so relatively small an area. Out of an 80-metre-thick layer cake of reddish-brown siltstone, grey sandstone and green-tinged claystones have come over 400 specimens of museum-quality dinosaur skeletons. Dinosaurs had already chalked up a 150-million-year history before they are recorded here but the Late Cretaceous was their heyday. More than 40 species lived in the area of Dinosaur Provincial Park alone, along with a rich variety of other fauna. Many of these left a record of their presence on Alberta's coastal plain.

Some periods of Earth's history are sparsely represented in the fossil record, while evidence of others is relatively abundant. The Late Cretaceous is one of the latter. Legacies from that time have been unearthed in widely separated parts of the contemporary world. In Central Asia, there once lived dinosaur groups very similar to the Red Deer River ones. Deposits from the Late Cretaceous have been found in Africa, India, Australia, South America, and Mexico. In the United States, Montana has rich fields, and less extensive repositories have been discovered in several other western states, including Alaska. There are sites in other parts of Alberta, in Saskatchewan, and in the northern Yukon. Even amidst such plenty, the Dinosaur Provincial Park area of the Red Deer River valley is distinguished; it is virtually wallowing in wealth. The fossils are generally in a fine state of preservation and the number of essentially complete skeletons has been high in proportion to the excavations carried out.

In recognition of this unparalleled richness within its boundaries, Dinosaur Provincial Park was named to the UNESCO World Heritage List in 1979. The List is administered by the World Heritage Committee, a body of fifteen United Nations member states, devoted to the promotion and protection of cultural and natural sites of "outstanding universal importance." Two additional considerations were cited by the Committee as qualifying the park for World Heritage status. One of these is the protection afforded the endangered riparian environment along the 26-kilometre run of the river through the park. The other is the aesthetic appeal of the extensive badlands terrain.

Conservation of the site is the foremost responsibility accepted at the time of inscription to the World Heritage List. In addition,

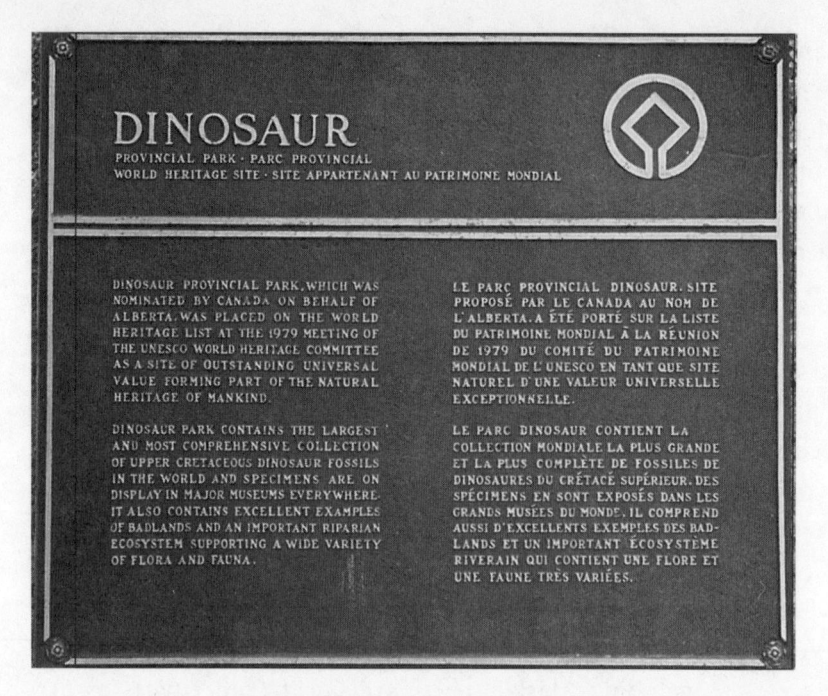

Dinosaur Provincial Park was inscribed on
UNESCO's World Heritage List in 1979

signatories agree to foster respect for the site through programs that interpret it for the public. To facilitate this part of the mandate, a Field Station was opened in 1987 to house displays that explain the prehistory of the park area. The Field Station operates under the wing of the Royal Tyrrell Museum of Palaeontology. It does in a localized way what its parent institution does on a more impressive and comprehensive scale.

The bronze-coloured forms of dinosaurs from the Red Deer River valley grace the exhibition halls of major museums around the world. The Canadian Museum of Nature in Ottawa, the Royal Ontario Museum in Toronto, the American Museum of Natural History in New York, the British Museum in London, and the Museum of Natural History in Buenos Aires are among those that give them pride of place. In these metropolitan centres, far from their badlands graves, the many types of duck-billed, horned, and armoured plant-eaters delight visitors with their diversity, while the flesh-eating dinosaurs lurk menacingly nearby.

Until recently, public recognition of the valley's dinosaurs was on a much more limited scale in Alberta than farther afield. It was a case of ignoring the value of what lies in your own back yard. This situation was finally remedied in 1985 when the doors of the Royal Tyrrell Museum of Palaeontology opened. Joining the ranks of the more prestigious natural history museums in the world, the Royal Tyrrell Museum is a major research centre for the study of prehistoric life. Housed in a fine new building on the banks of the Red Deer at Drumheller, the valley's dinosaurs are now on exhibition near where they lived and died, to acquaint visitors with the fascinating roles they played in the continuing story of evolution.

2

Drumheller:
A Town Fuelled by Fossils

The first dinosaur fossil from the Red Deer River valley to come to the attention of the scientific world was found on Kneehills Creek near Drumheller in 1884 by Joseph Tyrrell, a young employee of the Geological Survey of Canada. Although this event is now considered to be of great significance, at the time it paled in comparison with his other discovery during that fateful summer. Tyrrell had been sent from Ottawa to check into reports of coal in the area. He found that they had not been exaggerated, that there were large deposits of coal; and, furthermore, that they could be economically extracted. For a country poised on the brink of westward settlement, as Canada then was, Cretaceous fossil plant material in the form of coal held much greater immediate interest than fossilized animals from the same period.

Grass, however, was the natural resource that first attracted European settlement to the valley. Tyrrell reported coming upon a small band of buffalo during his survey of the area. There was poignancy in this sighting because it represented a tattered remnant of the economy that had sustained the Blackfoot tribes for generations but which, by this time, had been effectively destroyed. With the last of the buffalo, grass went begging. As the 19th century drew to a close, cattle interests began to trickle in to take advantage of it. Most of the ranches in what was to become the Drumheller area were small. The Two Bar, owned by the Winnipeg meat-packing firm of Gordon Ironsides and Fares, was an exception. It ran 5000 cattle from the Red Deer River south to Gleichen on the main line of the Canadian Pacific Railway. Gleichen, the supply centre for the Blackfoot reserve, extended its services to incoming ranchers and became the shipping point for a very large area.

The open range adventure was short-lived. Wildly fluctuating markets created chaos in a business that was uncertain at the best of times. Mange broke out among herds and treating for it was an expense that ate into already slim profits. The most serious problem, however, lay in not understanding the new country. One of the most appealing attributes of the southern prairie is that native grasses cure on the stem and are nutritious for grazing animals throughout the winter, provided they are accessible. Early ranchers counted on light snowfall and melting Chinook winds to keep the grass exposed. Hay making was given a low priority. When the killer winter of 1906-07 struck, it caught cattlemen completely unprepared for the extreme weather Nature held in reserve.

Cold set in early and blizzard followed blizzard. Cattle were pushed in front of the driving snow until they reached an immovable barrier where they bunched up and smothered. Even for those that were gathered home, there was not enough feed to last out the unremitting cold. When the weather finally broke in April it came too late for thousands of animals. "Carrion spring" is what Wallace Stegner calls it in <u>Wolf Willow</u> , his classic portrait of settling the west.

This natural disaster coincided with a development that had been looming on the horizon for some years: homesteaders began to arrive in the country north of the Red Deer about this time. All of the land south of the river belonged to the Canadian Pacific Railway, the final instalment of the land grant given to the company by the Dominion government for building the main rail line across Canada. It consisted of three million acres between Medicine Hat and Calgary, bounded on the south by the Bow River and on the north by the Red Deer. Plans for building a system to bring irrigation to the entire area were modified following detailed surveys that showed elevations in a large portion of the central section made the scheme impractical. Some 98,000 acres went on the market as dryland.

One who adapted quickly to the new situation was Thomas Greentree who had trailed a few cattle into the valley in 1902 and settled on the site that is now Drumheller. The very day the Canadian Pacific Railway surveyed the land he had squatted on, he made his downpayment. It was by way of the ferry he built and ran that many newcomers, travelling overland from Gleichen or Calgary with all their worldly goods, reached their homesteads. The first North West Mounted Police detachment in the area was barracked at Greentree Crossing. The Greentree Ranch was known for its hospitality and was an unofficial stopping place for some years.

One of the early wayfarers was Sam Drumheller. He was a well-established Washington businessman from a family with both agricultural and mining interests, He had been attracted to the area by a rumour going the rounds in mining circles of a soon-to-be railway connection between Calgary and Saskatoon that would run through the untapped coal fields of the Red Deer River valley. When

Thomas P. Greentree, passenger in Sam Drumheller's Cadillac, about 1912. Greentree's daughter, Beryl, on horseback. Skuce's livery barn, built in 1910, later destroyed by fire.

Thomas Greentree showed him the exposed coal seam that was the source of free fuel for the settlers, Drumheller immediately offered to buy the land from Greentree with the idea that he would develop a mine. His offer was generous; and rumour had it that the deal was expeditiously concluded when Sam Drumheller pulled the cash out of his pocket and offered it to Greentree on the spot. Upon his return to Calgary, Sam Drumheller went directly to the Land Titles office and took out a mineral lease on the property.

It was some time later that word of the coming railway reached Greentree. He thought he had been outfoxed by Drumheller and sued to get his land back. His chief argument was that the sale had been made on a Sunday which meant it was not legal. The Calgary judge who heard the case allowed that there *was* a law on the books precluding business transactions on the Lord's day. However, he pointed to the fact that Greentree had willingly taken the money in trespass of that law and, in view of that, was directed to split the land equally with the defendant and to return half the money Drumheller had given him. With that settled, and with a sense that just around the corner was an economic boom that both wanted a share in, there was no argument between them about locating the town site at Greentree Crossing adjacent to the spot where Sam Drumheller intended to build his mine. The name the town would go by was chosen on the flip of a coin.

Pick mining, Newcastle coal mine, Drumheller, 1914-15

The steel finally reached toward Drumheller in 1911 and there was a rash of activity to welcome it. Mines opened and the boom was on. Workers poured in and almost overnight a business centre was thrown up. Shack towns grew up on its perimeter and in the vicinity of the pit heads. By 1916, the population was 12,000 and growing. It was a rough and tumble place and soon earned the name of being the wildest town on the prairies, a reputation that stuck long after it had settled down and gained a degree of civility. During World War I, the town was facetiously christened "The Western Front." Labour unrest that led to nasty strikes in 1919

Jessie Gouge's Newcastle Coal Company opened the first valley mine in 1911. This photo, taken in 1928, shows a close-up of the tipple, with the Red Deer River in the background.

and again in 1925 did nothing to soften Drumheller's image.

Seam #1, from which most of the lignite in the valley was produced, is visible as a thick black layer in the badlands along the highway between Drumheller and East Coulee. It was formed from one of the many peat bogs that bordered Alberta's inland sea 72 million years ago. The coal is of domestic quality and demand for it kept the valley mines producing until the 1950s when oil and natural gas replaced it as the fossil fuels of choice for heating. One after another the coal mines closed and now the rhythm of days punctuated by piercing whistles announcing lunch breaks and shift changes at mines from Nacmine to East Coulee is only a memory. It is possible to catch informal glimpses into the past of some of the little places that grew up around a mine in the occasional small, asphalt-sided houses once so typical of these company towns.

Even when coal production was at its healthiest, summers were slack and miners were often forced to look for work elsewhere. Surrounding farms offered employment for some of them. Farming supplanted ranching on the land around Drumheller when settlers discovered how admirably suited the clay gumbo soil is for wheat growing. The large clay basin, which covers about 3000 square kilometres, marks the boundaries of glacial Lake Drumheller, a body of water that was created at the end of the Ice Age when meltwaters were trapped by a dam of ice between the Hand Hills to the east and the Wintering Hills to the west. Deposits from that time, perhaps carried under the glacial ice by streams from the west, constitute a rich soil, quite unlike the usual thin sandy soils of southern Alberta. Over the years, it has helped several Drumheller area farmers to win the coveted national title of Wheat King.

Only when it became quite obvious that the decline in the coal industry was not soon to be reversed did Drumheller's city fathers begin to assess the economic possibilities of Tyrrell's first discovery in the valley. Dinosaurs were of small concern to most early residents. Some might fancy having a big leg bone in the flower bed in front of the house but few recognized the scientific importance of their decoration. Even the arrival on the scene, in 1910, of bone collectors from the American Museum of Natural History in New York and, a few years later, from the Canadian Geological Survey in Ottawa failed to spark much awareness of the potential economic value that an area might gain from having a prehistoric world exposed on the back doorstep, as it were.

Yet, as is usual in human history, there were exceptions to the norm, those amateur fossil hunters who sensed the scientific significance of their discoveries and learned to preserve what they found on their trips to the dinosaur-bearing beds of the badlands. One of these was William R. Fulton, a clothing store owner who settled in the Drumheller valley in 1911. His particular interest was in fossilized botanical material. When trained palaeontologists and geologists began to visit the area, they made it a habit to stop by Fulton's home to see his latest finds. In 1934, he was honoured for his discovery of seeds of a pre-

Depth of coal seam on one level of the Atlas mine in East Coulee. The Atlas was the last mine to close and now operates as a mining museum.

DINOSAUR COUNTRY

C.F. Jungling, an early settler, with some of his large collection of dinosaur bones. Purchased in 1942 by the Drumheller Jaycees, the Jungling collection provided the foundation for the exhibits when the Drumheller Dinosaur and Fossil Museum opened in 1960.

viously unknown genus of plant by having it named after him. *Carpolithus fultonii* is thought to be a type of gingko and is currently under study by palaeobotanists at the Royal Tyrrell Museum of Palaeontology.

Leo J. Pluto came to Drumheller in 1948 as proprietor of the Dinosaur Hotel. He soon became interested in dinosaur fossils and, for some years, the window of his hotel lobby served as a display case for his growing collection. Pluto was one of several enthusiastic amateur collectors who tried to persuade their fellow townspeople that they should be concerned with collecting and preserving fossils with a view to creating a museum as a tourism resource, but their urging fell on deaf ears until the mid-1950s when serious economic recession hit the valley.

In 1955, temporary display space was found in the Rotary swimming pool club house and people with fossil collections stored in their basements or back sheds were prevailed upon to donate them to the new museum. The response was such that lack of space was soon a problem. Enough interest was generated by this activity to bring about the formation of the Drumheller and District Museum Society in 1957 with the purpose of fund-raising for a more suitable permanent location. A building was erected downtown and the museum moved into its new quarters in 1960. It was made possible by Drumhellerites' contributions of both time and money.

A local medical doctor, W.R. Read, and Mrs. Irene McVeigh, a keen collector and the museum's first curator, were responsible for setting up the museum displays. Judging from his strikingly literate writing for local histories and tourism pamphlets, Dr. Read was intellectually enriched by his surroundings and keen to share his knowledge. Attracting tourists had by now become the town council's major aim and visitors were urged to take in the museum before embarking upon the 50 km Dinosaur Trail Drive that is still a popular outing.

For the 25 years before the Tyrrell Museum was built, the Drumheller Dinosaur and Fossil Museum maintained a very important curatorial and educational function in interpreting the Cretaceous history of the area for the public. In the twelve years since the opening of the Royal Tyrrell, the Drumheller Museum has continued to operate, believing that the personal nature of its collections would bring in enough visitors to justify its presence. However, it is a bit like a mouse and an elephant being in bed together. The mouse is in danger even when the elephant is kindly disposed toward it. The Drumheller Museum Society is at present struggling to find ways to keep its small museum from being smothered to death.

3

Royal Tyrrell Museum of Palaeontology: Showplace on the Red Deer

When the decision was taken in 1980 by the Alberta government to build a museum in Drumheller that would showcase the fossil resource of the province and provide a sophisticated research facility to do justice to its study, the small palaeontology staff of the Provincial Museum of Alberta in Edmonton, headed by Dr. Philip Currie, was hived off to begin making plans. Following some preliminary work, it was realized that the magnitude of the undertaking demanded more than a competent scientific team and the resource people available through the Alberta Public Works Department. The expertise of a museum builder was needed to steer the project through to completion.

The Canadian judged to be best qualified for the job was Dr. David Baird who had gained his reputation through his work in the federal government museum system in Ottawa. At that time, he was Director of the National Museum of Natural Science and Technology, a job he left to come to Drumheller at the beginning of 1982. His arrival freed the scientific staff to collect and prepare specimens for exhibition. Dr. Baird is a man with confidence in his own vision and of single-minded purpose in its realization. Backing down in the face of any obstruction on the path to his goal was a course he never considered. Compromise was unattractive to him. Yet even those who sometimes ran afoul of his abrasive determination recognize his accomplishment. When he left Alberta in January of 1986, the Tyrrell Museum of Palaeontology was up and running. In four years, he had bulldozed it from hazy concept to completion and his vision of what a museum should be is now a reality enjoyed by its 500,000 yearly visitors. The museum was named for Joseph Burr Tyrrell. The animal whose skull he uncovered was also honoured when an *Albertosaurus*, Lillian, was adopted as mascot. Queen Elizabeth II conferred the title 'Royal' in 1990.

The relationship between the Royal Tyrrell Museum of Palaeontology and its badlands surroundings in Drumheller's Midland Provincial Park is one of those felicitous but relatively rare architectural unions in which each seems made for the other. Advancing towards the Museum between the erose hills that line the road, visitors may catch an occasional glimpse of the structure tucked

unobtrusively into the badlands but, once they arrive, the approach to the parking lot presents them with a comprehensive view of its facade. The low earth-toned building seems to have sprouted naturally from the land it sits on. Attractively landscaped earth berms roll up against it, burying the roofs of the lower portions of the building. This has the dual visual effect of anchoring the structure

Midland Collieries, 1925. Today, the original mine office functions as an interpretive centre. The site chosen for the Royal Tyrrell Museum is in the only part of Midland Provincial Park not undercut by shafts from the earlier mining operation.

in place while at the same time yielding it up in much the way the hills around release the fossils entombed within them.

The emphasis on the horizontal, which is inherent in any flat-roofed, elongated building, is further strengthened in this one by the construction technique and the material chosen for its exterior walls. Parallel bands of bleached reddish precast concrete, separated and accented by sandstone-coloured mouldings, echo the sedimentary strata of the badlands. Granite aggregate used for surface interest in the concrete bands has an organic quality and its dull terracotta colour is reminiscent of the ochre pigments gathered from these hills long ago by Blackfoot tribes and their predecessors on the prairie. Care was taken to maintain architectural balance by introducing vertical elements to the design. For example, the profile edges of the bands and mouldings are angled specifically to maximize the shadow line falling between and dividing them. This ornamentation, the facade's broken planes and elevations, and the dense plantings of trees and shrubs near the building combine to lend intermittent relief from its horizontal character and simultaneously relate it closely to the irregular landforms encircling it.

In creating the design for the museum, the architect, Paul Maas of the Calgary firm Bill Boucock Partnership, was guided by Baird's firmly-held belief that the museum experience for visitors of all ages should be totally enjoyable from arrival to departure. Clearly marked traffic patterns, inside and out, are intended to avoid the minor frustrations often faced by museum visitors.

About fifty percent of the interior space is allotted to galleries; research and storage areas account for the rest. The first consideration in planning the exhibition space was that very high ceilings were called for in the dinosaur hall in order to guarantee standing room for the tallest of these creatures. The main exhibition space was to be one large windowless "black box" with carefully controlled lighting. It sounds contradictory to say that it should feel airy and open and have no hint of a warehouse about it. The visitor should not be conscious of its underlying framework. In other words, form must follow function but not appear to do so. A tall order for the architect, and it is to his credit that the building so successfully marries the aesthetic with the practical.

Tyrannosaur logo at the entrance to the Tyrrell.

Consider the entrance as an example. On a large patio, the visitor is greeted by several models of alert active dinosaurs, a hint of what is to come inside. There is ample seating within hearing of the water playing in the nearby reed-encircled pond. Above the entrance, a canopy of glass supported by a lightweight metal frame steps out from the foremost plane of the building. Glinting in the light, it announces clearly that this is the way in and that visitors are welcome. The approach is marked by polished granite-clad pillars that open wide and then jog inwards to the door reinforcing the message.

Something else is going on as you walk under the canopy. Its glass panels are tinted, gradually darkening as you near the door, to condition your eyes for the dimly-lit interior. "A Celebration of

Life" was the theme chosen for the museum and no time is lost in introducing it. The story begins with a colour-filled changing collage of back-lit photographs. The large square entry way is linked to the building exterior by wall cladding of the same faded red granite as that used for the outdoor pillars. A wide red-granite archway opens onto a small, no-nonsense foyer, which houses services to accommodate visitors' practical needs.

The *raison d'etre* of the Royal Tyrrell Museum of Palaeontology is revealed, unarguably, in the Dinosaur Hall which occupies about one-third of the 40,000 square feet of exhibition space. With few exceptions, the 45 skeletons on display were found in the Red Deer River badlands. They give a wide sampling of the appealing diversity of the dominant land animals in this area during the Late Cretaceous period. Visitors with little time or very young children are well advised to take in this part of the museum first.

The exhibits that precede the Dinosaur Hall are geared to give perspective to the dinosaurs' place in the long continuum of life, and to explain the way in which many scientific disciplines, in addition to that of palaeontology, are involved in their study. In the Science Hall, for example, hands-on displays allow the visitor to

With floor to ceiling windows and a metal framework that appears weightless, the palaeoconservatory is a bright and airy contrast to the dimly lit adjoining galleries. A more marked contrast—between the landscape of the area as it once was and as it now is—comes from standing amid the lush humid vegetation of the conservatory and looking out at the parched badlands.

explore basic principles of science that contribute to an understanding of the anatomy of fossil animals. Time spent in these galleries deepens an understanding of the complexities of life in prehistoric time and, by extension, in the modern era.

Greeting *Triceratops*

As is true of any great museum, the Tyrrell's public programming and exhibitions reflect the research carried out behind the scenes, in field and laboratory. The results of intensified study by the palaeobotanists of seeds, pollens and fossilized specimens of plants found in the area can be seen in the palaeoconservatory. At the time of this writing, new plants are being set out to more closely emulate the Late Cretaceous landscape as it would have looked in the vicinity of the museum.

Near the entrance from the foyer to the gallery area, a window onto the preparation laboratory invites museum visitors to watch technicians at work as they clean encasing rock away from fossil specimens, readying them for study and display. Telephones just to the left of the window communicate messages from museum personnel outlining, in some detail, current field and research activities. Similar in-depth information is available at mini-theatres located throughout the building. Here and there, computer stations provide a chance to stop your tour for a dinosaur-related game.

In addition to a range of public programs conducted in the museum, there are several designed to give an experience of the earth scientists' work in the field. The most ambitious of these is the Dino tour which takes participants to several localities in Saskatchewan, Alberta and British Columbia where they prospect, excavate and collect fossils. The popular Day Digs offer a chance to work alongside Tyrrell staff and assist with fossil excavation in a quarry located a short distance from the museum. There is also a program called Field Experience in which members of the public can gain an in-depth feeling for the practice of palaeontology by working at fossil sites for a week or longer.

The museum's mandate is to manage, collect, research, display and interpret Alberta's fossil heritage. This directive is carried out by a permanent staff of 27, among which are seven curators. Dinosaurs, fossil vertebrates other than dinosaurs, invertebrate fossils, palaeobotany and sedimentary geology are among the subject areas investigated and studied by highly qualified scientists.

In July of 1997, in its 12th season of operation, the Royal Tyrrell Museum of Palaeontology registered its five-millionth visitor. Its popularity with the public has surpassed all expectations. The basic reason that tourists are happy to travel the not-inconsiderable distances from Alberta's main cities to Drumheller is certainly attributable to the calibre of the museum's exhibits. But there is another factor at work, and that is the current rage for dinosaurs.

Movies such as <u>Jurassic Park</u> and its sequel <u>The Lost World</u> have made household names of *Compsognathus* and *Dilophosaurus*. Dinosaurs are now among the coolest items around. And next to them in cool are the people who dig them up. Dr. Philip Currie, Head of Dinosaur Research at the Tyrrell, has become one of the darlings of the media and, as such, he is almost as valuable a resource for the museum as the fossils he studies. We open a copy of National Geographic Magazine and see his rangy form poised over a nest of hadrosaur eggs emerging from the Alberta badlands. Or we click the remote control to see what's on American PBS tonight and his blue eyes, strikingly pale in a sun-bronzed face capped by blond hair, are lit with excitement as he leads us to the discovery site of juvenile armoured dinosaurs in China's Gobi Desert. Who is the first scientist outside of China to be interviewed by the New York Times about the astounding feathered dinosaur fossil? Phil Currie. And when the huge flesh eater *Giganotosaurus* turns up in Patagonia, who shares the limelight with Dr. Rodolfo Coria, its Argentinian discoverer? Again, Dr. Philip Currie.

But there is much more to him than the outdoorsy good looks and easy boyish style so beloved of the press. His contributions to the field of dinosaur research have gained him a place of respect among his fellow scientists. He is considered one of the world's leading authorities on flesh-eating dinosaurs and their direct evolutionary link to birds. His professional success reflects well on the Royal Tyrrell Museum.

Dr. Philip Currie excavating baby *Protoceratops,* in China, July 1988.

In the mid-1980s, Dr. Currie played a major role in one of the most exciting expeditions in the history of dinosaur exploration. It was called the Canada - China Dinosaur Project. It took him and his Canadian colleagues to a place of mystical charm for dinosaur hunters—the Gobi Desert. It was to this inhospitable part of the globe that the fabled Roy Chapman Andrews travelled in the 1920s in search of early human fossils only to discover instead some of the best dinosaur fields known. Andrews's free-wheeling, gun-toting style had a distinctly 'wild west' flavour and the Gobi Desert was his Klondike. Many important skeletons were unearthed from its sands for the American Museum of Natural History. What most captured public attention, however, was the announcement that, at Flaming Cliffs, the world's first discovery of dinosaur eggs had been made. Andrews was an overnight sensation.

In 1980, when Currie and his then colleague Brian Noble conceived the notion of mounting an expedition to Mongolia, it had been virtually off-limits to Westerners for many years, divided as it was between the two Communist superpowers, the USSR and

China. Outer Mongolia has since gained independence but Inner Mongolia remains a part of China. After several false starts, it was to China that overtures were made. The Canadian Museum of Nature was brought into the project and the Ex Terra Foundation was set up, with Brian Noble as administrator. Negotiations resulted in an agreement being signed in 1985 and, with the blessings of respective governments, the Canada - China Dinosaur Project was ready to begin.

Dr. Currie and Dr. Dale Russell (then with the Canadian Museum of Nature, now at North Carolina State University) acted as co-directors of the Canadian contingent, the first team of western scientists to work in Central Asia in 50 years. The Chinese under the leadership of Dong Zhiming of the Institute of Paleontology

Field crews of the Canada - China Dinosaur Project, one of the largest international co-operative expeditions in the history of palaeontology.

and Paleoanthropology in Beijing collaborated with the Canadian team to examine the relations between North American and Asian dinosaurs during the Cretaceous Period. Together, they posed questions about continental land bridges, about possible migratory patterns, about the evolution of dinosaurs, about similarities and differences in the environments that supported dinosaur life on both continents. The search for answers consumed four field seasons from 1985 to 1990, with a hiatus in 1989 during the time of the Tianenmen Square troubles. They prospected, with great success, in the Junggar Basin of northwestern China, in the Gobi Desert of Inner Mongolia, in Alberta's badlands and in the Canadian high Arctic. In his book entitled <u>The Dinosaur Project: The Story of the Greatest Dinosaur Expedition Ever Mounted</u>, Wayne Grady does a fine job of capturing the intellectual excitement for all of the researchers involved in this very important international collaboration.

Some sixty metric tonnes of fossils were shipped from the China fields alone. The specimens collected will involve years of study but already scientific papers have been compiled in two special editions of the <u>Canadian Journal of Earth Sciences</u>. The Canada - China Dinosaur Project has shed a great deal of light on previously murky areas of dinosaur behaviour. These developments will be mentioned where applicable in the following chapters.

Collaborative efforts were made to mount a travelling exhibition to bring never-before-seen Canadian and Chinese dinosaurs to the public. The show was seen in Osaka, Singapore and Sidney as well as in four Canadian cities. In a modified form, the exhibit is expected to be on the road at least until the end of the century.

Perhaps the most important outcome of the Canada - China Dinosaur Project is the fact that it created an atmosphere of co-operation among the participating palaeontologists that will have ongoing benefits for future dinosaur research in both countries.

The Royal Tyrrell's mascot, Lillian, in a Late
Cretaceous setting in
the Dinosaur Hall.

4

The Age of Dinosaurs

Even though at its outset dinosaurs had not yet evolved, the Mesozoic Era is now commonly referred to as the Age of Dinosaurs. The era is bracketed by mass extinctions. The one used by geologists to mark the close of the Palaeozoic and the introduction of the Mesozoic is known as the Permian extinction. It occurred about 250 million years ago. It was a mass dying like no other in Earth's history, estimated to have wiped out 95% of all the species then populating the planet. By comparison, the extinction that killed the dinosaurs and brought the Mesozoic Era to a close 65 million years ago was mild, doing away with about 65% of species known to exist at that time.

The Mesozoic Era is divided into three periods. The first of these, the Triassic, lasted from about 250 to 206 million years ago; it was in the middle of this period that the first dinosaurs appeared. Once established, dinosaurs became a dominant force and continued their sojourn on Earth for 160 million years. This took them through the Jurassic Period which ran from about 206 to 144 million years ago and the Cretaceous which spanned the next 80 million years of time. The end of the Cretaceous Period and the end of the dinosaurs (at least for those that did not take wing) came 65 million years ago.

The Age of Dinosaurs

ERA	PERIOD		MILLIONS OF YEARS AGO	HISTORY OF LIFE RECORDED IN FOSSILS
			— 0 —	
CENOZOIC	Quaternary			Humans
	Tertiary	Neogene		
		Paleogene		
			— 65 —	Mass extinction — 65% of all known species
MESOZOIC	Cretaceous			Flowering plants
			— 144 —	Landscape: cycads, gymnosperms
	Jurassic			Birds
			— 206 —	Sea reptiles
	Triassic			Dinosaurs, crocodiles, pterosaurs
				Mammals
			— 250 —	Mass extinction — 95% of all known species
PALAEOZOIC	Permian			
			— 290 —	Reptiles
	Carboniferous			Amphibians
				Insects
				Seed ferns, rushes, shrubs
			— 360 —	
	Devonian			Land plants without roots/leaves
			— 410 —	Fish with jaws
	Silurian			
			— 440 —	
	Ordovician			Mosses and algae migrate to land
			— 510 —	
	Cambrian			Jawless fish with backbones
				Sea invertebrates: sponges, worms, mollusks, shrimp
			— 570 —	
	Precambrian			Cell with nucleus
				Blue-green algae
				Bacteria

Specimens preserved near Joggins, Nova Scotia in the hollow trunks of 310-million-year-old trees are of *Hylonomus*, the earliest known reptile.

Biogeography, the study of the location and distribution of plants and animals, aids in an understanding of the sequence of change undergone by continental land masses as a result of the shifting of Earth's oceanic and continental plates. The movement of terrestrial animals is restricted by the presence of large bodies of water; so if the animals on one continent are very similar to those on another, it indicates that there was a free exchange between the two, whereas a faunal assemblage peculiar to only one area points to it having developed independently and in isolation. The spread of marsupials unique to Australia, for example, indicates its isolation before placental mammals gained ascendancy as they did on the other continents. Fossil assemblages play a part in constructing maps of the ancient world.

An idea of where land connections existed during the Mesozoic Era is gained from comparisons of the kinds of dinosaur and other contemporaneous fossils found around the world in rock of similar age. There is a close similarity worldwide among the known Triassic fossils which reflects a time when climates were uniform everywhere and all of the continents were joined together to form a single supercontinent known as Pangaea.

Then throughout the Jurassic, the bonds were loosened and the cohesive land mass began to separate. Sometime during this period, rifting began to split Pangaea into the northern and southern hemispheres and the Tethys Ocean moved in. Central Asia was the first area to be cut off from Pangaea. It was also separated, by an epicontinental sea, from Europe. The Tethys Ocean continued to expand westward and, although land junctions between North

The Age of Dinosaurs

The Continental Dance

The 1967 theory of plate tectonics, demonstrating that Earth's surface is fractured into huge shifting plates, supports the much earlier hypothesis—that the continents originated from a single land mass which somehow broke apart.

Top: Rifting of super continent Pangaea began in the Late Triassic, about 200 million years ago.

Centre: In the mid-Jurassic Period, 175 million years ago, the Tethys Ocean separated Laurasia (the continent of the Northern Hemisphere) from Gondwana (the Southern Hemisphere).

Bottom: By the end of the Cretaceous Period, 64 million years ago, the continents were inching towards their present positions.

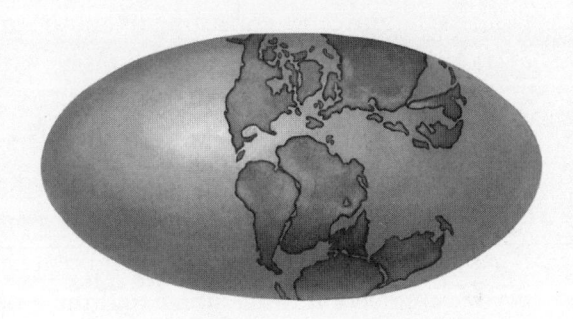

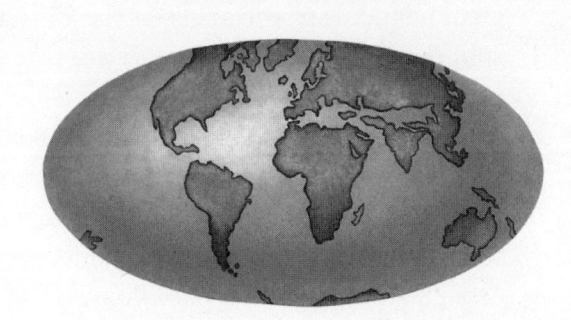

Dinosaur Country

The lineage of present-day mammals includes the famous sail-backed reptile, Dimetrodon, which lived during Permian times.

America and Africa and between Europe and Africa were protracted as evidenced by similarities in dinosaur genera, by the middle of the Jurassic period it had succeeded in creating two separate continents: Gondwana, consisting of South America, Africa, India, Australia and Antarctica; and Laurasia, which included Europe and North America.

During the Early Cretaceous, Gondwana drifted apart into separate continental plates. A spell of heightened tectonic activity, volcanic eruptions and mountain building marked the mid-Cretaceous period. The early Atlantic Ocean breached the North America/Europe connection in the north and the South America/Africa one in the south. By the close of the Mesozoic Era, the continental plates had reached positions very roughly approximate to those they occupy today. The ocean level rose and salt water flowed in, creating great inland waterways such as the Western Interior Seaway, which split the North American continent into an eastern and a western section.

The equator ran through the middle of Pangaea and, before its break-up, much of the interior of the continent is thought to have been arid, while the coastal areas were warm and humid, with seasonal monsoons. The dominant plants were primitive gymnosperms: drought-tolerant tufted palm-like cycads, seed ferns, and gingkos. Conifers made an appearance and thrived in the drier and cooler upland regions.

The Age of Dinosaurs

Gradually, the empty niches left by the Permian extinction began to be populated. Reptiles became the dominant land animals. It is interesting that at the outset of the Age of Dinosaurs, one of the most successful groups of reptiles was not the one from which dinosaurs eventually evolved but, rather, the one that gave rise to mammals. This group, called synapsids, seemed destined for continuing mastery but, as the period wore on, they diminished in numbers and stature; archosaurs, the "ruling reptiles," derived from a lineage that had survived the Permian extinction, came to the fore. Archosaurs gave rise to crocodiles, pterosaurs and dinosaurs. When true mammals appeared in the Late Triassic, they were tiny creatures, quite unlike their sturdy forebears. They were no competition for the dinosaurs that appear in the fossil record at about the same time.

Fossil animals from the Early Triassic, believed by some to be pre-dinosaurs and by others to be the basal forms of theropods, have been found in Brazil and Argentina: *Herrerasaurus*, *Staurikosaurus*, *Eoraptor*, and *Pisanosaurus*. The theropods, whose name means "beast foot," include all known flesh-eating dinosaurs.

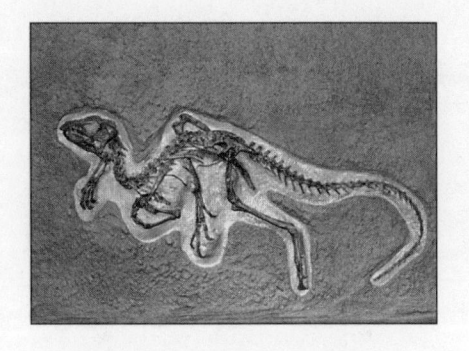

Heterodontosaurus was a turkey-sized bipedal herbivorous dinosaur known from Early Jurassic strata of South Africa.

There is a better fossil record from the end of the Triassic. Well-known from the Ghost Ranch site in New Mexico, where hundreds of individuals were killed *en masse* by some natural disaster, is the ostrich-sized theropod *Coelophysis*. About the same time, there was a proliferation of prosauropods whose remains have been found on all continents. *Massospondylus*, *Plateosaurus*, and *Anchisaurus* are included among them. In deposits containing prosauropods, their numbers dominate the fauna in the fossil assemblage and, although there has been much disagreement about their diet, most palaeontologists think they were herbivorous. They were generally big with very long necks, factors

Stegosaurus was a long, narrow-bodied plant-eater with a complex system of upright plates and spines along its back and tail. These plates were not for defence. They may have had a role in regulating the animal's temperature. *Stegosaurus* is best known from Late Jurassic deposits.

that would have allowed them to browse overhead on vegetation out of reach to most other animals. This exclusive food source may have brought about the apparent increase in their populations.

As Pangaea pulled apart, there were shallow rifts left between the plates and in time the sea moved in to fill them. The sea level rose during the Jurassic and water encroached upon the land, creating beach fronts where earlier there was inland desert. The climate got steadily warmer and more humid, and seasonality lessened. Polar ice disappeared.

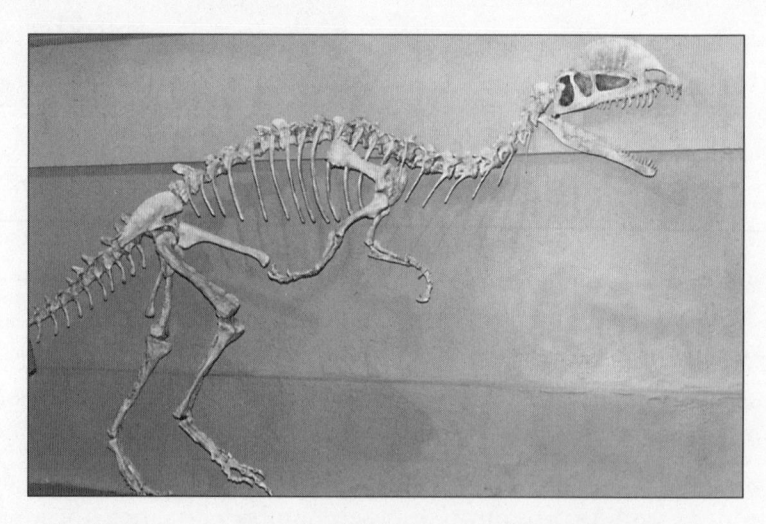

The slender, six-metre-long *Dilophosaurus* (named for its thin paired crests) was a meat-eater of the Early Jurassic period. It had strong sharp-clawed hind limbs and flexible hands with four fingers, one opposable like our thumbs.

The Age of Dinosaurs

Dilophosaurus dates from the Early Jurassic Period. Its fame has spread since the novel <u>Jurassic Park</u> was made into a movie. Who can say with certainty that *Dilophosaurus* did *not* spit poison? There is more credible evidence to suggest it was a bipedal seven-metre pack hunter about the weight of a small horse.

Closely related to the well-known North American sauropod, *Diplodocus*, *Mamenchisaurus* lived in China 140 million years ago. It weighed about 16 metric tonnes and was over 20 metres long.

Jurassic flora was similar to that of the Triassic but changing conditions stimulated lush growth. Perhaps in response to an abundant food supply in these subtropical parklands, herbivorous dinosaurs waxed in size. One thing seems certain and that is that the very large quadrupedal sauropods co-evolved with the spread of gymnosperms. The small bipedal *Heterodontosaurus* from the early Jurassic was later eclipsed by these animals that measured up to 25 metres, their necks accounting for at least half of that length. *Diplodocus*, *Apatosaurus* (earlier known as *Brontosaurus*) and *Brachiosaurus* are among their number. The well-known plated *Stegosaurus* and its Chinese relative *Tuojiangosaurus* were low-slung armoured plant eaters.

Some of the meat-eaters of this time were also very large. The bipedal *Allosaurus*, known from North America, and possibly Africa, was about 12 metres long and weighed over two metric tonnes. At the extreme other end of the dimensions chart was *Compsognathus*, a chicken-sized carnivore.

The controversial transitional bird, *Archaeopteryx,* appeared toward the end of the Jurassic. Other ancient bird fossils have been found dating from this time. They shared the atmosphere overhead with pterosaurs, the only reptiles and the largest vertebrates ever to fly. The warm seas teemed with a variety of life. Many different fish shared the waters with plesiosaurs, ichthyosaurs, marine crocodiles, ammonites, squid, sharks and rays. Mammals were developing and diversifying during the Jurassic. Early in the Cretaceous Period, the first placental mammals made an appearance.

This was the time when Gondwana was breaking up. Warm shallow seas surrounded the new continents, which lay at or near sea level. Laurasia, too, was low lying. There was a spread of steamy near-tropical forests. The first flowering plants, angiosperms, evolved. These plants so dominate our landscapes today that it is hard to imagine Earth without them but it was to be millions of years before they offered real competition to the well-established gymnosperms.

Animals kept pace with plants and their numbers and diversity increased too. In the first half of the Cretaceous, many new groups arose from earlier dinosaur lineages. Specimens of the most interesting of these were recently discovered, *Unenlagia* from Argentina, and *Sinosauropteryx* from China. The shoulder structures of these chicken-sized bipedal animals show clear connections to birds. More noteworthy, in the Chinese fossil there are traces of what appear to be downy feathers along the spine and sides. Those palaeontologists who have long supported the dinosaur - bird connection believe that feathers are the final confirmation of its validity.

Deinonychus made an appearance somewhat earlier than either of the above two theropods. About three metres long and weighing 80 kg, this small animal was named for the fearsome large claw it used to slash its prey. Bones of several of these animals found in conjunction with those of a large plant-eating dinosaur suggest pack behaviour. Descriptions of this animal in the 1960s and 70s by Yale University's John Ostrom began the reassessment of dinosaurs' physiology and renewed awareness of their structural similarities with birds.

The Age of Dinosaurs

Lambeosaurus, a large duck-billed dinosaur, under attack by a pack of dromaeosaurs. These fierce little carnivores were Late Cretaceous relatives of the earlier *Deinonychus*.

It was in the middle of the Cretaceous Period that the largest of all known meat-eaters lived. Hard as it may be to imagine, *Giganotosaurus* outstripped the later *Tyrannosaurus rex* in size. It weighed about eight metric tonnes and stood four metres tall.

Representatives of the herbivorous dinosaurs presaged those that are so plentiful in the Red Deer River area. *Iguanodon,* dating from about 130 million years ago, has a close ancestral tie to the hadrosaurs. *Psittacosaurus* appeared about 95 million years ago and is the precursor of the many horned dinosaurs that arrived on the scene in the second half of the Cretaceous Period.

Big changes, which began the planet's make-over to its present geographical configuration, took place about the middle of the period. Plate tectonics is often referred to as a waltz but, during this time, the dance seems to have been more on the order of rock and roll with each plate boogeying off on its own. Lots of volcanic action accompanied this stepped-up crustal activity. Mountains were thrown up in several parts of the world. The ancestral Rocky Mountains were among these although it would take another period of intense mountain building, long after the dinosaurs were extinct, to bring them to their present height and position.

At about the time that the North Atlantic ruptured the connection between North America and Europe, lifting forces created land bridges between North America and central Asia. The latter area had existed in isolation since Triassic times. This connection was to have a major influence on animal life in Alberta. The very close similarities remarked upon in the Late Cretaceous dinosaurs of these two areas suggest pedestrian traffic over the Bering Land Bridge between central Asia and western North America. By the end of the Cretaceous, the continents had drifted to positions approximate to those they hold today. The sea level rose again, submerging about one-third of the land area under water.

The climate generally continued warm and humid, very conducive to plant growth, and the herbivorous dinosaurs flourished. Hadrosaurs, ceratopsians, ankylosaurs and pachycephalosaurs from this time exhibit interesting diversification. Nipping at their heels came dinosaurs with a taste for flesh. Carnivores, large and small, prospered. In our view of their time, dinosaurs are such imposing beasts that they tend to eclipse all other forms of animal life. But, of course, ecosystems then were at least as complex as those of today. Dinosaurs shared their world with a multitude of others. Turtles, lizards, crocodiles, tiny mammals, bony fishes and shell fishes, marine reptiles, flying reptiles, insects and birds were all a part of the teeming scene.

The foregoing brings us back to the badlands of the Red Deer River valley: from the general to the more specific, in terms of both time and place. Geologically speaking, the 12 million or so years represented here is only a tiny chapter in the long dinosaur saga. It is, however, a fascinating and detailed account—thanks to the rich fossil lode of the valley.

Often the question is asked: why are so many dinosaurs found here? There is more than one answer. The most immediately obvious one is that a substantial population of dinosaurs seems to have found conditions on this Late Cretaceous coastal plain very much to its taste. No other site in the world yields up such a diversity of well-preserved dinosaur skeletons in so relatively small an area. There is, however, a certain bias in the dinosaur fossil record everywhere in the world. Many specimens come from lowland seaside palaeoenvironments such as the one that existed in this area. So it is not surprising that dinosaur remains are found here. But the animals may have been equally successful in other areas where all traces of an earlier time is either buried away from human eyes or completely erased. The fact is that the vast majority of organisms simply rot away after death. Lack of fossilized remains does not mean that particular plants or animals never lived in an area but, conversely, their once-living presence can be confirmed only from fossil evidence. What makes the Red Deer River valley one of the world's most important repositories of Cretaceous life is the fortunate coupling of two chancy processes—first, the fossilization, and then, the exposure of the skeletons.

For much of the Late Cretaceous, high rates of sediment accumulation in the area through which the Red Deer River now flows favoured the rapid burial of carcasses. To suggest a scenario with optimum conditions: an animal died near the edge of a shallow stream and slipped beneath the surface of the water's flow where the soft bottom muds washed over it before scavengers had an opportunity to scatter its parts hither and yon. Over millions of years, after the organism decayed, layers of sediments continued to be deposited over this burial place exerting pressure and heat that, together with the chemical action of mineral-rich ground water, fossilized the bones and turned the sediments to rock.

The original shape and internal microscopic structure of the animal's bones were preserved in these processes, so that millions of years later, scientists are able to accurately recreate the beast's appearance in life using its fossilized remains as a guide. Analyses of the rock give information about the environmental conditions under which deposition took place. These data, combined with an examination of all of the other plant and animal fossils present, are clues to the interrelated elements of ancient ecosystems.

5

Alberta's Late Cretaceous Landscapes

Had they lived here 225 million years ago during the Early Triassic Period, Albertans from the Red Deer River valley would not have had to travel very far to reach the seacoast. The Pacific shoreline lay just to the west. The waters were teeming with a wide variety of life. At Wapiti Lake in the northern Rockies, fossils from that time are abundant. Many different kinds of fish, small coiled ammonites and squid-like creatures are a few of the 1500 specimens that have been collected from the site. Among the most interesting forms of life were marine reptiles. They had adapted themselves for an aqueous existence presumably to take advantage of empty niches left by the Permian extinction which had been particularly devastating to life in the oceans. The nothosaurs looked a bit like long lizards; thalattosaurs had beaks and seem to have lived an amphibious sort of existence. Dental apparatus of the placodonts suggest a diet of clams and snails. All of these animals were among those that disappeared at the end of the Triassic, when another mass extinction occurred, perhaps brought about by asteroids bombarding the Earth.

In the early Jurassic, the ocean moved inland, entirely submerging what are now the three prairie provinces. North America floated nearer to its present position. Then came an attack of west coast

Alberta's Late Cretaceous Landscapes

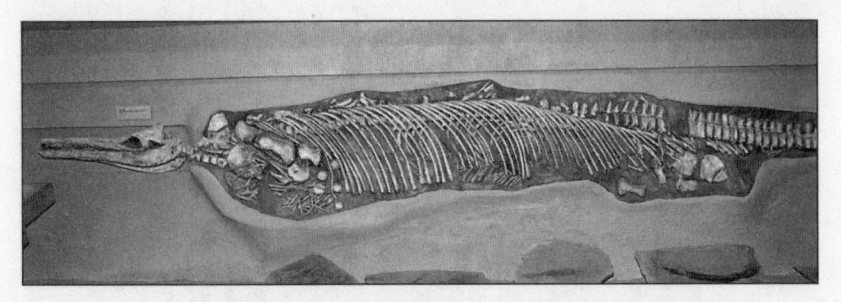

The only marine reptiles to escape extinction at the end of the Triassic were the ichthyosaurs. Fast dolphin-like fish-eaters, they survived through much of the Cretaceous but died out before the dinosaurs did.

tectonic turbulence that was a determinant in the preparation for the migration of the dinosaurs into our area. Rocks from offshore volcanic islands began to smash against the continental land mass, thrusting it up and eventually cementing themselves onto its western margin as newly formed mountains. The ocean retreated to the north and, for a time, rivers ran from the south to join it.

During the Cretaceous, periodic bombardment from the island arcs in the Pacific continued and the continent accreted westward. With each series of collisions, the mountain building that had begun earlier was furthered. Eventually, this rising action caused a corresponding leeward dip; the long narrow depression of the Alberta basin sank under the weight of sediments pouring eastward from the young unstable highlands. Similar events were taking place all along the western margin of North America, creating interior troughs that stretched from the Arctic to the Gulf of Mexico. About 100 million years ago, water flowed in from both north and south to fill the basins and create the Western Interior Seaway.

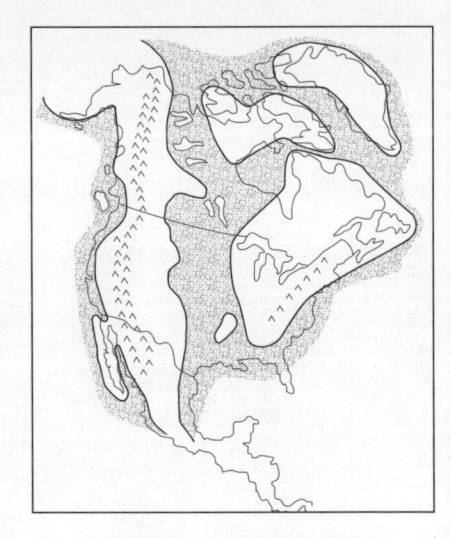

For almost 40 million years, until near the end of the Age of Dinosaurs, the Western Interior Seaway split North America in two.

43

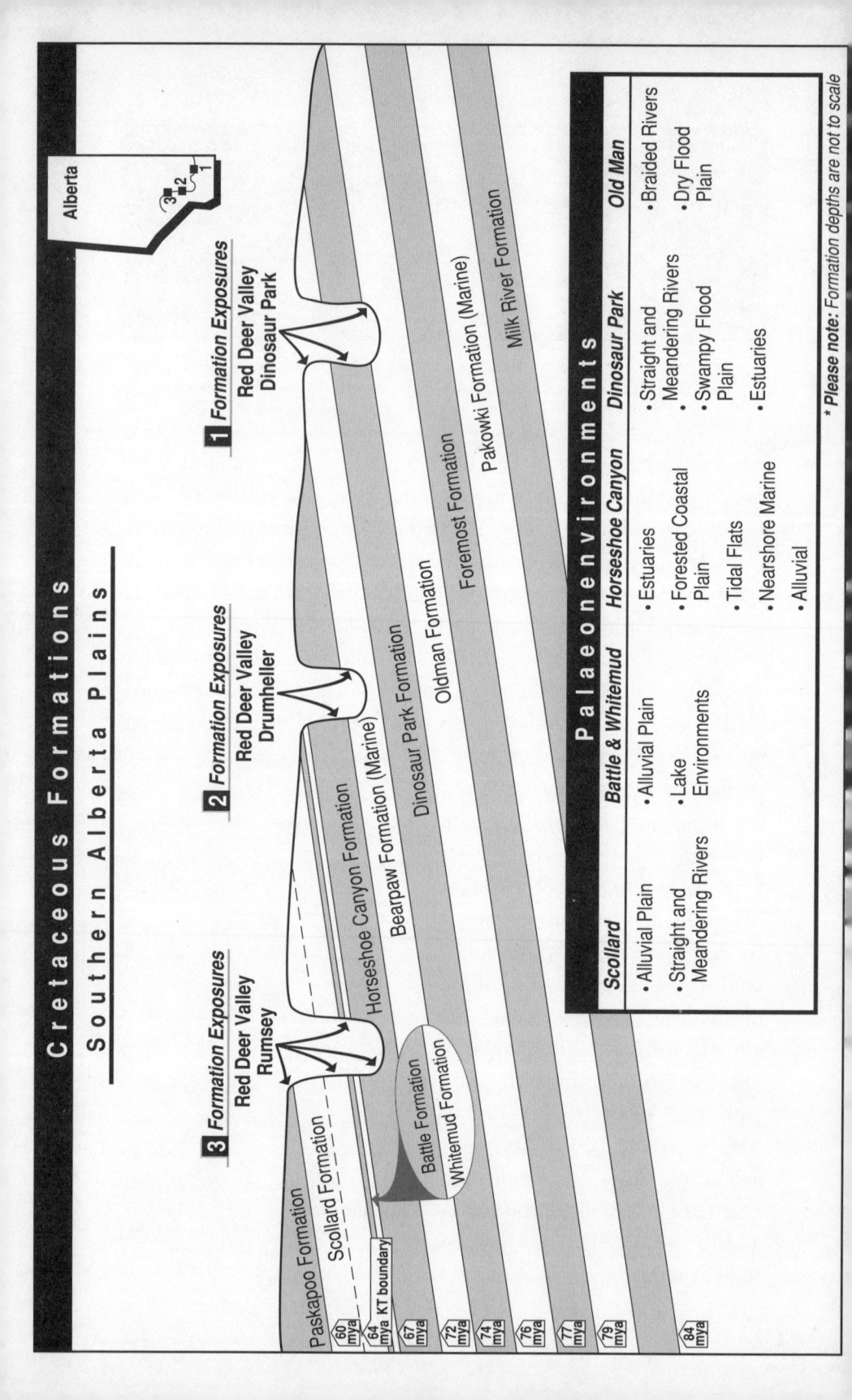

Cretaceous Formations
Southern Alberta Plains

Formation Exposures 1: Red Deer Valley — Dinosaur Park

Formation Exposures 2: Red Deer Valley — Drumheller

Formation Exposures 3: Red Deer Valley — Rumsey

Formations (top to bottom / youngest to oldest):
- Paskapoo Formation
- Scollard Formation
- Battle Formation
- Whitemud Formation
- Horseshoe Canyon Formation
- Bearpaw Formation (Marine)
- Dinosaur Park Formation
- Oldman Formation
- Foremost Formation
- Pakowki Formation (Marine)
- Milk River Formation

Time markers: 60 mya, 64 mya KT boundary, 67 mya, 72 mya, 74 mya, 76 mya, 77 mya, 79 mya, 84 mya

Palaeoenvironments

Scollard	Battle & Whitemud	Horseshoe Canyon	Dinosaur Park	Old Man
• Alluvial Plain • Straight and Meandering Rivers	• Alluvial Plain • Lake Environments	• Estuaries • Forested Coastal Plain • Tidal Flats • Nearshore Marine • Alluvial	• Straight and Meandering Rivers • Swampy Flood Plain • Estuaries	• Braided Rivers • Dry Flood Plain

* Please note: Formation depths are not to scale

The subtly-hued strata that chronicle events in the life and times of Late Cretaceous Alberta are organized by geologists into two groups of formations. The term 'formation' does not refer to the erose contours of the badlands. Rather, it is the term used by geologists to delineate a geological unit in which various strata are related to one another in a particular way. Several similarly related formations may be assembled, as they are here, into a larger unit called a group. The exposures seen in Dinosaur Provincial Park are part of the Judith River Group. In ascending order, from the river up, are the Oldman and Dinosaur Park Formations. An earlier member of the group, the Foremost Formation, is not exposed here but is known from other areas of southern Alberta. Events recorded in these strata took place during the Campanian age of the Late Cretaceous Period.

The Bearpaw Formation, also of Campanian age but of marine rather than continental origin, overlies the Dinosaur Park Formation. It acts as a chronological divider between the Judith River Group and the Edmonton Group, which is visible in the Drumheller area north. There the story continues in the Horseshoe Canyon Formation and the Whitemud, Battle and Scollard Formations.

Rock records show an age-old struggle between land and sea for dominance of Alberta. About 80 million years ago, the land was pushing back the waters once again. With each successive upward paroxysm of the coastal mountains, tonnes of sediments were produced. Rushing east-flowing rivers, fed by heavy rainfall, brought these loose sediments tumbling into the depression of the seaway. The rate of deposition was high and, although the seaway trough continued to sink throughout this time, the shoreline advanced along its western edge. The Foremost Formation, exposed southeast of Dinosaur Provincial Park, contains both marine and non-marine deposits which register a low-lying estuarine environment in very close proximity to the inland sea. Oyster beds abound and sharks' teeth, turtle shell and crocodile teeth are its more common fossils.

The layered bedrock exposed in Dinosaur Provincial Park, from the level of the Red Deer River to the prairie above, was formed

Aquatic, crocodile-like champsosaurs had narrow jaws lined with very sharp teeth. They were heavy boned and may have preyed on fish and amphibians at the bottom of streams.

from the silts, sands and clays of these and subsequent deposits. It contains a record of about two and a half million years of events under the influence of the inland sea. The lowest formation, which can be seen as striations of yellowish sandstones and dun-coloured mudstones in the area of the Field Station, is the Oldman. It is about 30 metres thick and, at its base, is dated at about 77 million years. It documents a time when, after a few million years of materials being transferred from the west, a broad alluvial plain was established. It was about five hundred kilometres wide and extended at least as far south as present-day New Mexico. For about twenty-five hundred kilometres from north to south, the dinosaurs were at home.

A drainage network of shallow fast-flowing rivers and sandy tributary streams ran north-eastward across the plain. Intermittent wet and dry periods occurred. Vegetation on the floodplains probably consisted of brush and small stands of trees. Non-marine molluscs are common fossils in this formation indicating the presence of ponds and fresh water lakes. It is rare to find well-articulated dinosaur fossils in the Oldman Formation but there is an abundance of fragmented plant and animal material. Taphonomists, who investigate factors affecting an organism from the time of its death until it is exhumed as a fossil, have found evidence of various reasons for the damage. It was a period when the Alberta Basin was not sinking very much and the wide shallow rivers were not carrying heavy burdens of sediments. Burials were probably superficial, making it likely that carcasses were disturbed when rivers dried up during spells of drought or altered their channels when huge amounts of water arrived in the form of flash floods.

Above the Oldman lies the Dinosaur Park Formation. Events dating from 76.5 to 74.5 million years ago are deciphered from its 80-metre-thick grey sandstones, reddish siltstones, green-grey claystones and narrow black bands of coal. The shore line of the coastal plain was always unstable. The presence in the park of sharks' teeth and marine plesiosaur fossils suggest that, during this

This sunlit hill in Dinosaur Provincial Park shows clear demarcations between the sedimentary rock layers that constitute the geological formations of the badlands.

time, the area was connected by major river channels to the nearby sea. In the soft sands and silts through which the rivers now ran in a southeasterly direction, they altered their courses often. Shallow lakes formed in the channels they abandoned. Frequently, at times of high water in the rainy season, they overflowed their banks. Where the coarser materials of the flooding waters collected, levees formed. Finer muds and silts were deposited beyond the levees and covered huge areas of the broad floodplains.

Lapped by the shallow waters of the sea, the area no longer experienced dry seasons. Warmth and humidity encouraged the growth of abundant vegetation. In general character, the climate and landscape bore comparison with today's northern Florida and the Gulf States of the United States. Many of the plants were early versions of those familiar today. It seems to have been an environment very suitable to the needs of dinosaurs. Over forty different species have been identified from the strata of Dinosaur Provincial Park.

These fossilized cones and imprints of seed pod and leaf are from
a metasequoia, a tree closely related to California's redwoods

---

It is from the lower half of the Dinosaur Park Formation that the majority of complete and well-articulated dinosaur skeletons has come. Understanding the geological events that promoted this successful preservation is one of the professional interests of Dr. David Eberth, Curator of Sedimentary Geology at the Royal Tyrrell Museum of Palaeontology. His studies suggest that, during the period recorded in these strata, tectonic activity was once again stirring up large volumes of sediments which were accumulating on a sinking estuarine plain. The shoreline had retreated from Saskatchewan into Alberta and the effects of tidal backwaters were felt far upstream in coastal rivers. Seasonal storms brought extensive flooding. In combination, these conditions were very favourable to the quick and thorough burial of carcasses. The most important factor assuring the fine condition in which the skeletons are found is the fact that once buried they stayed put. This is explained by the fact that the subsidence rate of the Alberta Basin was higher than that at which the river channels were cutting down into underlying sediments. The result was that opportunities for moving the skeletons about were reduced. This one-step interment also accounts for the frequent finding of skin impressions in dinosaur quarries.

Alberta's Late Cretaceous Landscapes

The shorelines advanced and retreated many times during the long period under discussion. At least twice during the mainly terrestrial time registered in Dinosaur Provincial Park, water covered the area. Its final flooding took place about 74 million years ago when southern Alberta was submerged under the shallow waters of the Bearpaw Sea, the ultimate manifestation of the Western Interior Seaway.

From the park's 10-metre-thick Bearpaw Formation exposures of brown and grey marine sediments comes a complement of fossils that show life in the sea was remarkable and varied. Two sorts of plesiosaurs, survivors from Jurassic times, plied the waters. There

In a manner similar to today's sea turtles, this short-necked plesiosaur used its strong flippers to propel itself through the waters of the Bearpaw Sea.

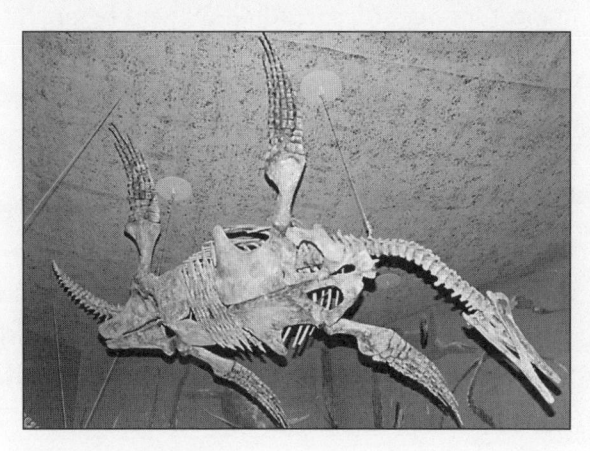

were long-necked elasmosaurs and short-necked pliosaurs, both equipped with strong paddles. Another type of marine reptile was the large, long-bodied, tough-toothed mosasaur, a relative of modern lizards. Fish of all sorts, including shark, were there, along with beautiful coiled ammonites, tubular baculites and many other molluscs.

In the introduction to this book, in order to take in the lay of the land, we floated down the Red Deer River into this, the oldest burial ground in the valley. It is useful now to reverse and go upriver towards Drumheller. Fifteen kilometres below the city, where Willow Creek flows into the Red Deer is the site of the famous hoodoos on which a striking transition can be seen. The lower portions of the pillars are made up of the grey-brown marine deposits of the Bearpaw Formation. Then, as though set with precision on top of this, is a layer of whitish grey siltstone of continental origin. This layer belongs to the Horseshoe Canyon Formation. Registered in this part of the valley, from below Drumheller to as far north as Big Valley, are the events of the Maastrichtian Age of the Cretaceous Period, from 72 to 64 million years ago.

Throughout the time the Bearpaw Sea covered what is now southern Alberta, dinosaurs and other animals moved northwards and westwards in advance of the encroaching waters. Heavy plant cover in Alberta's bush country hides most fossil evidence of them. Between 72 and 71 million years ago, rivers on this land mass fanned out southward, spreading deposits before them. The northern shoreline eventually reached to where Drumheller is situated to day.

For thousands of years, the area was covered by boggy swamps. In still, poorly-drained backwaters, plants died and decayed, muds washed over them, new vegetation sprang up, and the process began anew. Heavy peat deposits piled up. These were to form some of the thick coal seams on which Drumheller's mining industry was founded. The lower third of the 200-metre-thick Horseshoe Canyon Formation dates to this time.Conditions under which plants become fossils are often not conducive to the fossilization of bone. Animal fossils are not plentiful in the sediments left by these bogs.

The sea was a constant presence, continuously altering the coastline. North of Drumheller in Horsethief Canyon, there are lime-rich oyster beds indicative of a major rise in the sea level which brought about the infringement of salt water bays upon the land.

As more sediments accumulated, drainage improved and the swamps began to dry up. They were replaced by dense hardwood forests that sheltered thick undergrowths of ferns and wild flowers. Tree ferns, redwoods, needle-leaf pines, and palm-like cycads were all a part of the varied landscape. The upper two-thirds of the Formation are rich in evidence of plant and animal life on the coastal plain, with dinosaurs dominating the faunal assemblages.

The diversified habitats of the forested coastal plain supported members of every group of dinosaurs known to have existed in the earlier time represented in Dinosaur Provincial Park. The quality of skeletons found in the upper two-thirds of the Horseshoe Canyon Formation approaches those from the Dinosaur Park Formation. To date, fewer genera of dinosaurs have been found in the Drumheller area. Fewer small animals and fish fossils have been located here, too. This has persuaded some palaeontologists to the view that the dying off of the dinosaurs was gradual and may have taken place over several millions of years. However, this seeming decline may be more illusory than real. Research is now being carried out to determine its significance.

Thin white strata of the Whitemud Formation are visible above the Horseshoe Canyon sediments at Drumheller. They tell of the activity of volcanoes in Montana and the subsequent deposition of their sediments over the flat low-lying coastal plain of Alberta and Saskatchewan. Frequent volcanic eruptions are registered too in the layers of dark clays that make up the Battle Formation. These two formations reflect a time of very low rates of subsidence and sediment deposition, conditions not conducive to the fossilization of dinosaur skeletons. Although few animal remains are found, coprolites (fossilized feces) attributed to dinosaurs are present. It has been suggested that both the absence of shells and bones and the abundance of coprolites may have been caused by chemical processes involved in consolidating the deposits. Plant fossils are important in these strata. The popular panoramic view of Horseshoe Canyon is a good place to observe the three lower members of the Edmonton Group.

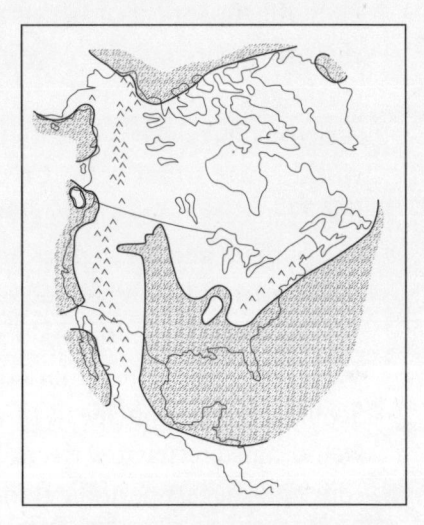

Near the end of the Age of Dinosaurs, the global sea level was dropping and the shoreline of the plain lay over 700 km southeast of the Red Deer River valley.

Further upstream, from Tolman Bridge north to Dry Island Buffalo Jump Provincial Park, the largest expanse of Scollard Formation exposures occurs. In some places, the thickness of the beds is 80 metres. The bottom half of this unit dates from the Late Maastrichtian Age of the Late Cretaceous Period, about 65 million years ago. These exposures, which yield the youngest Cretaceous fossils of the Red Deer valley, are less extensive than the ones in either the Drumheller or Dinosaur Provincial Park areas. This has meant that the rewards for dinosaur hunters were harder won. Historically, less time has been devoted to exploration here but as the emphasis in the fossil hunt has changed in the last few decades, current enquiries have turned the spotlight on it.

The two approximate halves of the formation are divided by a thin tan-coloured layer of clay that occurs just below the Nevis coal seam, one of 13 coal horizons in the Edmonton Group. Unremarkable in appearance, this narrow layer of clay holds important clues to events taking place at the time of the mass extinction. It marks the Cretaceous/Tertiary boundary. Above it, no dinosaur skeletons have ever been found. There are very few places in the world where strata of the Cretaceous are overlain by deposits from the Palaeocene Age of the Tertiary Period. It happens that this is one of them and, as such, is an extremely important area for investigations into the extinction event.

The thick layers of pale sandstones and thin layers of dun-coloured and brown mudstones that make up the lower interval of the Scollard Formation speak of a time when this was a broad plain, well-drained by narrow rivers The mudstones derive from floodplain soils and suggest periodic flooding and wet and dry climatic cycles.

The diversity of the dinosaurs recovered from these beds is diminished as compared with the varieties found in the valley's older formations. Whether this is indicative of diminishing strength among dinosaurs as a group or is simply a result of poor fossil records attributable to environmental conditions or biases in collection is part of the ongoing research program at the Royal Tyrrell, referred to above. Articulated dinosaur specimens are quite rare but about 12 different taxa have been identified from microfossil sites. These are sites that feature accumulations of skeletal fragments, some of which are sufficiently intact to be diagnostic of the

Alberta's Late Cretaceous Landscapes

Life in the Bearpaw Sea

Top: Left - the internal shell of a squid. Centre - Clams burrowed in soft bottom muds. These impressions of opened shells are evidence of a time when some disaster forced them from their burrows and they met with a mass death. Right - Trace fossils of shrimp burrows.

Centre: Shell fish and other organisms are preserved in ironstone concretions found in marine deposits. The long tapering baculite, on the left, was probably free-floating but may have moved short distances by water-jet propulsion.

Bottom: The mosasaur was more than 15 metres long. Its strong jaws and sharp teeth indicate it was a fierce predator in the Cretaceous sea. It was a relative of today's monitor lizard.

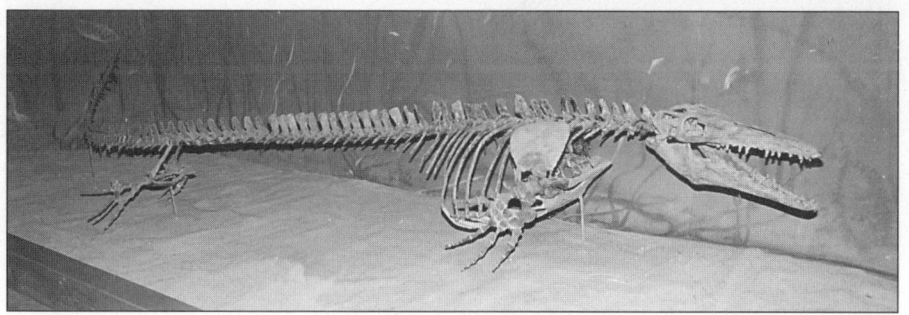

animal they came from. Mammal fossils are of more evolutionarily advanced groups than those found in the older sediments of the valley. The remains are mostly of placental mammals, whereas those collected from the Dinosaur Provincial Park beds are predominantly of marsupials.

Each of the above descriptions is like the backdrop of a diorama in a museum, an effort to describe, with some small degree of truth, a moment in the millions of years it represents. Before adding suitable dinosaurs to animate the ancient plains, the next chapter takes a look at how perceptions of the animals have developed and changed in the 150 years since humans first became aware of their existence.

6

Dinosaurs Reborn

Dinosaurs made their first public debut in 1854 when models of an *Iguanodon* and a *Megalosaurus* were unveiled on the grounds of the Crystal Palace in Sydenham, south of London, as part of a geological exhibit. It was little more than a decade earlier that the noted scientist Richard Owen had named and described dinosaurs on the basis of a few fossilized bones and teeth found in the English countryside. From the limited knowledge of the beasts' appearance provided by this paucity of material, the sculptor Benjamin Waterhouse Hawkins, under Owen's direction, painstakingly fashioned the *Iguanodon* and *Megalosaurus* and unveiled them to scrutiny. Not surprisingly, the populace was enchanted. Interest in the natural sciences was widespread among the intelligentsia. This was the decade that saw the publication of Darwin's On the Origin of Species. For the general public, the notion of prehistoric reptiles swarming over the land prior to the biblical flood had all the appeal of novelty.

One of the social events heralding the arrival of the New Year in London was a dinner held in the interior of the partially completed *Iguanodon*. The party must have had some of the flavour of Jonah's miraculous sojourn in the belly of the whale! Space in the torso for tables and chairs and milling guests was provided by dint

This 19th-century concrete *Megalosaurus* may still be seen in a park in London, England.

of the fact that the reconstruction was entirely inaccurate. The animal was firmly planted on four approximately equal, massive sprawling legs with elephantine feet. A decorative flourish was added by a small, sharp spike on the end of the snout. It was almost a quarter of a century later that several *Iguanodon* skeletons were uncovered in a Belgian coal mine. It soon became apparent, from this wealth of fossil material, that the living animal had been decidedly bipedal and the spike was an accoutrement of the hand, not of the nose.

The unlikely product of a model based upon a few bones and a lot of imagination is a thing of the past. It is now more than a century and a half since dinosaur bones were first recognized; and in this time, many complete skeletons have been collected and masses of fossil specimens added to the shelves of museum laboratories for study. The physical structures of many of the known dinosaurs are determined on ample evidence. The size and shape and the articulation of the bones provide the clues to the framework of the skeleton. How the muscles and tendons were attached to this foundation is observable from marks left on the bones. The outer covering is fashioned following the lead taken from skin impressions preserved in rock. Dinosaurs left their footprints, now set in stone. These tell not only where they went, but how, and at what pace.

In the early years of dinosaur palaeontology, intense energies were channelled into the search for new genera and species. These

Dinosaurs Reborn

A large number of dinosaur trackways were preserved from the Peace River Canyon of northeastern British Columbia. These were left by a duck-billed dinosaur. Nearby, but not in the picture, are footprints of a carnivorous dinosaur and the earliest known tracks of birds in Alberta.

were the halcyon days of bone hunting when museums were competing feverishly for first-rate exhibition specimens. In the furor of the hunt and the subsequent concentration upon recreating the appearance of the animals in life from the recovered bones, questions about how the dinosaurs lived took third place. This is not to say that no attention was paid to this problem; it was simply a matter of emphasis. Skull anatomy identified dinosaurs as reptiles so it was assumed that they would have behaved as reptiles, even though they were noted to have skeletal features that were birdlike and their limbs did not quite fit the reptile pattern. But then, there was the matter of food. The amount necessary to sustain an animal of dinosaur size boggled the imagination. For this reason, it seemed that only with geared-down reptilian metabolism could the largest dinosaurs hope to eke out an existence.

And so emerged the traditional view of the dinosaur as a lethargic, sprawling hulk, basking in the sun on the bank of a tropical swamp, waddling in and out of the water as the need arose. It hardly seemed surprising such sluggishness was punished by extinction. Once our awe at their enormous size melted away, dinosaurs remained for us something of an evolutionary curiosity but public fascination with them slipped away beneath the waters of the archaic swamp.

Fortunately, scholars are not quite so fickle as the general public. Although dinosaurs may have suffered some loss of popularity, they were never completely abandoned. Working quietly, palaeontologists continued to amass knowledge about dinosaurs and their world. The 1969 description of the light-bodied, agile little predator, *Deinonychus,* introduced a spirited reappraisal of the animals. New looks were taken at the old bones. Accepted theories were reassessed and refined. Intense activity in the field kept pace with laboratory investigations. More than half of all the dinosaurs known have been described since 1970. Changing ideas that had been percolating in scientific back rooms bubbled up to the level of public attention and dinosaurs, once again, moved into the spotlight. It seemed that while our attention was diverted elsewhere, facts were assembling to topple our long-held view of the dinosaur. The stereotype of the stupid, oversized, solitary slug was cast out in exchange for a bright, gregarious, active, graceful warm-blood, a creature that escaped eternal extinction by evolving into a bird. If it all sounds a bit like Ovid's <u>Metamorphoses,</u> rest assured that much good evidence is put forward to support the case for the new dinosaur.

Many palaeontologists now believe that the linkage of dinosaurs with reptiles, in fact the very name "terrible lizard," has cast them in a blinkered light. In many important ways, dinosaurs are more similar to mammals and birds than they are to reptiles. One feature that distinguishes them from modern reptiles is their upright carriage. The limbs of all dinosaurs to a greater or lesser degree support the body from beneath whereas today's reptiles squat on legs that project sideways from the torso. An erect posture implies mobility.

Preoccupation with the giants among the dinosaurs has been tempered in more recent years by a closer study of the smaller members of the race. Skeletal structures that these exhibit include such things as hollow bones, large brain capacity and long legs, the faculties of active, fast-moving animals. Recent reconstructions of some of the larger dinosaurs indicate that, in spite of their tonnage, they too probably enjoyed locomotor freedom similar to that of large modern mammals.

Adaptations for mobility and, especially, for rapid movement suggest to some palaeontologists that dinosaurs were possessed of much higher body metabolisms than were their reptile cohorts. In fact, declares one widely discussed theory, they were not cold-blooded at all but fully warm-blooded.

In his book <u>Dinosaur Hunters</u>, David Spalding credits Loris Russell, who was associated with the Royal Ontario Museum and the National Museum of Canada (as director of the latter from 1957-63), with being the first to suggest, in 1956, that dinosaurs were warm-blooded. There was little reaction from his colleagues to what may be seen as a startling departure from orthodox thinking about dinosaurs. Perhaps, it was an idea born prematurely. Its time had apparently come two decades later, when an article arguing forcefully for its acceptance was published in <u>Scientific American</u> by Robert Bakker of Johns Hopkins University. Very soon thereafter, warm-bloodedness became something of a hot potato in palaeontological circles. Those who are adamant in its defence argue that the success of the dinosaurs was based upon endothermy. They say the mammals would have superseded the dinosaurs far sooner had the dinosaurs not been metabolically equipped for their dominant life. They marshal several pieces of empirical evidence in support of this theory of warm-blooded dinosaurs.

For one thing, the Mesozoic Era as 185 million years of uninterrupted tropicality is no longer tenable. Examination of the deposits in which dinosaurs have been found indicates climatic conditions were much more variable. Remains of most groups of Late Cretaceous dinosaurs have been discovered above the Arctic Circle; and while temperatures then would not have been as cold as they now are, they were considerably cooler than in the lands farther south. The length of the days varied much as they do now. A cold-blooded reptile probably could not have survived so far from the equator through prolonged periods of darkness. It has been suggested that the dinosaurs may have migrated seasonally. Either one of these courses, life within the Arctic region or migration, would be easier for an animal with internal heat regulation.

Studies in which fossilized bone tissue has been compared microscopically with the bone tissue of living animals show that, in its fine structure, dinosaur bone is similar to mammal bone. The bone tissue in both is rich in canals that aid in the transfer of calcium from the blood stream to the skeleton. This tissue is not found in most living reptiles, although there are exceptions. Critics of this theory point to the exceptions and argue that the connection between the presence of this bone tissue and endothermy is questionable. They suggest it may be related to something else entirely, such as body weight or the strength needed to support the skeleton.

Perhaps no argument put forth by the proponents of endothermy is quite so contentious as that of predator/prey ratios. Comparisons made within communities of living animals have shown that a predatory mammal requires a much larger number of kills to support its active life than does a reptilian predator of the same size. The ratio of predators to prey in a mammal community is 1:20. Extrapolating from this knowledge, palaeontologists have conducted similar studies on fossils and found that the ratio of carnivorous to herbivorous dinosaurs corresponded closely to the predator/prey ratio of living mammals. From this evidence, they conclude that dinosaurs, at least carnivorous ones, were warm-blooded. But, say the detractors, the results of these studies are dubious because of the many variable factors in the fossil record. Some types of dinosaurs are fossilized more readily than others and fossil counts may not accurately reflect the once living populations. Coupled with this is the contention that samples are prejudiced by the possibility of collecting biases. Concentrating upon large well-preserved specimens, earlier counts tended to ignore the fragmentary evidence of other individual dinosaurs.

The idea that such a study has value has not been abandoned. Palaeontologists working at the Royal Tyrrell Museum of Palaeontology, for example, now make note of all specimens discovered, whether or not they are collected. The intent is to produce, over several years, an unbiased sample that will give a more accurate measure of the predators and prey present in the sediments. Perhaps studies of this sort will help to resolve some of the current uncertainties about dinosaur metabolism.

Those who trumpet warm-bloodedness are diametrically opposed by a diminishing group of palaeontologists who hold to the thesis "all dinosaurs are reptiles, therefore no dinosaurs are warm-blooded." Between the two camps is a much larger group who counsel caution and a rigorous scrutiny of available data. They say that to substitute a new orthodoxy for the old would do nothing to further an understanding of dinosaur life. The moderate position is that while some dinosaurs were probably endothermic, it does not follow that all were. Gaining ground is the idea that dinosaurs may have possessed their own unique physiology, somewhat different from that of either reptiles or mammals.

Intertwined with, and supporting, the theory of the warm-blooded dinosaur is the more interesting one that dinosaurs never really became extinct. Rather, they evolved and are still with us—in the form of birds. At first glance, the connection between *Tyrannosaurus* and the hummingbird seemed to stretch credulity. However, with the passage of twenty years during which accumulating evidence has lent weight to the hypothesis, it no longer seems quite so preposterous. After all, it is not from the largest of dinosaurs that birds are believed to have descended but from a small theropod like *Deinonychus*.

The bird connection has had a profound effect upon the way in which the dinosaur family tree is assembled because it led scientists to take a more rigorous look at relationships between birds and the various groups of dinosaurs, and then between one group of dinosaurs and another. Classification of the enormous variety of organisms that have inhabited the Earth since life began has been a pursuit of scientific interest since the 1700s. The Linnaean system was

Dromiceiomimus measured about three metres. It had a light build and could run very fast. Its long tapering fingers may have been used to clear away brush to reveal a meal of tasty insects.

instituted at that time and has been used ever since, with many modifications over the years. Very recently, it has been largely supplanted by a new filing process known as phylogenetic systematics or, alternatively, cladistics.

The theory of evolution presupposes that life arose once and only once and that reproduction from that beginning accounts for all ensuing life. It follows, then, that all living things are related in some way to all others. Biological systematics strive to clarify these relationships.

Proponents of cladistics believe that its approach more accurately reflects evolutionary change by viewing it as a branching process (using the metaphor of a tree) rather than as a progression from the lowliest form upward (metaphor of a ladder) as the Linnaean system does. Cladistics groups organisms on the basis of shared genealogical traits derived from their most recent common ancestor. The group thus defined is called a taxon or clade. The word clade means branch and a treelike cladogram is used to illustrate relationships of organisms and the relative time of their branching from the ancestral stem.

Dinosaurs Reborn

The methodology for hypothesizing the make-up of a clade is quite exacting and the most problematic aspect of phylogenetic systematics. It depends upon the analysis of skeletal diagnostic features and, although computers are used extensively in this work, it is sometimes difficult to reach consensus about which features legitimately define the group under consideration. It is fair to say that the whole subject of dinosaur classification is in flux. One thing certain is that many of the details in the tidy charts you might meet with in earlier publications (the first edition of this book included) no longer prevail. As an example, that most famous of all dinosaurs, *Tyrannosaurus rex*, recently moved from the company of the carnosaurs to join the coelurosaurs, a group of small, fierce theropods. Bone-headed pachycephalosaurs have revealed that they are more closely related to horned dinosaurs than to the duck-bills,

Although outwardly very different, tyrannosaurs are now thought to be closely related to ornithomimids, of which *Dromiceiomimus* is a member

as was formerly believed. And so it goes. Perhaps part of the deep fascination dinosaurs have for us is tied up in the fact that, in spite of being so long dead, they are still energetic and full of surprises.

There are some biologists who are not completely won over to the cladistic system of classification, although the voices of protest seem to be growing fainter. We outsiders may think that the differences are negligible in that the classification business is really just a filing system, but the case of the dinosaur - bird connection serves to demonstrate that there is an underlying philosophical difference between the two systems.

It is important to say, first of all, that although there are exceptions, most palaeontologists, certainly those who specialize in dinosaurs, accept the descent of birds from small theropods. Under the cladistics system, it follows that birds must form a clade with this particular group of dinosaurs before being taken branch by branch into all the parent clades to which theropods belong: back to Dinosauria, Reptilia and beyond.

Traditionalists balk at the classification of birds as reptiles when living examples of each are clearly so different in a functional sense— this in spite of skull and limb structures that establish a close relationship between them. They feel that, after branching, birds diverged profoundly from their dinosaur ancestors and made a huge evolutionary transformation. Birds learned to fly while dinosaurs remained earthbound, so taking biological structure and behaviour into account and giving those factors equal weight with direct ancestry, it seems right to these systematists that dinosaurs be left with reptiles and birds retain their separate group, Aves.

The opposing camp counters that physiology is a separate concern from that of classification, which should be based solely on direct ancestry. One of the drawbacks to establishing connections such as the dinosaur - bird one is the fact that fossil bones tell only a limited story about the biology of the living entity of which they were once a component. One imagines that, if the thesis that dinosaurs were warm-blooded were to gain general acceptance, including birds in a clade with dinosaurs would seem no more odd than recognizing bats as mammals.

After a century and a half of the "terrible lizard" slouching along, he has become old hat. An active dinosaur poised on the evolutionary brink of flight has tremendous appeal. But remember the Crystal Palace *Iguanodon*. Palaeontology is a creative science; its practitioners work to piece together a cohesive whole from a gathering of scattered parts. There are still many questions about how the animals lived and died, so it seems the fervour to find the answers will continue. What this means is that an hypothesis that meets with favour today may be thrown aside tomorrow. This may come about because of new fossil discoveries. It may also result from the fact that there are many more people working in specialized areas in the field of palaeontology today than there were a few decades ago. The more information brought to the subject and the more minds that sift through and interpret it, the more dynamic, and therefore always changing, the topic of dinosaurs becomes.

The following chapters discuss the Red Deer River valley dinosaurs and their family connections to other parts of the world. According them their place in the food chain, herbivorous dinosaurs—hadrosaurs, ceratopsians, pachycephalosaurs and ankylosaurs—lead off, followed by the carnivorous tyrannosaurs and a complement of their small, fierce relatives.

7

Hadrosaurs:
The Duck-Billed Dinosaurs

Hadrosaur fossils are the most widespread and plentiful of any dinosaur group. Their remains have been found in almost all parts of the world, from Alaska and the Yukon in the north to the southern extreme of Antarctica. The rock formations in which they are buried were formed from sediments of quite diverse ecosystems, implying that they were adaptable to a range of habitat. The Red Deer River valley fields are particularly rich in hadrosaurs. Their skeletons here are numerous and well-preserved.

Gigantic members of the hadrosaur family have been found in other sites but not, to date, in the Red Deer River region. Bear in mind that the term "giant" has a somewhat coloured meaning when dinosaurs are being discussed. The hadrosaurs found in the fossil beds of the Red Deer could hardly be termed diminutive. As adults, they are estimated to have weighed from two to four metric tonnes and measured six to ten metres in length. Size and numbers secured a dominant presence for them in the Late Cretaceous landscapes.

One of their number, an *Edmontosaurus*, provided the first dinosaur skeleton mounted for exhibition in Canada. It is affixed to a wall in the Canadian Museum of Nature in Ottawa. The fossil bones are arranged much as they were discovered in 1912 in the Horseshoe Canyon Formation on Michichi Creek, north of Drumheller.

Hadrosaurs: The Duck-Billed Dinosaurs

Describing his son's find, the paleontologist Charles H. Sternberg wrote, "The animal lay like a dead dog. I thought I had never seen anything so pitiful and forlorn." The skeleton curls in upon itself, the hind legs drawn up to shield the belly, the front limbs limply disposed toward the knees. The head hangs low. Found complete, but for the tail which was reconstructed from bones of another of the same species, the skeleton measures nearly ten metres in length. So large and yet so vulnerable, the essence of the living creature is poignantly distilled in the pathetic pose of death.

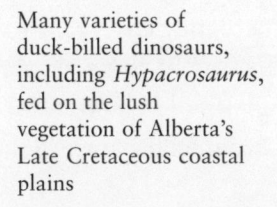

Many varieties of duck-billed dinosaurs, including *Hypacrosaurus*, fed on the lush vegetation of Alberta's Late Cretaceous coastal plains

In life, the hadrosaur was a gentle being. Of all the dinosaurs known, it seems the least equipped for aggression. It possessed no lethal weapons in the line of claws or horns. It has been suggested the hadrosaurs probably played a role similar to that assumed today by the deer family. The large head of the hadrosaur was supported by a long, flexible neck. The flat, elongated jaw was wide and rounded at the front like the beak of a duck, hence the name, "duck-bill."

Theories of how the hadrosaurs lived have come full circle since the first discoveries of their remains in the mid-1800s. When you consider that studies of patterns of behaviour in living animals in their natural habitats often leave questions unanswered and yield conflicting interpretations among naturalists, it should come as no surprise that the habits of animals known only from their fossilized remains are elusive. The approach to the truth about these ancient beasts is halting and subject to change as new information surfaces.

It was first proposed, based upon the disparity in the size of the limbs, that the hadrosaur was something of a hybrid between a kangaroo and a giraffe. According to this model, the animal hopped from place to place, and when it stopped to stretch its neck up to nibble on the foliage overhead, its heavy tail served as a prop. It was supposed, since it seemed otherwise defenceless, it must have had some sort of armour to keep it safe from predators.

At the beginning of this century, the discovery in Wyoming of a mummified specimen, with extensive impressions of skin preserved in the rock, excited great interest among palaeontologists. Not armour plate but a mosaic of tubercles on a leathery hide covered the animal. They were too thin to offer much in the way of protection. Since that time the skin impressions of many duck-billed dinosaurs have been found in the deposits of Dinosaur Provincial Park.

Now in the American Museum of Natural History, this skeleton of the previously unknown hadrosaur, *Corythosaurus*, was excavated near Steveville in 1912 by Barnum Brown.

Hadrosaurs: The Duck-Billed Dinosaurs

It was noted from the Wyoming specimen that what seemed to be a mitt of skin encased the fingers of the hand. Smooth hide, webbed fingers and a broad flat tail, which could have been designed to propel a swimming animal, led to the theory that the hadrosaur spent most of its life in the lakes and marshes dotting its landscape. In keeping with this mode of existence, the beak, it was thought, was designed to clip the soft vegetation that grew in the hadrosaur's watery home.

"What's in a name?" one might ask. Could it be that, once this animal was labeled as "duck-billed," there was a tendency to carry the association with a duck further than the evidence could support? In any case, much of what was known from the fossils of hadrosaurs did not jibe well with the aquatic lifestyle theory. For

One of the flat-headed group of hadrosaurs, *Kritosaurus* is believed to have lived in well-drained terrain away from the coast. This specimen, from Dinosaur Provincial Park, is in the Royal Ontario Museum in Toronto.

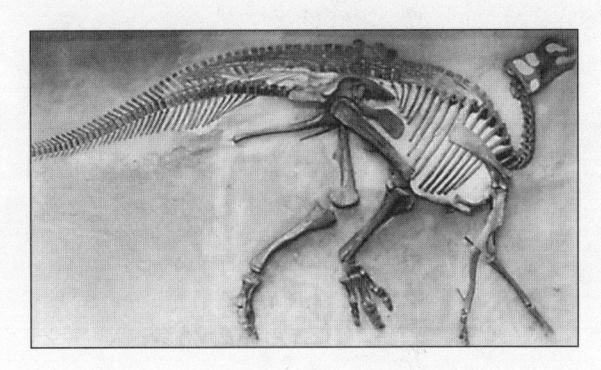

one thing, there were the hands and feet. Two of the three fingers of the hand ended in small hooves and the three-toed feet had hoof-like nails. What had earlier been interpreted as webs of skin between the fingers is now thought to have been impressions left by hoof pads. Hooves are an unlikely adaptation for life in the water.

Perhaps the most persuasive evidence to move palaeontologists back toward their first intuitions about the hadrosaur—that it was, indeed, a land-dweller—was its dental apparatus. The upper jaw was covered in a horny sheath. The 'beak' was toothless but the muscular cheeks contained row upon row of prism-shaped grinding teeth, densely packed in a pavement pattern. Below the functional teeth, as many as four complete sets were growing up to replace worn ones. An adult could have had over 1000 teeth in the mouth at any one

> ## Hadrosaurs from the Red Deer River Valley
>
> <u>Flat-Headed Hadrosaurs (hadrosaurines)</u>
> From Dinosaur Park Formations:
> *Brachylophosaurus* "short crested lizard"
> *Gryposaurus* "hook-nosed lizard"
> *Kritosaurus* "noble lizard"
> *Prosaurolophus* "before Saurolophus"
>
> From Horseshoe Canyon Formation:
> *Edmontosaurus* "Edmonton lizard"
> *Saurolophus* "ridged lizard"
>
> From Scollard Formation:
> *Edmontosaurus*
>
>
> <u>Hollow-Crested Hadrosaurs (lambeosaurines)</u>
> From Dinosaur Park Formations:
> *Corythosaurus* "helmet lizard"
> *Lambeosaurus* "Lambe's lizard"
> *Parasaurolophus* "beside Saurolophus"
>
> From Horseshoe Canyon Formation:
> *Hypacrosaurus* "high ridge lizard"

time. Presumably, such a dental battery could process much tougher plants than those commonly growing in water.

Its ability as a swimmer has not been strongly debated. Based upon the fact that hadrosaur remains have been found in deposits of quite diverse origin, different species probably favoured different living conditions. Some may have lived near the water and been semi-aquatic whereas others may have been fully terrestrial. The front limbs were strong but slighter than, and about half the length of, the back limbs. Strongly muscled limbs and bony tendons at the base of the tail, which could allow it to serve as a horizontal balance, suggest the hadrosaur was capable of efficient locomotion on land. It is likely that it walked about on all fours browsing at what was within easy reach from this position, saving a bipedal stance for reaching up to nibble the leaves of trees or to sprint for a short distance at high speed to escape its enemies.

Highly developed senses alerted the hadrosaur to danger. A large eye socket suggests keen eyesight, and intricate inner ear canals attest to its ability to hear well. There is evidence, as we shall see, to suggest it had an acute sense of smell, also.

Although hadrosaurs had been discovered elsewhere before expeditions to the Red Deer began in earnest in 1910, the numbers and, more particularly, the diversity of hadrosaur fossils uncovered in these fields amazed the scientific world. The bodies of the beasts were all relatively similar to the description given above, but bone hunters were now unearthing a veritable potpourri of skulls. Flat headed ones and ones with hooded skulls were known but now, an array of hadrosaurs sporting fantastically shaped crests began to emerge. The crests were extensions of the skulls, sheathed in skin.

Understandably, palaeontologists were captivated by these beasts with their seemingly endless variety of decorative headdresses. As discovery followed upon discovery, each new species to join the known phalanx of hadrosaurs contributed another question mark to the puzzle of their existence. Why did some hadrosaurs appear to manage perfectly well with flat heads while others developed such extravagant features? If the raised crest was functional, why were there so many variations on the theme?

These questions were being mulled over when a specimen that added yet another dimension to

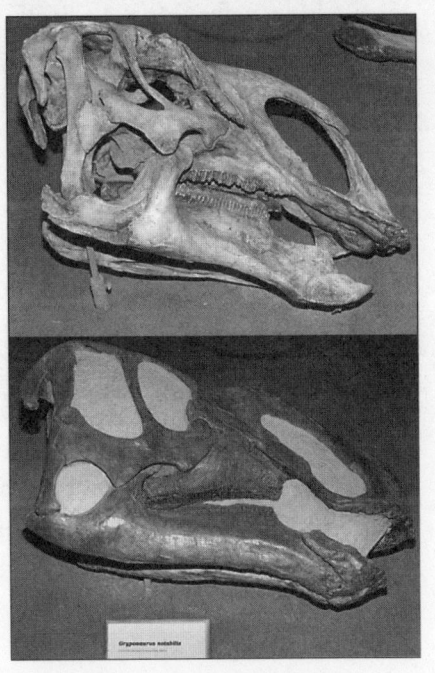

Flat-headed *Brachylophosaurus*, top, and *Gryposaurus*, bottom.

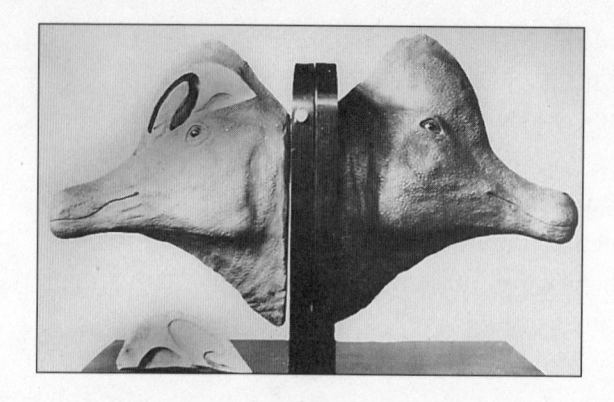

Model of a *Corythosaurus* with a cut-away skull showing the nasal passages characteristic of hollow-crested hadrosaurs.

the inquiry was discovered in the Dinosaur Park area. This was a skull of a *Corythosaurus*, of which one-half had been eroded. Nature's fortuitous bisection revealed that the ornate crest contained a hollow passage leading from the nostrils, following along the contours of the crest, and finally, looping back through the throat. It was subsequently learned that, although some of the hooded conformations were solid, others were designed along the lines of the hollow crest of *Corythosaurus*.

Over the years since the internal structure of these crests became known, speculations about their purpose have engrossed palaeontologists. A number of the theories put forth would apply only if it is assumed that these particular hadrosaurs not only lived in water but spent a good part of their time completely submerged and, therefore, required a device to allow underwater breathing. The hollow crest has been variously interpreted as a snorkel, as an air storage chamber, and as an intricate air lock to prevent water from entering the lungs. Problems were detected with each of these ideas and they all lost applicability once it was again accepted that the hadrosaur spent most of its life on land.

Now, conjectures about the possible purposes for the hollow crest altered. Given the need of a passive animal for means of self-preservation, it was suggested that the extended nasal passages were an adaptation to increase the amount of membranous lining tissue and, thereby, to enhance the sense of smell. What a pleasant notion this is. It is reassuring to imagine the docile hadrosaur thus equipped for a head start in a race with a fearsome carnivore bent on a kill.

Hadrosaurs: The Duck-Billed Dinosaurs

Given that the elongated cavity was, indeed, an organ of smell, the question still remains—why did so many different crest designs develop? One suggestion deals with an aspect of the dinosaur world rarely considered: that is, what sounds echoed through the populous swamps and forests? Perhaps, the passages in the crests were resonating chambers to produce characteristic calls by which each species recognized its own. Like a range of brass musical instruments, each tubular conformation may have produced its unique set of bellows to communicate fear or warning, pain or pleasure. Another possibility, one that could apply to both the flat-headed and hollow-crested varieties of hadrosaurs, is that the distinctive crests may have been the signposts by which the individual knew his close kin amongst the dense hadrosaur populations of the coastal plain.

Lambeosaurus was the first hollow-crested hadrosaur found in North America. It was named for Lawrence Lambe of the Geological Survey of Canada who, in 1898, discovered a partial skeleton near Berry Creek. The pictured skeleton was discovered and excavated by Charles M. Sternberg in 1937.

Many other early theories of dinosaurian behaviour have undergone change in the light of amassing evidence. All dinosaurs were once envisioned as solitary creatures but most palaeontologists now believe that at least some groups were of a more sociable nature. The numerous variations and the large numbers of hadrosaurs found

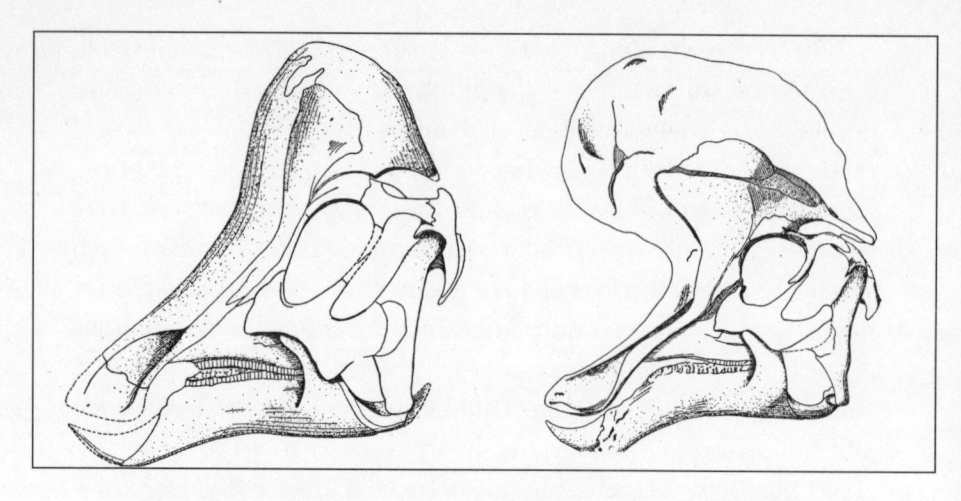

The hollow-crested *Hypacrosaurus* (left), known from the Horseshoe Canyon Formation, is probably a descendant of the earlier *Lambeosaurus* (right) from the Dinosaur Park Formation.

in the Red Deer River valley suggest they were herding animals. This theory gains support from footprints found in other parts of Alberta and British Columbia. There are hundreds of prints made by hadrosaurs of various sizes, arranged in trackways. Remains of hadrosaurs have been uncovered in the northern Yukon and Alaska, and the possibility has been put forward that the trackways are a trace of herd migration.

Another belief, long held, was that family life was nonexistent among dinosaurs. However, it seems now that there is considerable evidence to cast doubt on the model of the solitary reptile, devoid of concern for its offspring. As an example: small prints in proximity to larger ones in the hadrosaur trackways suggest that some degree of parental care was administered to youngsters in the herd.

It is one of those curious accidents of discovery that, although clutches of hadrosaur eggs had been found in other fields, in Alberta where the skeletons of hadrosaurs are more plentiful than anywhere else in the world, only fragments had shown up. Then in 1987, an important and exciting discovery was made, not in Dinosaur Provincial Park as might have been expected but in a small patch of badlands on the Milk River Ridge at Devil's Coulee, in the far southern part of the province. The discovery might have been

Hadrosaurs: The Duck-Billed Dinosaurs

delayed had it not been for the fact that the previous year, the Royal Tyrrell Museum had been called upon to conduct a palaeontological impact assessment prior to the building of a dam on the Milk River. Dr. Philip Currie and his staff were aware, from this visit, of evidence of baby dinosaur bones and thought there was a good possibility that further exploration, which they planned to undertake in the next field season, would lead them to some eggs. The depositional material, quite different from what is found in Dinosaur Provincial Park or Drumheller, was very similar to that in which an egg site had just that summer been located on the Montana side of the United States/Canadian border. The eggs were found in association with shellfish in deposits with an abundance of caliches, hard little balls of minerals that form in well drained, alkaline soils—soils with the right chemistry to preserve eggshell.

Just before the field party from the Museum was to set out, they were informed that Wendy Sloboda, a high-school student working in the area, had found a site with hundreds of broken egg shells. The search for intact eggs was undertaken with great enthusiasm but, alas, nothing but fragments of eggs and bones was turned up. Then, only a few days before the field crew was to return to Drumheller and other pressing commitments, they found three nests and a hillside of baby duckbill bones. And the best was yet to come; amidst a mass of broken eggs and more baby bones, one of the group, Kevin Aulenback, came upon eggs sectioned by erosion to expose tiny embryos within. "Exquisite preservation" is Currie's phrase for the find. Several more nests were

In this display, a meat-eating ornithomimid dinosaur is about to eat the eggs from the nest of an *Hypacrosaurus*. The eggs are from the Devil's Coulee site.

75

The route of complex internal passages in the tubular crest measured up to two metres in some *Parasaurolophus*.

discovered, some material collected for display in the museum at Drumheller and protection of the Devil's Coulee field assured by declaring it a Provincial Heritage Site. It now has an interpretation centre and is a stopping point on the Great Canadian Dinosaur Trail.

Research into material collected from Devil's Coulee has revealed that the nests belonged to a species of *Hypacrosaurus*. The many nests made by one type of animal indicate the site was probably a colonial rookery which saw repeated use. The nature of the rock is indicative of ancient arid or semi-arid habitat. This may mean that it was not very hospitable to many of the hadrosaurs' enemies and therefore offered a relatively safe place to which they retreated periodically to lay their eggs. The nests appear to have been in exposed places, another plug for maternal care in that large numbers of adults would have been required to protect the hatchlings from those predatory dinosaurs who did venture into the rookery and whose teeth have been found among the baby bones. Hatchlings from a similar site in Montana were found to have wear on their teeth, supposedly from chewing on regurgitated food brought to them by an adult. This implies a period of post-natal care.

It is interesting to note that no *Hypacrosaurus* species are known from the 76-million-year-old Dinosaur Park Formation which cor-

Hadrosaurs: The Duck-Billed Dinosaurs

relates in age to the deposits on the Milk River Ridge where the nests were found. However, *Hypacrosaurus* is known from the 71-million-year-old beds of the Horseshoe Canyon Formation at Drumheller.

Another inhabitant of Drumheller's forested coastal plain was *Saurolophus,* one of the flat-headed group of hadrosaurs. It had a broad, spatulate jaw which rose ramplike to a spike with a slightly forward concavity. A ridge running along the back inspired its name which means "maned, or ridge, lizard." A member of the genus *Saurolophus* holds the historical distinction of being the first nearly-complete dinosaur skeleton to be unearthed from the Red Deer River valley. It was excavated from a quarry near Tolman Bridge by a team from the American Museum of Natural History in 1911. The fact that *Saurolophus* is known from Late Cretaceous beds in Mongolia is intriguing to researchers who believe that hadrosaurs emigrated from Asia to North America.

Remains of *Edmontosaurus,* a model with no skull adornment of any kind, are the most commonly found in the Horseshoe Canyon strata. An inhabitant of the damp lowlands near the sea, it was the largest hadrosaur known to have lived in Alberta, reaching 15 metres in length. It was an *Edmontosaurus* whose acquaintance we made on the museum wall at the beginning of this chapter. Long

The bones of this *Edmontosaurus* are arranged on a wall of the Canadian Museum of Nature much as they were discovered in 1912 on Michichi Creek, north of Drumheller.

after the more elegant and exotic crested genera had had their fling and departed from the scene, these conservative, flat-headed versions carried on until near the end of the Age of Dinosaurs.

Remains of *Thescelosaurus* ("pretty lizard"), above, have been found at several western North American sites. The first one collected in the Red Deer valley, in 1926, was a partial skeleton from the Scollard Formation west of Rumsey. Alive near the end of the Age of Dinosaurs, it was also around much earlier, as shown by teeth found in Dinosaur Provincial Park.

The three-metre-long *Thescelosaurus*, if not a member of the immediate family, is closely related to a group of bipedal herbivores, the "ridge-toothed" hypsilophodonts. Both groups have strong jaws, with sharp cone-shaped teeth in front and broader grinding teeth in the cheeks; stout bodies; strong legs; and long tails stiffened by a lattice of tendons. Similar to *Thescelosaurus* is *Parksosaurus*, known from the Horseshoe Canyon and Scollard Formations.

Unlike this earlier one, a modern-day model of *Thescelosaurus* would show the tendon-supported tail off the ground in a line horizontal with the torso and head.

8

Ceratopsians: The Horned Dinosaurs

Ceratopsians were one of the last groups to make an appearance on Earth during the long reign of the dinosaurs. The first evidence of them comes just at the end of the Early Cretaceous Period. In spite of their late start, they soon cornered an impressive share of available habitat. Fossils of ceratopsians in the Red Deer River valley number second only to those of hadrosaurs.

An interesting phenomenon in the annals of ceratopsian development occurs in the most northern badlands of the valley. It is one that hints at the fascinating complexity of life in the penultimate years of the Late Cretaceous and exemplifies the riddles palaeontologists work to solve. In these beds, *Triceratops* remains are found. *Triceratops,* "three-horned face," is perhaps the best known of the horned dinosaurs because of the many skulls that have been found in the dinosaur fields of western North America. While evidence of its existence in this area just prior to the extinction of dinosaurs is interesting, it is not, of itself, the most remarkable aspect of the fossil story. What gives it that extra dimension is the discovery, along with *Triceratops,* of skeletal material from the protoceratopsid *Leptoceratops.*

Reconstructions of *Triceratops* show that it was a very imposing beast. Its approximately eight metric tonnes was firmly planted on four strong limbs. Viewed straight on, its enormous head had a

DINOSAUR COUNTRY

The small protoceratopsid *Leptoceratops*, (left) is closely related to the big horned and frilled ceratopsid *Triceratops* (right). Both are ceratopsians.

roughly triangular shape, rising up from a narrow beak to a wide frill growing out from the back of the skull. Two very long horns were positioned above its large eyes. It was equipped with a short nasal horn, as well.

By contrast, *Leptoceratops* weighed about as much as a large pig, was low-slung and measured only about a metre and a half from tip to tail. It had no elevated frill nor horns. The two animals must have appeared to be quite different one from another and yet

Triceratops was the last and largest of the horned dinosaurs. Its huge head was almost one third of its total length. No complete skeleton has, to date, been found in the Red Deer badlands. This specimen, in the Royal Tyrrell Museum, is from Montana.

there is a close familial relationship between protoceratopsids, represented here by *Leptoceratops,* and ceratopsids, of which *Triceratops* is a member. Most experts believe that the protoceratopsids were a step in the evolution from an earlier form, *Psittacosaurus,* towards ceratopsids. *(Psittacosaurus,* "parrot beak," is well known from Early Cretaceous deposits in China and Mongolia). Others, while agreeing that *Psittacosaurus* was the common ancestor, argue that protoceratopsids and ceratopsids developed parallel to one another. To date, all protoceratopsid remains have come from sediments of Late Cretaceous age, while ceratopsids have been discovered in earlier strata. To a nonprofessional, this would seem to confound the issue somewhat. However, for a palaeontologist, lack of fossils is proof of little more than that they remain to be found.

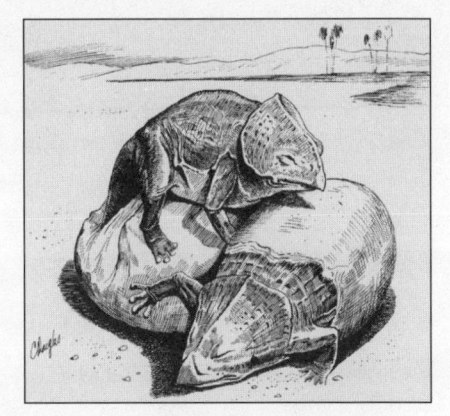

The first dinosaur eggs were discovered in Mongolia by Roy Chapman Andrews in 1922. They belonged to a protoceratopsid.

Those who expound the theory that ceratopsids derived from protoceratopsids say that later frill developments in the ceratopsid line were incipient in the bony solid arc along the neck to which the jaw muscles attached in *Leptoceratops*. And the teeth, although not so large or developed as those of *Triceratops,* were of the same structural type. Proportionately, the head was even larger than in ceratopsids. It accounted for about a quarter of the total length of the body. Because of the bony ridge mentioned above, the animal seemed to lack a neck, an appearance characteristic that is also present in ceratopsids.

Whichever view eventually prevails, the archaic *Leptoceratops* and the evolutionarily derived *Triceratops* were equally successful. The alpha and omega of horned dinosaur design shared joint occupancy in time and place near to the end of the dinosaurs' time on Earth.

Ceratopsians from the Red Deer River Valley

Protoceratopsids

From Dinosaur Park Formations:
Leptoceratops "narrow-skulled horn face"
Montanoceratops "horn face from Montana"

From Scollard Formation:
Leptoceratops

Ceratopsids

Centrosaurines

From Dinosaur Park Formations:
Centrosaurus "sharp-point lizard"
Styracosaurus "spiked lizard"

From Horseshoe Canyon Formation:
Pachyrhinosaurus "thick-nosed lizard"

Chasmosaurines

From Dinosaur Park Formations:
Chasmosaurus "open lizard"

From Horseshoe Canyon Formation:
Anchiceratops "close-horned face"
Arrhinoceratops "hornless-nose face"

From Scollard Formation:
Triceratops "three-horned face"

Ceratopsians: The Horned Dinosaurs

Leptoceratops remains have been found in the much earlier strata of Dinosaur Provincial Park, as have those of another protoceratopsid, *Montanoceratops*. "Horn-face from Montana" was so named because it was in Montana that it was first discovered. Like *Leptoceratops,* it had a bony crest and pointed beak but no noticeable horn development. Also like *Leptoceratops*, it coexisted with more advanced forms of horned dinosaurs.

The more modest ceratopsids belong to the centrosaurine line. These animals were relatively small, perhaps about five to six metres in total length, with skulls of one to two metres. They had relatively short, high faces and the frills they sported were generally quite restrained. The nasal horn was usually dominant; the ones over the eyes were often little more than bony ridges. *Centrosaurus*, well known from Dinosaur Park strata, is a good example of the foregoing description. *Centrosaurus* was first discovered here early in this century and many well-preserved skeletons have turned up since then. So far, this is the only place these animals have been found. *Styracosaurus* was a contemporary of *Centrosaurus* and very similar. It is differentiated by the six bony spikes that edge its frill.

The only member of this line known from a later time is the *Pachyrhinosaurus,* which was considerably larger than either *Centrosaurus* or *Styracosaurus*. Until very recently, *Pachyrhinosaurus* was known from a single skull, excavated in 1960 from the Horseshoe Canyon Formation near Munson. The specimen is in the Drumheller Dinosaur and Fossil Museum. Then in 1987, a bone bed was discovered in the Grande Prairie area in which the remains are predominantly of *Pachyrhinosaurus*. Excavation of the bone bed has been undertaken by a team from the Royal Tyrrell. *Pachyrhinosaurus* appeared to be an anomaly among horned dinosaurs in that, in place of horns, it had a thick pad of bone, running from between the nostrils to the forehead, that bulged up in a knobby protuberance. Heavy ridges of bone formed the eyebrows. The thickness of this bone mass, about that of an automobile tire, made it eligible to serve as a battering ram but a more recent interpretation, deduced from individuals

The large frill and horns of Chasmosaurus *may have been used for ritual sexual display or for species identification.*

excavated at the Grande Prairie site, is that it may have been the base for an oversized epidermal horn. The image that springs to mind is of a unicorn to end all unicorns.

Chasmosaurus, "open lizard," got its name from the large eyelets in its frill. It shares this characteristic with the other members of the chasmosaurine branch of ceratopsids. These animals were generally larger than their centrosaurine relatives. The earlier ones were, however, smaller than *Triceratops*, their last representative. Based on fossil findings up to the present, it seems that the centrosaurine line died out while the chasmosaurines continued into the last days of the dinosaurs. In general, they had long low faces and very large frills composed of extensions of skull bones. In the horn department, the ones on the brows were more pronounced than was the one on the nose. Numerous skulls of *Chasmosaurus* have been found in the Dinosaur Park Formation, many of them with body parts. The first one excavated, at Steveville in 1913, was found with a patch of fossilized skin, not an uncommon occurrence here as bone hunters were to discover. The leathery hide was

Ceratopsians: The Horned Dinosaurs

composed of large circular plates set in irregular rows and spaced sufficiently to allow for smaller many-sided scales to fit between. *Chasmosaurus* seems to have ranged quite widely, as its remains are known from Alberta to Texas.

From the time represented by the Horseshoe Canyon Formation came *Anchiceratops* and *Arrhinoceratops,* both of which were furnished with horns of lethal proportions on their brows. *Arrhinoceratops* is known to palaeontologists from only one nearly complete skull, which was unearthed from a quarry near Bleriot Ferry in 1923. Its name means "hornless-nose face" but it was misnamed because it did in fact have a nose horn, albeit a very small one. *Anchiceratops's* nose horn was similarly stubby.

Centrosaurus is well-known from several skeletons found in Dinosaur Park. To date, this is the only place the animal has been found.

The duck bill of the hadrosaur was remarked upon in the previous chapter. The ceratopsian is also linked, in simile, with a bird. It had a beak shaped like that of a parrot. This would have served to pluck up tough fibrous plants; and powerful jaw muscles operated a battery of shearing, chopping teeth to masticate them. The diet of the ceratopsian was far from easy on the teeth. Like the hadrosaur, it was equipped with replacement sets.

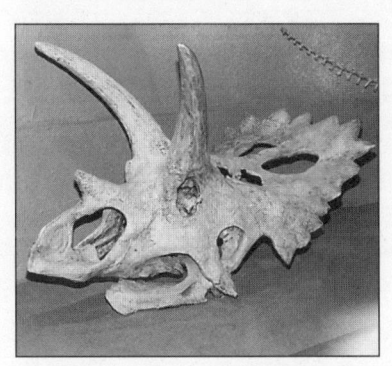

Anchiceratops, a chasmosaurine ceratopsid from the Horseshoe Canyon Formation.

One of the many theories put forward about ceratopsid frills is connected to the animals' eating apparatus. It postulates that the

This recently-discovered Pachyrhinosaurus *skeleton in the Royal Tyrrell Museum is from Grande Prairie. For many years, this animal was known from a single skull, which can be seen on display at the Drumheller Dinosaur and Fossil Museum. Discovered in 1960, the skull was excavated from near Bleriot Ferry by museum volunteers.*

---

frill was the framework for jaw muscles, but others have pointed out that a muscle does not become stronger by being elongated. Also, if the reason for the frill were so straightforward, the question leaps out: why the variety? Like the hadrosaurs' elaborate crests, ceratopsids' fancy frills have stimulated lots of discussion in palaeontology circles. For many years, they were seen as safety devices, used along with the horns, to guard the head and neck from the potentially life-threatening teeth of tyrannosaurs. They were referred to as 'shields' as often as they were called 'frills'. Today, many believe that, while the need for protection may offer a partial explanation, the diversity of design in both frills and horns has to be interpreted another way. This leads to the postulation that they had more to do with ritual than with day-to-day necessity. Comparisons with groups of living animals, such as the African antelope, seem to support the thesis that frills and horns were developed within a species to serve the purposes of sexual display and male-supremacy puffery.

Ceratopsians: The Horned Dinosaurs

The quantity of ceratopsid fossil remains found here suggests that, 75 million years ago in the Red Deer valley, they accounted for about one-quarter of all the animals in their community. Bear in mind that there may have been many species included in the groups of ceratopsids named above. It is believed that horned dinosaurs herded. This may mean that frills and horns evolved to differentiate the various species so that an individual was able to recognize one of its own kind amongst the many species populating the coastal plains.

Evidence of an extensive degree of herding is supported by the frequent occurrence in the badlands of bone beds in which the remains of one species of ceratopsid predominates. Staff from the Tyrrell Museum spent almost 12 field seasons systematically excavating Quarry 143, a *Centrosaurus* bone bed in Dinosaur Provincial Park. There is a distinct variance in size among the specimens retrieved. They represent a range of age groups: adults, juveniles and babies. The study of the bone bed is providing important clues to the stages in the life cycle of the *Centrosaurus*. This is information that is scarce because, for some unknown reason, although adult ceratopsid skeletons are relatively abundant in North America, those of younger ones are very rare. One inference borne out by the evidence of the bone bed is that ceratopsids did not cast their babies off to fend for themselves once they were hatched from their eggs but nurtured them within the encompassing protection of the herd.

A dinosaur of moderate proportions like all centrosaurines, *Styracosaurus*, a contempory of *Centrosaurus*, had spikes sticking out from its frill. *Styracosaurus* is well-known from the 76,000,000 year old strata of Dinosaur Provincial Park.

At this particular site, several hundred animals met their deaths together. The number of individual animals present when disaster struck is established by counting the occurrences of a particular portion of skull. The deposits have been found to be consistent with those of a flooding river channel, suggesting the herd may have been in migration and was drowned while attempting to ford the river. This sort of event is sometimes observed today among migrating animals, such as caribou.

Excavation of bone beds has for some time been a priority with the research department of the Royal Tyrrell. In Dinosaur Park, several other *Centrosaurus* bone beds at the same stratigraphic level as Quarry 143 are being investigated. They show that, time and again, herds of these animals met with similar catastrophes. This leads to the question of whether, as a group, ceratopsids were somehow vulnerable to natural disasters or epidemic diseases.

To date, fossils of protoceratopsids (*Leptoceratops* and *Montanoceratops* were introduced earlier) have been confirmed only in Asia and North America, and those of ceratopsids only in North America and Kazakhstan. The areas in Mongolia where protocertopsids are found indicate that the palaeoclimate was hot, semi-arid and seasonal. They are found in North America in deposits, such as those in the Scollard Formation, that were laid down in cooler, drier areas back from the inland sea. They seem to have habituated the uplands; only rare evidence of them has come from the rich coastal lowland strata where many ceratopsids are buried. Judging from the wealth of material in bone beds and other quarries, most palaeontologists think ceratopsids were so plentiful that different species would have occupied different environmental niches—witness *Triceratops* who shared the uplands with *Leptoceratops*. The biodiversity they sought would surely have been available in the great range they covered, from the North Slope of Alaska and the Northwest Territories south to Mexico.

9

Pachycephalosaurs: The Thick-Domed Dinosaurs

More than one hundred fragments of skull caps, remarkable for their thickness, have been collected over the years from the Red Deer River badlands. They belong to a rather odd and mysterious group of herbivores known as pachycephalosaurs. Because each skull cap represents an individual, it is estimated that this group may have constituted about ten percent of the area's Late Cretaceous dinosaur population.

The skull pieces are like large water-worn pebbles and most are found in channel deposits. For this reason, it is believed that the majority of the pachycephalosaur species in this area were streamside dwellers whose carcasses were carried some distance by flowing water. The thickened bone of the skull cap made it less susceptible to destruction than other parts of the skeleton.

Although pachycephalosaur remains are scarce, they reveal that the animals were widely distributed from the steppes of Asia to western North America. All of the pachycephalosaur specimens found, with the exception of one from Early Cretaceous rock on the Isle of Wight in England, date from the Late Cretaceous. In the Red Deer valley, evidence of pachycephalosaurs is found in Dinosaur Provincial Park, around Drumheller, and further north in the Scollard Formation.

The thick dome of the male *Stegoceras*, "horned roof," suggests it may have taken part in ritualistic butting, in the way that mountain goats do today.

Because of skeletal likenesses, in particular the thick ridge on the back of their skulls, pachycephalosaurs are thought to be closely related to ceratopsians. The fancy frills of the latter group developed from a similar raised thickening. From the relatively large size of the eye socket, it is inferred that pachycephalosaurs had keen sight. A sense of smell was also well-developed, judging from the large olfactory lobes observed in casts made from the interiors of skulls. These would have been good adaptations for smallish plant eaters which their small sharp cheek teeth suggest they were. Their forelimbs were much shorter than their hind ones so they were decidedly bipedal. There was little flexibility in the long heavy tail that was supported by ossified tendons. Rigidity was also a feature of the broad stocky trunk and thick short neck. When in motion, the animal was probably in a near horizontal position, with the tail acting as a counterbalance for the rest of the body. Some palaeontologists suggest that the rather thick body of the pachycephalosaurs means they were slow moving, probably relying upon acute senses to detect danger.

The presence of pachycephalosaurs in the Dinosaur Provincial Park area was recognized from fossil material collected prior to 1900 by Lawrence Lambe, an employee of the Geological Survey of Canada. The remains were of *Stegoceras*, the best-known North American genus, thanks largely to a well-preserved skull and partial skeleton found in the Red Deer field some years later. *Stegoceras* was quite small, only about two-and-a-half metres long. *Pachycephalosaurus,* its contemporary, was more than twice this size. A bony fringe projected out from the back of the skull of *Stegoceras. Pachycephalosaurus* had a much thicker skull which was ornamented by spiky protuberances at the back and all over its short snout.

Although the raised dome of these animals gave them a somewhat professorial countenance, it was deceptive. Relative to size, *Stegoceras* had a larger brain than did *Pachycephalosaurus* but, with most of the space devoted to bone, brain size was necessarily limited in all of their kind. So what was the purpose of this peculiar thickening? It has been suggested that it was a specialization connected with mating rituals in which male supremacy was decided by the outcome of a butting contest. Some say that the rigidity of the backbone directed the powerful impact that such sport implies directly to the remarkably stong pelvic region where it was

The upper skull of *Pachycephalosaur*, "thick-headed lizard," was ornamented by spiky protuberances at the back and all over its short snout.

absorbed. Others have suggested that the neck pleated like an accordion to soften the blow. Still others believe that it would have been too dangerous for the animals to throw the full force of their sturdy bodies at each other and that the butting may have been ritualistic. If serious injury was the intent, it would seem that ribs would be a more vulnerable area to ram than the competitor's equally thick head.

However, not all of the known skull caps belonged to males. Researchers who have closely examined many *Stegoceras* skull caps note that there is quite a diversity among them and interpret this as sexual differentiation. Some domes are larger, thicker and more convex than others, fittingly adapted to the butting activities of the males of the species. Females would not have participated in this behaviour and, therefore, thinner and less convex domes probably belonged to them.

In addition to the high-domed pachycephalosaurs, one with a skull equally thick, but of a flat table-like conformation, was discovered in the Dinosaur Provincial Park area in 1981. It was named *Ornatotholus*, "ornate dome," for its knob-bedecked skull. A partial skull cap found east of the park near the hamlet of Jenner was originally thought to be that of an unknown species and was given the name, *Gravitholus*, "heavy dome." It is now thought possible that the fossil is from a juvenile *Pachycephalosaurus*.

10

Ankylosaurs:
The Armoured Dinosaurs

One group of Red Deer River dinosaurs was very different from the others we have met so far. These were the ankylosaurs, remarkable for the fact that their bodies were barricaded within heavy suits of bony armour. They were closely related to stegosaurs, but are distinct from them because their armour does not include a series of erect plates along the spine. Most stegosaurs are known from deposits of the Jurassic Period whereas ankylosaur remains are mostly Cretaceous in origin. It is thought that both groups may be descended from an animal like *Scelidosaurus,* known from 206- to 200-million-year-old Early Jurassic deposits in England. *Scelidosaurus* was a three- to four-metre-long, heavily limbed quadruped, an early experimenter with armour in the form of rows of projecting studs along its back.

Until recently, ankylosaurs have been pictured as low-slung, slow-moving tanks pursuing their solitary, ponderous reptilian ways about the lowland plains of the Late Cretaceous. The solitary behaviour was suggested by the fact that North American ankylosaur remains, always of adults, have consistently been found as single specimens, never in association with others of their species. Important discoveries made in China, during the Canada - China Dinosaur Project, somewhat altered this appreciation when several

Ankylosaurs from the Red Deer River Valley

Nodosaurids

From Dinosaur Park Formations:
Panoplosaurus "fully-plated lizard"
Edmontonia "from Edmonton"

From Horseshoe Canyon Formation:
Panoplosaurus
Edmontonia

Ankylosaurids

From Dinosaur Park Formations:
Euoplocephalus "well-armoured head"

From Horeseshoe Canyon Formation:
Euoplocephalus

From Scollard Formation:
Ankylosaurus "fused lizard"

clutches of juvenile ankylosaurs were found. This discovery implies that the animals lived communally for at least a period in the early years of their lives. Another fact noted is that the armour plates that are found in mature ankylosaurs are missing from these skeletons. The armour must have developed as the ankylosaur grew; therefore, young ankylosaurs would have been vulnerable. If this was so, rather than striking out on their own soon after hatching, they remained together for protection until they were equipped to defend themselves. No adult fossil material was found at any of the mass graves. That does not necessarily preclude the possibility of parental care of the young. It is thought the animals were buried by sand that was either windblown or from a collapsing dune. The adults, if there were any with the young, may have been able to escape the disaster.

As to the pace of the adult ankylosaur, its weight and the structure of its short massive legs indicate that it was habitually slow. The front limbs were about two-thirds the length of the hind ones; in motion the hind legs had a near-vertical orientation but the elbows of the front ones angled slightly outward. Some experts believe an anylosaur may have been capable of short bursts of speed but, obviously, its main defences lay in impenetrable armour and a wide, heavy, virtually untippable body.

Among ankylosaurs, body armour patterns vary somewhat from species to species but, in general, small rounded plates were embedded in the thick skin of the upper body to form a shield that covered almost the entire surface of the broad arched back. In some species, hollow horns projected from any spaces on the back not taken up with dermal plates. The long, tapering tail, half the total length of the body, was wrapped in armour. At the other end, the throat and flat, trapezoid-shaped head were protected in like fashion. Cheek plates and ridges of bone shielded the face and hooded the eyes. The only vulnerable spot on these living tanks was the soft underbelly, and plates extended out along the sides to afford protection to that body part.

There are two major kinds of ankylosaurs. Although both adhered to the above description, the nodosaurids were, relatively speaking, lighter and slimmer than the ankylosaurids. The most distinctive difference between them was that the nodosaurids lacked the tail club brandished by the ankylosaurids. The fossil beds in Dinosaur Provincial Park have yielded up several specimens of the nodosaurids *Panoplosaurus* and *Edmontonia*. Both of these groups were wide-ranging; their remains are known from as far south as Texas. *Panoplosaurus*, whose name means "fully-plated lizard," is particularly well described. In addition to all of the armour common to its kind, its defences were increased by hard knobs fused into the skin on the underside of a short thick neck. To date, no complete skeletons have been found but it is estimated that the animal was about seven metres long.

This artist's rendering of armoured dinosaurs shows (left) an ankylosaurid with a ball-club on the end of its tail. The nodosaurid (right) lacked this feature but was otherwise equally well protected.

Named for the formation in which it was first discovered in 1924 near the town of Morrin (in what was at that time called the Edmonton Formation, now known as the Horseshoe Canyon Formation), *Edmontonia* was about the same size as *Panoplosaurus*. Later, the remains of an earlier species unearthed in the Dinosaur Park Formation showed that the *Edmontonia* genus was a presence on the Alberta coast for over five million years. It seems to have died out about 70 million years ago, as no evidence of it has been found in later deposits. From the fossil record worldwide, in fact, it seems to have been the last of the nodosaurid ankylosaurs. *Edmontonia* was probably less streamlined in appearance than *Panoplosaurus*. They both had fairly long narrow skulls but *Edmontonia* was more snub-snouted than its relative. It supplemented its armour with forward-projecting spikes on either shoulder.

The line of ankylosaurs with tail clubs is represented in the 76.5-million-year-old sediments of the park by *Euoplocephalus*, "well-armoured head." This epithet was, indeed, apt for most of the skull, covered as it was with bony plates. However, the rather wide arched beak was devoid of armour. More skull specimens have been found of this genus than of any other ankylosaur. The top part of the animal's flat skull was as broad as the whole skull was long. The head was quite small in comparison with the body, which was especially broad in the rear region. The rounded back was lined with rows of ridged plates. While passive resistance may have been the habitual defence employed by ankylosaurs, this group's long, heavily-muscled, flexible tails—that terminated in big ball-shaped bone clubs— speak of more aggressive tactics. A carnivorous enemy, bent on flipping one of these two-tonne beasts in search of the chink in its armour, risked a damaging clout from a lashing tail. *Euoplocephalus* is known only from Alberta and Montana. Its remains have been found in the Horseshoe Canyon Formation so, like *Edmontonia*, it survived in this area for at least 5 million years.

Unlike *Edmontonia*, *Euoplocephalus* was **not** the last of its line. Its descendant, *Ankylosaurus,* survived until the end of the time of the dinosaurs. Everything about this last ankylosaur was more pronounced than those that preceded it. For one thing, there was its size. It was eight to nine metres in length, weighed four to five metric tonnes and had a skull 60 percent larger than that of *Euoplocephalus*. The tail club was less defined than that of the earlier animal but it was of massive proportion. The body of *Ankylosaurus* was heavily armoured. Bands of bony oval plates embedded into its leathery skin were intersticed with hard projecting spikes. The skull armament was similarly exaggerated. Dermal plates covered the entire head, including the beak, leaving only small circular openings for the nostrils. Bony plates jutted out above the eyes and others formed hornlike projections further back on the skull. Near to impenetrable, *Ankylosaurus* carried on into the waning of the Cretaceous Period.

Unlike the other plant eaters of their time, ankylosaurs had small weak teeth and poorly developed jaw muscles. This suggests a number of possibilities about eating habits and digestive systems. Ankylosaurs were comparatively slow moving. This may mean that they also had sluggish metabolisms, low food requirements and, hence, little need for the sort of dental apparatus found in hadrosaurs and ceratopsians. They may have eaten only soft, easily chewed plants like ferns or flowering weeds. It used to be thought that the flexibility of the front limb joints implied they mined the coastal plain for soft roots but recent studies indicate the foot is not really adapted for digging. If they grazed on the same sort of woody food preferred by the other plant-eating dinosaurs of their time, they must have had a more efficient mechanism than mastication for breaking it down. To some researchers, the enormous size of the back portion of the torso has suggested the body may have housed complex fermentation chambers in which enzymes carried out the major digestive process.

Another mystery about ankylosaurs concerns the function of very extensive and intricate nasal sinuses. Some people have thought they must serve to enhance the animal's sense of smell, but comparisons with living creatures known for this faculty do not support the hypothesis. Nor do casts made of the interior of ankylosaur skulls, which show no enlargement of the olfactory lobes. Speculation is made that the sinuses may have operated as air filters or as resonating chambers. Another possibility, that has nothing to do

In this display, the tyrannosaur, *Albertosaurus* threatens the ankylosaur, *Euoplocephalus*. In life, the stature, armour and fearsome tail club of *Euoplocephalus* kept predators at bay.

Ankylosaurs: The Armoured Dinosaurs

directly with the intake of air, is that the bony structure of the passages may be necessary as a support for the exceptionally wide skull. The jaw also houses a secondary palate which, in addition to separating the nasal air intake from the mouth, acts as a brace for the upper dental shelf.

Ankylosaur finds are most common in Asia and North America. Only a few specimens have so far been found in what was Gondwanaland. They come from Australia and Antarctica and, although they are accepted as ankylosaurs, they represent quite different animals from those found in the northern hemisphere. The Asian ones are generally from earlier formations so it is postulated that the group may have evolved in Asia and dispersed into North America through the land bridge of the Arctic. Studies of the strata in which ankylosaur fossils are found show that they adapted to a variety of biomes—a hot humid coastal climate in North America and a much drier, though no less hot, one in Asia. Many of the skeletons from the Red Deer River badlands were found upside down in channel deposits, perhaps because they bloated and floated downstream from where they died. By contrast, most Asian specimens have been buried where they died.

This introduction to the armoured dinosaurs brings us to the last entry on the roster of herbivorous dinosaurs once alive in the area where the Red Deer now flows. Imagine what an entertaining diversity these plant-eaters of the Late Cretaceous must have bestowed upon the landscape: roving herds of ceratopsians shaking the very foundation of the ancient coastal plain beneath the weight of their combined bulk; pachycephalosaurs screening themselves in the dense forest undergrowth; cumbrous ankylosaurs going about the business of providing for their sustenance, unconcerned and impervious in their armour; migrating hadrosaurs trekking to their seasonal feeding grounds. Nature being what it is, they were, of course, not allowed unbridled prosperity. Their plenty on the earth summoned up a full complement of carnivores to keep the balance of all living things in check.

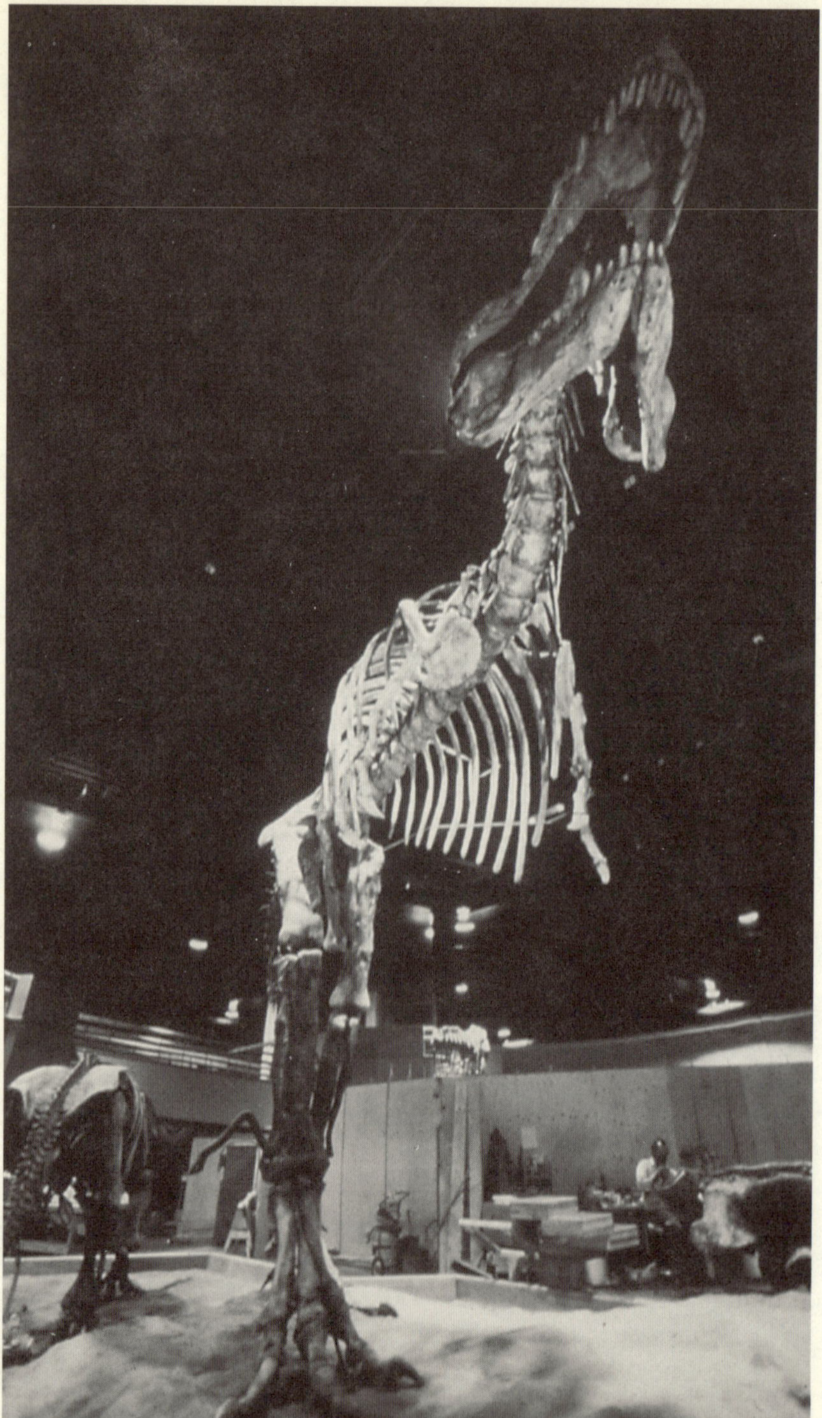

11

Tyrannosaurs: The Big Flesh-Eaters

Traditionally, at the mention of dinosaurs, the image of *Tyrannosaurus rex* would spring immediately to mind. The "king of the tyrant lizards," or a fantastic facsimile, lurched through the mouldering swamps of a multitude of pulp novels and sci-horror movies, slavering after the kill. More often than not, human sacrifice was offered at the altar of *Tyrannosaurus's* insatiable lust for blood. For a very long time, the reign of *T.rex* over the popular imagination went supremely unchallenged. Then, rumblings were heard that there was a serious contender and they proved to be all too true when, in 1993, the Jurassic Park 'raptors' vaulted to the centre of the ring. These small theropods with wit, stealth and speed, to say nothing of unadulterated viciousness, made *T.rex*'s style seem clumsy and dated, in spite of its being accorded a fast-forward film speed in the movie.

Even in the real world, its reputation was suffering setbacks. The discovery in Morocco of the fossil remains of an enormous skull of *Carcharodontosaurus* was followed shortly by an Argentinian find of an even larger skull, that of *Giganotosaurus*. It seemed clear that *T.rex* had been robbed of its championship status as the largest flesh-eater ever to have walked the Earth. Then news broke from Montana in 1997 of the discovery of a tyrannosaur that would reclaim the title. It was said to be even larger than *T.rex* Sue, the dinosaur that had been in the news off and on from the day in 1990 when it was discovered in South Dakota. Litigation over the skeleton was finally resolved when ownership was awarded to the rancher who leases the land under which *T.rex* Sue was buried. He put the skeleton up for sale and no less prestigious a firm than Sotheby's conducted the auction at which it was purchased for the Field Museum of Chicago at the astounding sum of eight million dollars. The news captured headlines worldwide. What a great day that was for *T.rex* Sue and others of the species. Because of the connection between fortune and fame, even people with little or no interest in palaeontological finds or prehistoric animals are now bound to think of '*T.rex*' as synonymous with 'dinosaur'. Until something even more extraordinary happens in the fomenting world of dinosaur mania, *T.rex* is once again the public's Numero Uno.

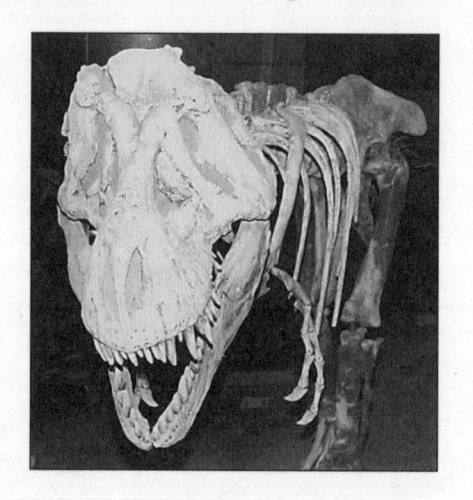

This frontal view shows the narrowed snout that allowed tyrannosaurs a clear view forward, as well as sideways

Over the years since bone-hunting expeditions to the Red Deer began, many well-preserved specimens of tyrannosaurs have been found and, still, new material surfaces almost every field season. The same may be said of several other dinosaur fields in North America and Asia where tyrannosaurs are found. As fresh evidence is brought to bear on the study of tyrannosaurs, it adjusts perceptions about their familial relationships. As a result, classifications are undergoing shifts. What this means to the public is that an exhibition skeleton they have known earlier by one name may be found, on a subsequent visit to the museum, to have undergone a name change. Tyrannosaur species from the Dinosaur Park Formation

Tyrannosaurs from the Red Deer River Valley

From Dinosaur Park Formations:
Albertosaurus "Alberta lizard"
Daspletosaurus "frightful lizard"
Gorgosaurus "Gorgon lizard"

From Horseshoe Canyon Formation:
Albertosaurus
Daspletosaurus

From Scollard Formation:
Tyrannosaurus "tyrant lizard"

(*Albertosaurus, Daspletosaurus, Gorgosaurus*) may soon figure in just such a shuffle. In most respects, save being smaller, all of these 76-million-year-old tyrannosaurs follow a design very similar to their relatives from the later Horseshoe Canyon and Scollard Formations.

T.rex lived just prior to the Cretaceous extinction. A skeleton of this animal on display at the Royal Tyrrell Museum of Palaeontology came from Late Maastrichtian sediments in the river valley near Huxley. The specimen was almost complete but for the head, which is a cast from a skull in the possession of the American Museum of Natural History in New York. Viewing this extraordinary display animal, it is easy to imagine using it as the raw material out of which to fashion the wicked fire-breathing dragon scourging the lands of folk myth. It was a towering giant. Could a very tall (and, one might add, foolhardy) man have stood alongside *Tyrannosaurus*, he would have reached only to the beast's knee. Anyone with a grain of sense, of course, would hardly put himself in such a mortally threatening position, especially if

Leg bone of a tyrannosaur from the 76-million-year-old Dinosaur Park Formation. Collected in 1917 by C.H. Sternberg for the University of Alberta

he looked up to catch a glimpse of a demented grin that displayed the lethal weaponry of as many as 60 strong, serrated, 15-centimetre teeth, so arranged that all of them could have clamped down at one and the same time on its prey. The teeth are adapted for tearing, stabbing, and cutting, rather than for chewing. A keen sense of sight is implied by the generous size of the eye sockets and optic nerve channels. Its olfactory tracts were large, suggesting a sharp sense of smell. It had heavily muscled legs supported by huge feet bearing three sharp talons designed for ripping. From its wide-based tail, along the extent of its broad back, to its boxy rectangular head braced by a short stout neck, every feature of this animal translated to a fearful array of power. Every one, that is, except a pair of tiny arms.

The arms represent a curious paradox in the growth patterns of the tyrannosaur line. While their general girth got progressively larger during the twelve million years of evolutionary time recorded in the valley, the size of the arms diminished. The seventy-six-million-year-old tyrannosaur had arms of human dimensions; its seventy-one-million-year-old counterpart's arms were smaller. On *Tyrannosaurus rex*, the sixty-five-million-year-old member of the family, the arms were minute. Another strange aspect of this upper limb development is that skeletons of younger *Albertosaurus* individuals had proportionately longer arms than did their elders. As *Albertosaurus* matured, the growth of its arms seems to have been arrested.

Tyrannosaurs: The Big Flesh-Eaters

In the words of Alice in Wonderland, this arm business is "curiouser and curiouser." What use could this powerful giant have for such appendages? When the forelimbs were first discovered, the answer to this question was "None." Because they were too short even to lift a morsel of food to their owner's mouth, they were dismissed as vestigial relics that would have disappeared completely had fate decreed further evolution of the group.

Then, as so often happens in the annals of palaeontology, a contradictory bit of evidence, which had been conveniently ignored, demanded explanation. If the animal made no use of its hands, one would expect that its shoulder development would be negligible. But careful study of the tyrannosaurs' anatomy showed that the deltoids must have been powerful.

One question that has always puzzled researchers is: how did the giant beast rise from a resting position? Given the structure and weight of its body, righting itself was an undertaking comparable to raising a four story building from its side onto its base. Perhaps, it was suggested, the little arms had a role to play in this feat. They may have been used to lever the forward part of the body slightly off the ground and to support it while the animal gathered the hind limbs into a crouch. Then, with the arching of the neck and massive upper back, the final heave to a vertical position was accomplished. Other palaeontologists dismiss this theory as mere whimsy. They say that longer arms would have been a more logical adaptation for such a function.

Collected from Dinosaur Park in 1991, this specimen of a juvenile tyrannosaur measures about half the size of a full-grown member of its species.

The serendipitous discovery of this tyrannosaur skeleton occurred when a dropped camera case came to rest on its exposed skull. The skeleton is 90% intact, displayed much as it was found emerging from the rock of Dinosaur Park.

A more likely explanation for the tiny arms is based upon the teeter-totter principle. As the skull of the tyrannosaur grew larger (as it did over millions of years), it added a lot of weight to the front of the body. Truncation of the front limbs was probably an adaptation to reduce weight and, thereby, to retain body balance.

The claws of the two-fingered forelimbs are comparatively large and could have served as grappling hooks to anchor the tyrannosaur's prey while the claws of the hind limbs dealt a killing blow. They could have served, as well, to hold the carcass while ripping its flesh off with the teeth. Think back to the plant eaters of the previous chapters. Holding such large beasts immobile would require all the power that strong shoulders could provide.

But was the tyrannosaur an active predator or did he just scavenge for the flesh of the already dead? Because of the preponderance of large herbivorous dinosaurs in the Red Deer fields and the absence of heavy wear patterns on the teeth of some tyrannosaurs, one of the earliest theories put forward on this sub-

Tyrannosaurs: The Big Flesh-Eaters

ject was that they moved about hardly at all but stayed near to the ground, like large lizards, and scavenged the soft, decaying flesh of animals that had the good grace to die of natural causes in close proximity. This model of the giant carnivore seems strangely at odds with its built-to-kill appearance.

Participants in the Royal Tyrrell Museum Day Digs program get a first-hand idea of life as it played out on the ancient coastal plain near the museum. They assist with mapping and collecting from a large bone bed in which remains of the hadrosaur *Edmontosaurus* predominate. Bone beds contain the disarticulated remains of many individuals. Study of bone beds involves the science of taphonomy which investigates how ancient organisms died and were buried to become a part of the fossil record.

There is ample evidence that tyrannosaurs were definitely involved to some extent in the events recorded in the bone bed. Some diagnostic bones and teeth are found. The presence of *Albertosaurus* teeth and of their tooth marks on the *Edmontosaurus* bones mean they may have been the killers of the *Edmontosaurus* herd. Because there were so many victims, it seems more likely that the tyrannosaurs were on the scene as opportunistic scavengers. The feast must have been of some duration as over 50 per cent of the *Edmontosaurus* bones (upwards of 500 bones have so far been examined) show evidence of having been chewed upon prior to burial. The shaley sandstone of this burial site is typical of a riverbank deposit. The *Edmontosaurus* herd may have been drowned in a flood. Most palaeontologists today

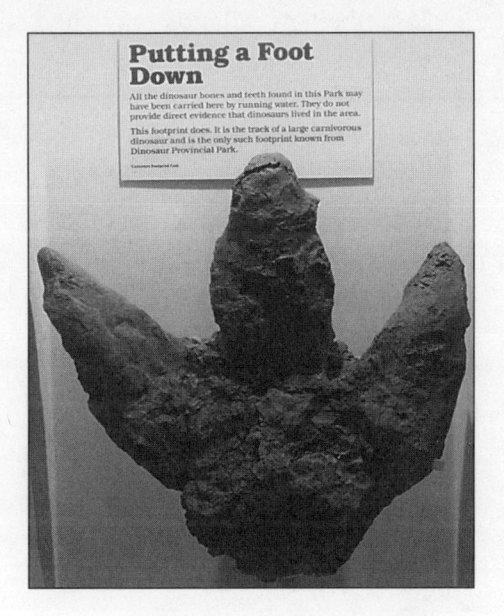

Cast of a tyrannosaur footprint found in Dinosaur Park.

believe that tyrannosaurs would have been unlikely to spurn a meal set out for them, as in the mass death occurrence registered in the bone bed, but, failing such hospitality, they would have hunted and killed their own prey.

The question of whether they were lone or pack hunters remains unresolved, although the recent discovery or, to be more accurate, rediscovery of an *Albertosaurus* bone bed in the Drumheller badlands may shed some light on this and other aspects of tyrannosaur behaviour. When Barnum Brown came from New York in 1910 to prospect this area for the American Museum of Natural History, he noted the bone bed but was not very interested in it. His mission was to look for big well-preserved skeletons that would be suitable for exhibition. Perhaps twenty years ago, Philip Currie learned of the existence of the bone bed from Dale Russell of the, then, National Museum of Natural History. No one knew its location. On one of his frequent visits to New York to review the collections amassed from the Red Deer fields by the American Museum, Currie came upon drawers of articulated *Albertosaurus* specimens gathering dust in storage. As he examined them, he became increasingly excited because he realized that what he was seeing represented a group of eight or nine individual tyrannosaurs, all from the same place. Where other than the *Albertosaurus* bone bed? But where was it? Brown's field notes, never very detailed, were not a lot of help. The only promising leads were a few photographs. Armed with these, and knowing the general range of Brown's 1910 explorations, a joint expedition of the Royal Tyrrell Museum and Dinamation, an independent American organization from Colorado, set forth late in the 1997 field season to recreate Brown's prospecting trip. Within a day or two, they had found the bone bed. Initial assessments are that the bed is extensive and that an enormous amount of information is to be had from the mass of material still to be collected. All of the specialized and meticulous work that is involved in making sense of the disorganized mess that comprises a bone bed will begin in the summer of 1998. On the basis of a preliminary appraisal, Dr. Currie is "willing to bet" that *Albertosaurus* was a pack hunter and, judging from the size variance of the bones of individuals, that the social organization of the pack may have involved an association of several age groups.

Older re-creations of tyrannosaurs often show them in an upright position, sometimes with tails dragging on the ground. This posture is contradicted by the fact that trackways show no imprints of tails; and, besides, anatomical investigations point to the entire body from tail tip to snout being held almost horizontally. It would seem that this stance would allow for better balance and more efficient locomotion but just how fast they moved is under debate. Some say size would preclude anything faster than a quick walk. Other estimates of tyrannosaur speeds based upon trackway studies and biomechanics, which is the application of principles of physics to living things, range from 35 to 70 km per hour. Perhaps if these alleged increased speeds were possible, they could be maintained for only short bursts. Hadrosaurs are thought to have been their chief source of food. One imagines

George Sternberg with a tyrannosaur skull
collected in 1921 for the University of Alberta

that, given a head start, an otherwise defenceless hadrosaur could possibly have outdistanced its enemy.

The logo chosen for the Royal Tyrrell Museum of Palaeontology leaves few doubts about the leanings of the dinosaur experts there on the question of tyrannosaur locomotion. A stylized *Albertosaurus* brings to mind the words grace, fluidity, swiftness, agility. In fact, it connotes all the features we have come to accept as belonging to the small theropods, the 'raptors'. There is good reason for this as a recent reclassification of tyrannosaurs bears out. Because of their size they had been placed with other large flesh eaters known as carnosaurs. Reassessment of their anatomy suggests they have much more in common with the coelurosaurs, the group that includes all the theropods who have been put forward as candidates for the position of ancestor to the birds. Maybe the joke about looking out the window to see *Tyrannosaurus rex* at the bird feeder is not as far fetched as it once seemed.

12

Small Flesh-Eaters and The Bird Connection

A 1969 scientific paper published with none of the media fanfare that today greets new discoveries and theories about dinosaurs proved to be the spark that ignited a revolution. The dinosaur world has not been the same since John Ostrom of Yale University introduced it to *Deinonychus*. A three-metre-long carnivore found in Montana, the creature was named for the "terrible claw" that extended from the second toe of its three-toed hind foot. Ostrom reasoned that, in order to use the sickle-shaped claw as a slashing weapon of attack or defense, the animal would have required speed, dexterity and good balance, on a par with one of today's large flightless birds. His argument was compelling and threw the traditional reptilian model of the dinosaur into disarray. In 1973, Ostrom resurrected a theory that had been toyed with about a hundred years earlier, that birds evolved from dinosaurs. Thus began a period of enquiry that has entirely altered our perceptions about dinosaurs. In less than 30 years they have been released from the swamp to gallop across the coastal plains and finally to soar overhead. Central to this metamorphosis are the small theropods, a group that went almost unnoticed until *Deinonychus* brought them to the forefront of the collective, and collecting, consciousness of bone hunters.

In spite of all the attention focused upon them, small theropods are elusive. Random under the best of circumstances, the odds against fossilization are even longer against them, given their delicate air-filled bones. Although their remains are scarce, those that have been unearthed represent numerous species. While this implies that small theropods were successful inhabitants of the Mesozoic world, it has the negative effect of presenting all sorts of problems for scientists attempting to arrange them in orderly groups. Be warned that the proposed relationships of these active animals often prove unstable. Characters that have been used to diagnose a close kinship may be recognized subsequently as a case of convergent evolution, that is an evolutionary development that occurs as a common adaptation to environment, in two genera not linked by a near common ancestor. This is what happened with dromaeosaurs (which were placed with troodontids because of the second-toe claw) and with ornithomimids and oviraptors (both of which have toothless beaked jaws). Now, neither of these pairs is believed to be as closely related to one another as each is to some other form. New discoveries and/or new looks at old material make classifications subject to continual revision. For the moment, all of the small theropods (ornithomimids, troodontids, oviraptors, elmisaurs, therizinosaurs and dromaeosaurs) are grouped with tyrannosaurs as coelurosaurs ("hollow-tailed reptiles"). Some include birds in this group and refer to them as avian coelurosaurs/dinosaurs. The best known coelurosaurs are found in Late Cretaceous rock but their evolutionarily advanced features lead palaeontologists to believe their history dates from well before that time.

Leaving tyrannosaurs and birds out of the mix for the moment, it is fair to say that smaller coelurosaurs share many outward appearances. The well-known groups are long-legged, light-bodied, quick and agile. Most had long necks and tails. Their skulls were small and light, characterized by many air passages, with large eye sockets that imply keen vision, perhaps stereoscopic or even nocturnal. Brain-to-body-size ratios are higher for these dinosaurs than for any other groups. Relatively long arms end in three long dexterous fingers.

Small Flesh-Eaters and the Bird Connection

Now, nothing in the above paragraph seems to describe a tyrannosaur but, as different as they seem in style and presentation from the smaller coelurosaurs, skeletal similarities recognize a close relationship between tyrannosaurs and the clade known as Bullatasoria which is made up of troodontids and ornithomimids. Ornithomimids and troodontids share many characters with each other as well as with other theropods but what seems to be unique to only the two of them is a feature of the skull's interior sinuses, a large system of cavities behind and beneath the eye socket. Bullatasoria means "inflated lizards."

Troodontid skulls show that the animals shared many characteristics with birds. They had large brains relative to their body size.

The meaning of *Troodon's* name is "wounding tooth"; its name was based upon a single triangular serrated tooth found in Montana in 1855. Amazingly, the name has survived and *Troodon formosus* has the distinction in North America of being the oldest dinosaur species name still considered valid. This in spite of the fact that troodontids spent many years tucked up with the thick-skulled pachycephalosaurs or with another, more unusual, herbivorous group called hysilophodonts. A paucity of specimens was partly to blame for this; it was not until the end of the 1960s with a scientific description of a *Stenonychosaurus* (later found to be synonymous with *Troodon*) from Dinosaur Provincial Park that distinguishing features were proposed by which troodontids could be recognized as carnivorous dinosaurs.

Deinonychus had been discovered in 1964 and, although it had not yet made its formal debut to the scientific society, the buzz about small theropods had already announced its arrival. That some of these little carnivores were hidden in the Alberta badlands was known from the fact that fragmented specimens had been collected from time to time since the earliest days of bone hunting here. In 1968, Dr. Dale Russell led a team from the National Museum of Natural Sciences in Ottawa (now the Canadian Museum of Nature) with the purpose of flushing them out. The bone hunters devoted six weeks of long, hot days prospecting in the Dinosaur Park area for clues that would lead them to their quarry. It was exhausting work, the more so because clues, in the form of a few fragmented bones, were exactly what they found— clues that led nowhere. Dispirited, Dale Russell lamented to Hope Johnson, the first Dinosaur Provincial Park curator, about the singular lack of success he and his party had experienced. Their time had run out and they would have to return to Ottawa empty-handed. As they chatted, Russell told Johnson what he knew of the animal they were looking for. Johnson was very knowledgeable about dinosaur fossils and the description of the small meat-eater triggered a memory of a Velveeta cheese box, containing a fossil foot that might be just what they were after.

The owner of the cheese box was Irene Vanderloh, a local woman with an interest in fossil hunting. She was contacted and willingly made the trip to the park, bearing her fossils with her. There was a stirring of hope in Russell's heart as he examined the bones and recognized them for those of a small theropod. But hope subsided when Mrs. Vanderloh admitted that six years had passed since her discovery. She was now unsure exactly where the bones had come from. It was agreed,

Small Flesh-Eaters and the Bird Connection

however, that she would go with the group from Ottawa the following morning to make a stab at finding the site.

Early the next day, they set off for a spot on the north side of the river, downstream of the park. Erosion had done its work and much had changed in the six years. The area where Mrs. Vanderloh thought she had been when she discovered the bones looked very different to her now. She kept repeating that the ground had been more crumbly and eventually decided that she must have made a mistake, that this was just not the right spot. They were about to move on to another area she considered a possibility. Just then, Gilles Danis, a member of the Ottawa team, bent down to brush the sediments aside. Lo and behold, eroding out of the ground was part of the skull of the coveted little theropod! Excavation was begun at once. In addition to the foot in the cheese box, they now had the back part of the skull, a few ribs and an assortment of miscellaneous other parts.

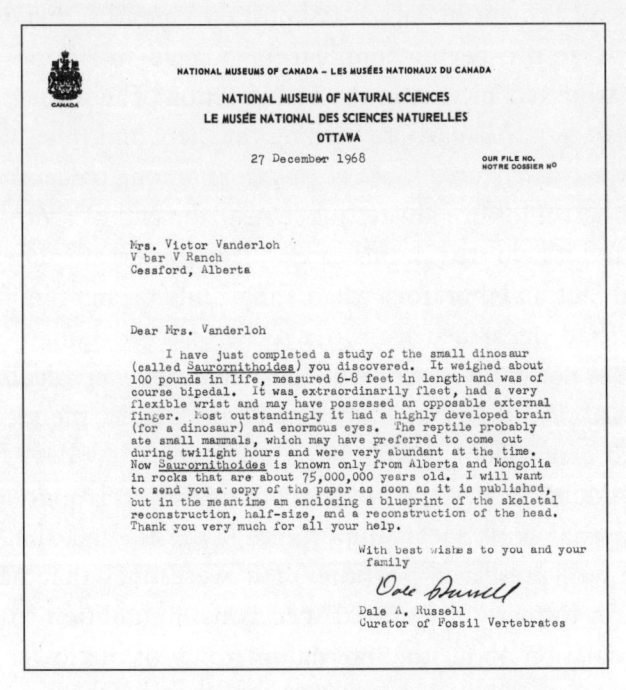

> NATIONAL MUSEUMS OF CANADA – LES MUSÉES NATIONAUX DU CANADA
> **NATIONAL MUSEUM OF NATURAL SCIENCES**
> **LE MUSÉE NATIONAL DES SCIENCES NATURELLES**
> OTTAWA
>
> 27 December 1968
>
> Mrs. Victor Vanderloh
> V bar V Ranch
> Cessford, Alberta
>
> Dear Mrs. Vanderloh
>
> I have just completed a study of the small dinosaur (called *Saurornithoides*) you discovered. It weighed about 100 pounds in life, measured 6-8 feet in length and was of course bipedal. It was extraordinarily fleet, had a very flexible wrist and may have possessed an opposable external finger. Most outstandingly it had a highly developed brain (for a dinosaur) and enormous eyes. The reptile probably ate small mammals, which may have preferred to come out during twilight hours and were very abundant at the time. Now *Saurornithoides* is known only from Alberta and Mongolia in rocks that are about 75,000,000 years old. I will want to send you a copy of the paper as soon as it is published, but in the meantime am enclosing a blueprint of the skeletal reconstruction, half-size, and a reconstruction of the head. Thank you very much for all your help.
>
> With best wishes to you and your family
>
> Dale A. Russell
> Curator of Fossil Vertebrates

The animal referred to in Dr. Russell's letter was later renamed *Stenonychosaurus* and is now believed to be synonymous with *Troodon*.

Russell's description of the animal was published near to the same time that Ostrom's paper on *Deinonychus* came out and from this time forward, concentration on small coelurosaur theropods came to dominate the study of dinosaur palaeontology. Throughout the next two decades, important finds of troodontids were made in Late Cretaceous beds of Alberta and Mongolia, the fields that have to date yielded most of the known specimens of these animals.

The Canada - China Dinosaur Project greatly advanced the understanding of this group of small flesh-eaters. In 1986, the first field season of the joint project, several Chinese scientists and technicians joined Canadian colleagues for an introduction to North American Late Cretaceous fossil repositories. Tang Zhilu, chief technician from the Institute of Vertebrate Paleontology and Paleoanthropology in Beijing, and Li Rong, head of vertebrate palaeontology from the Inner Mongolian Museum, had been working in Dinosaur Provincial Park for almost two months, dividing their time between prospecting and learning Canadian laboratory procedures from technicians in the Field Station. The former activity had not been particularly rewarding for them and time was nearing for their departure. There is an axiom among palaeontologists that the best finds are always made near the end of a prospecting season and it held true in this case. There was great excitement in the Field Station laboratory when Tang Zhilu brought in the small skull he had unearthed from the rocks of Dead Lodge Canyon. They were not entirely sure whether what they were dealing with was a bird or a dinosaur but when Philip Currie, the recognized theropod expert, saw the prepared specimen a few days later, he had no doubt. It was the lower brain case of a *Troodon*. It was only a partial skull but its importance lay in the fact that the extremely well-preserved portions of it were ones that had been crushed in formerly discovered specimens. In addition to providing information about the internal anatomy of the lower part of the brain case, this little beauty showed the complex air ducts of the inner and middle ear. The pneumatic system is described as having a close correlation with that of birds. Also present in this specimen was evidence of a sinus passage that was previously thought to exist only in birds and crocodiles, not in dinosaurs. This invalidated one of the arguments that had been used to dismiss the dinosaur - bird evolutionary connection.

What proved to be an even more important troodontid discovery was one that might just as easily have been missed. Found in the Ordos Basin of Inner Mongolia in 1988, it was assessed in the field as yet another small skeleton of the primitive horned dinosaur *Psittacosaurus*, too common in Inner Mongolia to be of great interest. Fortunately, it was collected but many times specimens thought not to contain any new information will be left for years in storage, and this is what might have happened with this one but for the fact that, after lying for a year in Beijing, it was inadvertently included in a shipment to the Canadian Museum of Nature in Ottawa. In 1990, when a technician finally got around to unwrapping the package marked **"Psitticosaurus"** and began to remove the rock surrounding the skeleton, he was happily shocked. No sturdy little *Psittacosaurus* this, but a bird-like small coelurosaur, the most complete troodontid skeleton ever discovered anywhere. It was very tiny, measuring a little over one metre, with about 50 percent of the length accounted for by the tail. Although it had lived in Early Cretaceous times, it closely resembled known troodontids from millions of years later in the Cretaceous. It differed sufficiently in skull shape, in the orientation of the bone forming the optic rim and in hind limb morphology to be described with a new name, *Sinornithoides*.

All of the troodontid material found in the Red Deer River beds has been identified as belonging to one species, *Troodon formosus*. Traces of its occupation of Cretaceous Alberta are found in many parts of the province. Teeth, for example, have been collected from the *Hypacrosaurus* nesting grounds in Devil's Coulee. The most complete specimens have come from the Red Deer River badlands. Although there is evidence of *Troodon's* presence throughout the 10 or 12 million years recorded in the valley, it is at present too fragmentary to give any picture of evolutionary change throughout that period.

The pneumatic skull of this animal shows a high arch sloping down to a U-shaped snout. It seems to have been filled with air moving through a complex system of sinuses, bearing close approximation to the skull anatomy of birds. It had the largest brain-to-body-size ratio of any dinosaur yet known which, coupled with the keen sight of its enormous eyes and acute multi-frequency hearing in its large well-developed middle ear, implies the advanced motor-sensory control needed by a fast moving predator. Interestingly, *Troodon* has long, narrow olfactory tracts so probably its sense of smell was not outstanding.

Mrs. Vanderloh, she of the foot in the Velveeta cheese box, had spent her life in the badlands and fossil hunting was one of her great hobbies. Yet in all her years of combing through the Steveville hills she had never encountered anything like the foot that so excited Dale Russell. It had a retractable second-toe claw. This claw was much larger than those of the other two toes; and, unless it was needed, it was held up off the ground, presumably to protect it from wear and keep it sharp for action. Dromaeosaurs had a similarly specialized second digit in the foot. The sharp second-toe claw of *Troodon* is thought to have been much less efficiently lethal than that of the dromaeosaurs. This is because the metatarsals in troodontids were long, slender and flexible, attributes of a fast runner, while those of the dromaeosaurs were more stout and fixed. *Troodon's* claw was probably used for finer work.

Troodontids had more teeth than most other theropods. One *Troodon's* tooth count was 122, a lot of teeth for a small jaw. Size and shape varied according to the position in the jaw, but overall the teeth were small, tapered, serrated and recurved. They seem fitted for sawing rather than ripping which suggests to some researchers that troodontids ate small things such as tiny mammals or baby hadrosaurs. Long forelimbs were equipped with supple grasping fingers that could have caught and held prey.

In the last couple of decades, Egg Mountain, an aptly named site in western Montana, has yielded hundreds of dinosaur eggs. Until very recently, the nests were attributed to a hypsilophodont herbivorous dinosaur, based upon the fact that much of the accompanying skeletal material at the site belonged to this animal. A re-examination of the embryos contained in some of the eggs has revealed that they were incorrectly identified and, in fact, were developing into baby troodontids. The eggs were deposited in a hollow with a rim of earth built up around it. There are so many nests of this same design that the area is believed to have been a rookery. One nest found with a *Troodon* skeleton above it suggests that the parent probably sat on its eggs to hatch them.

The adjective that best describes troodontids' sister taxon, the ornithomimids, is "long": long necks, long tails, and long hands that measured more than one-third of the total length of the long forelimbs which were one-half as long as the long hind limbs. It has been estimated that in addition to looking rather like an ostrich, an ornithomimid's brain may have been as large as that of the bird. Another similarity is suggested by the flexible structure of the hip, leg and foot which indicates that an ornithomimid could probably have kept pace with a running ostrich. Speed and agility were undoubtedly the main defense mechanism of ornithomimids; they manifest no others.

Most ornithomimids have been excavated from Late Cretaceous deposits of Asia and North America but Mongolia has provided good skeletons from the Early Cretaceous. Like all small theropods, their fossils are not abundant. Some of the best skeletons are from the Red Deer River badlands, showing that they were occupants of Alberta throughout the 10 or so million years leading to the time of dinosaurian extinction. The first footprints ever found in this valley belonged to a member of one of the three genera of ornithomimids known from these beds.

Dromiceiomimus, "emu mimic", was the smallest of this group of dinosaurs, about three metres in length. Its eyes were the largest of any land animal. In the Drumheller badlands, skeletons of an adult *Dromiceiomimus* and two babies were discovered near one another. The pelvic canal of the adult ornithomimid was very broad, leading to some speculation that it may have given birth to live young. This would really make her odd woman out among the dinosaurs, as eggs have now been connected with most other major groups. Sort of like a snake among modern-day reptiles. There is a hint of family life in the intimate arrangement of the three *Dromiceiomimus* skeletons. It is charming to think of these lithe and elegant creatures as concerned parents. *Dromiceiomimus* is known from the strata of Dinosaur Provincial Park and from Drumheller's Horseshoe Canyon Formation.

This is true also of the slightly larger, four-metre-long *Ornithomimus,* "bird mimic." The third ornithomimid known from

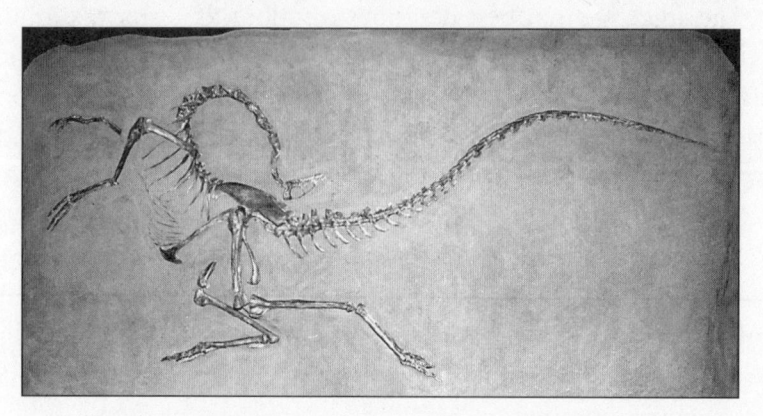

The most complete skeleton known of an ornithomimid was collected for the American Museum of Natural History in the early 1900s from Dinosaur Park. The classic death pose, with the head pulled back and the tail forward, is a result of the drying of ligaments along the back after death.

the province is *Struthiomimus,* "ostrich mimic." It was a bigger, heavier animal than either of its relatives and the only one for which there is indisputable evidence, from the Scollard Formation, of having survived until the very last stage of the Cretaceous.

Different ideas have been advanced about what these animals might have eaten. The thin tapering fingers, almost equal in length and ending in relatively straight claws, seemed configured for stealth and it was suggested that ornithomimids might have insinuated them into other dinosaurs' nests to steal eggs. Or they may have used them to delicately clear underbrush from the forest floor in search of insects or small lizards. Some palaeontologists are hesitant to link ornithomimids closely with troodontids partly because the former had a much less sophisticated wrist structure than the latter. Comparatively speaking, an ornithomimid's hand movements would have been much more restricted than a troodontid's.

Pelicanimimus is an ornithomimid known from Early Cretaceous deposits in Spain. Its jaw had lots of sharp teeth. The toothlessness of the relatively weak-jawed Red Deer River forms has been seen by some researchers as an indication that the line reverted to eating plants but present-day barnyard hens will leave off feeding on grain to catch and swallow baby mice or grasshoppers whole. Most experts are agreeable to the idea that, like chickens, ornithomimids were omnivorous. It had been accepted traditionally that the animal's shallow snout was covered by a horny beak but there was no real proof of this until 1995 when the evidence was found imprinted in the matrix surrounding an *Ornithomimus* skeleton.

Excavated in Dinosaur Provincial Park, this is one of the best preserved ornithomimid skeletons yet known. One noteworthy observation regarding this skeleton is that there seem to be unusual patterns on the bones and there has been some consideration that these may be traces of feathers. Ah, the bird connection, one supposes, but no, interestingly enough, it is not these ornithomimid dinosaurs whose hollow bones, toothless beaks and general outward appearance earned them the name of bird mimics that are put forward most forcefully as the closest thing to birds. For the moment, dromaeosaurs, the 'raptors' of Jurassic Park fame, lead the field of contenders for that position although in the minds of some experts, troodontids are still very much in the race.

Dromaeosaurs are, at present, grouped as Maniraptora ("hand seizers") with a number of other small coelurosaur theropods; traces of most of these have been found in the Red Deer valley. Oviraptors, elmisaurids, therizinosaurs, caenagnathids, segnosaurs are names they go by. The specimens that compose these groups are too rare and incomplete to make much sense, and assigning relationships to them is a challenge for researchers. The stories that follow of the introduction to the scientific world of two never-before-encountered creatures exemplify the problem.

One of these is known as *Caenagnathus,* which means "recently jawless." This seems an odd choice of name, in light of the fact that it was described by R.M. Sternberg (the son of Charles M.) on the basis of a fossilized lower jaw, the part best preserved. Nowadays, it sometimes seems that the dinosaur/bird connection has become a fashionable hobby horse in danger of being ridden to death by palaeontologists but in 1940 when *Caenagathus* was first discovered, no one was talking about dinosaurs being the ancestors of birds. When Sternberg identified the jaw as that of a bird, his vision was unclouded by popular theories. The mistake was an honest one and points out the astonishing similarities in the anatomy of birds and dinosaurs. Another bone was collected that confirmed Sternberg in his identification of the fossil and that was the wish bone. It was thought then that this was present only in birds but now it is recognized in several groups of dinosaurs. It was not until 1976, more than 30 years later, that *Caenagnathus* was re-examined and re-assigned as a dinosaur.

More than 80 years have passed since the first specimen of a creature with the beautiful name *Chirostenotes,* "slender hands," was collected in the Red Deer River beds and still there is uncertainty about where the animal belongs. This is because it is known almost exclusively from its hands and feet; and, speaking of its feet, they for many years went under the alias of *Macrophalangia,* "big toes." With the discovery of a partial skeleton in the latter part of the 1980s, it became clear that the slender hands and big toes belonged together and *Macrophalangia* merged into *Chirostenotes.* No cranial material has been found in conjunction with these specimens nor for an animal with similar hands and feet found in Mongolia, so with only the observation that the hands and feet are dissimilar to those of any well known dinosaur family, the two have been housed in a slot labelled elmisaurids, "foot lizards." They are definitely not permanently settled there because the odds are that they are synonymous with *Caenagnathus*. Even as you read this, another shuffle or merger may be taking place.

Significantly more is known about dromaeosaurs. It is clear from the discovery of several articulated skeletons that, like the

Small Flesh-Eaters and the Bird Connection

Small Theropods from the Red Deer River Valley

Troodontids

> From Dinosaur Park, Horseshoe Canyon and Scollard Formations:
> *Troodon* "wounding tooth"

Ornithomimids

> From Dinosaur Park Formations:
> *Dromiceiomimus* "emu mimic"
> *Ornithomimus* "bird mimic"

> From Horseshoe Canyon Formation:
> *Dromiceiomimus*
> *Ornithomimus*
> *Struthiomimus* "ostrich mimic"

> From Scollard Formation:
> *Struthiomimus*

Dromaeosaurs

> From Dinosaur Park Formations:
> *Dromaeosaurus* "running lizard"
> *Saurornitholestes* "bird robber"

Other Small Theropods

> From Dinosaur Park Formations:
> *Caenagathus* "recently jawless"
> *Chirostenotes* "slender hands"

troodontids, they took care to keep their lethal slashing claws up off the ground while walking about. This claw was knife-edged and came to a sharp point. It was almost hook-shaped and more than two times as long as the claws on the other two toes. It is believed that, when the muscles of the toe contracted, the claw

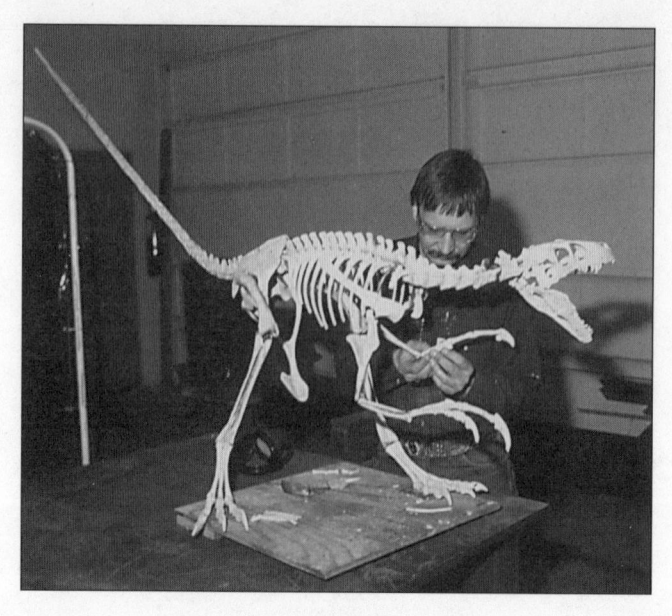

Preparing a Dromaeosaurus skeleton
for display.

slashed down in a killing arc. Dromaeosaur means "running lizard" and they were probably fast, although without the stretch that gave the longer-boned ornithomimids their speed. The legs of a dromaeosaur had heavier bones and muscles and were set lower to the ground. Its feet had much shorter bones than are noted in most theropods, features that would slow it down but compensate by giving it the strength needed to perform what has become its familiar trademark—a leap through the air at its prey. A tail that could be stiffened probably aided its balance, while it used its large, grasping, sharp-clawed hands to tear the flesh from its victim and bring it to its mouth where sharp, serrated teeth continued to process the meal.

Deinonychus is an Early Cretaceous member of the dromaeosaur clade and the reputation he has bestowed upon his family of being killing machines was strengthened in the public mind by the appearance of *Velociraptor*, "swift seizer," in Jurassic Park. The factual *Velociraptor* is known from Late Cretaceous deposits in Mongolia and China. It is a participant in one of the most interesting tableaus ever fossilized. Buried with its victim in a sandstorm on the Gobi Desert, *Velociraptor* is caught in a struggle to the death, its killing hind claw in or near the neck and one of its slashing forelimbs trapped in the beaked jaws of a small horned dinosaur, *Protoceratops*. In life, *Velociraptor* was about the size of a large dog but his movie persona was much enlarged. Nothing particularly untoward about the use of creative license. What is remarkable is a subsequent development. It became a somewhat bizarre example of life following art when, during the filming of Jurassic Park, *Utahraptor*, a very large dromaeosaur skeleton, was discovered. Or should it be viewed as art following life? The big dromaeosaur, after all, lived millions of years before the author created it. Perhaps its image was phylogenetic material stored in Michael Crichton's unconscious!

There is some evidence from the Cloverly Formation in Wyoming to support the movie rendition of dromaeosaurs hunting in packs. Several individual skeletons of a *Deinonychus* species were found together in close proximity to a large herbivorous dinosaur. The teeth of one of the dromaeosaurs known from Alberta have been found with the bones of much larger dinosaurs. Given the size discrepancy, it seems unlikely that a lone dromaeosaur would have carried out the attack. Scavenging cannot be completely ruled out, of course. Pack hunting presupposes the degree of intelligence necessary for quite complex social behaviours.

Both of the dromaeosaurs known from the Red Deer River badlands were found in the Dinosaur Provincial Park area. No better specimen of *Dromaeosaurus* has yet been found than the one discovered here in 1914 by Barnum Brown of the American Museum of Natural History. It consists of an incomplete skull and some body skeleton fragments. Some 60 years later, while prospecting with a field crew from the Royal Tyrrell, the inimitable fossil-finder Irene Vanderloh came upon a fragmented specimen. It was recognized as a dromaeosaur and named *Saurornitholestes*, "bird robber." This animal fell at the opposite end of the size scale from the big 'raptors', measuring only about two metres. It is the smallest adult dinosaur known from Alberta.

What are the features that make dromaeosaurs the leading candidates as precursors of the birds? One of the most important is the birdlike hip structure. The word "hip" is a reminder of how muddled the uninitiated are by a filing system using headings that may once have seemed clearly descriptive but because of the addition or alteration of information have become semantically misleading. This is what has happened with terms that were introduced in the 19th century and are still in use to describe the two stem taxa of Dinosauria, "Ornithischia" (meaning bird-hipped) and "Saurischia" (meaning lizard-hipped). All dinosaurs belong to one or the other. They are grouped according to a large number of shared evolutionary characters, their pelvic anatomy being but one of them. However, where the confusion arises is in the fact that the Ornithischia clade contains many of the least birdlike of the dinosaurs: the duck-billed, horned and armoured dinosaurs. Dromaeosaurs and all other theropods, the most like birds and least like lizards, are Saurischians. Convoluted as it may seem, a dromaeosaur hip is said to be more birdlike than that of any other dinosaur.

There are many other features pointed to as confirming the descent of birds from dromaeosaurs. One of the chief among these is the feet. The proportions and alignment of the three main toes are very similar. A recently discovered bird from Madagascar has a big, sharp claw resembling that of the dromaeosaur. They also share a feature of the wrist, carpal bones fused into a half-moon-shaped compound bone that allows for folding of the wings. Along with other specializations to the forelimb of the dromaeosaur, it has been proposed that its reaching/grasping motions probably followed a pattern not unlike that of the flight stroke in birds.

While the controversy swirling around the question of whether or not dinosaurs are the ancestors of birds seems very up to the minute, it is hardly new. In the middle of the 19th century, about the same time that Darwin's theory of evolution was in the news, *Archaeopteryx* was discovered in a limestone quarry in Solnhofen, Germany. Skeletons of the coelurosaur, *Compsognathus*, were also found in the Late Jurassic sediments. Had feather imprints not been

Small Flesh-Eaters and the Bird Connection

Ornitholestes, like *Compsognathus*, was a very small bird-like meat-eater of the Early Jurassic Period, a forerunner of the small theropods known from the Red Deer River.

observed with the *Archaeopteryx,* the remains might have been interpreted as belonging to different individuals of the same species. Even with the feathers, *Archaeopteryx* was seen to be remarkably like *Compsognathus*. T.H. Huxley, a colleague of Darwin's and an outspoken proponent of the theory of evolution, viewed the little dinosaur as the link between reptiles and birds. Although *Archaeopteryx* has been widely accepted as the earliest bird fossil, some researchers are of the opinion that it is really a dinosaur with feathers. It seems that no sooner does someone put forth what seems a revolutionary idea than some evidence crops up to support it. In 1997, two small dinosaurs with feathers, or perhaps proto feathers is more accurate, were discovered in northeastern China. Christened *Sinosauropteryx,* they also bear a close resemblance to *Compsognathus*.

Most prestigious museums around the world, the Royal Tyrrell Museum of Palaeontology among them, are aiding and abetting dinosaurs to take flight. There are, however, some voices raised in protest. They hold that dinosaurs and birds sprang from a common archosaur ancestor at least 200 million years ago and that the similarities between them are coincidental—a case of evolu-

The skeleton of *Archaeopteryx* is very similar to that of a small theropod, so similar that some believe it was a feathered dinosaur.

tionary convergence. The development of flight is the central problem they see with the theropod to bird evolution. They believe that lifting off the ground is the least likely way to begin to fly, that the ancestor of the birds was probably similar to a flying squirrel, developing flight by learning to glide from tree to tree. This may seem perfectly logical, but there is little evidence in the fossil record to support it. The lack of hard proof, however, plays both ways in the debate. Those on the arboreal ancestor side point to the fact that the most bird-like theropod fossils so far discovered are millions of years younger than *Archaeopteryx*, so they could hardly be its ancestor. This is countered by the argument that such evolutionarily derived groups as the coelurosaurs obviously had a long history even if there are as yet no fossils to prove it. Any theory may be said to be just a fossil short of gaining dominance, although it also seems fair to say that what seems to one interpreter to be proof positive may be seen as quite otherwise by another. Even the long held position of the 'dino-bird' *Archaeopteryx* has recently been challenged, with the contention that it was not on its way to becoming a modern bird but rather came to a dead end, leaving the field to less dinosaurian early birds.

Public fascination with the tortuous connections between long-ago life forms and those we see around us today has never been quite so fevered as it is about the debate over the dinosaur - bird link. Fanned by media hype that glamorizes the opposing participants, many of whom seem to have eagerly forsaken the ivory tower

Small Flesh-Eaters and the Bird Connection

of a science laboratory for the television stage, each new development is avidly awaited. Interest in dinosaurs themselves has rarely been higher than it is today. Jurassic Park grossed the largest box office in movie history. Twenty years ago, psychologists could be heard to muse about why dinosaurs so entranced children, especially little boys. Now, it seems they need to expand the discussion to include all of us. It is as if almost everybody's 'inner child' has emerged to share in the fun of watching denizens of a lost world re-awakening, albeit in altered form.

13

Extinction

Warm-blooded, cold-blooded, or an assortment of each, the dinosaurs were remarkable. Measured against the comparatively insignificant 4-million-year span of human existence on our planet, the reign of the dinosaurs was an unparalleled success. For 160 million years, they were the dominant form of life on land. Then, about 65 million years ago, they were overtaken by events of such destructive magnitude that they, along with possibly as much as three-quarters of all contemporary life, were obliterated from Earth.

Dinosaurs may have assumed the guise of birds to slip through the dragnet of death and carry on into the new dawn of the Tertiary Period, but the forms that stamped the character of the Mesozoic Era were no more. Gone forever, too, were the soaring pterosaurs. The great aquatic mosasaurs and plesiosaurs and the beautiful intricate ammonites disappeared from the Late Cretaceous seas, along with microscopic plankton species and many varieties of one-celled oceanic organisms. There were some survivors, too. Many fish, turtles, crocodiles, and various small reptiles were among those that made it. Among plants, ferns not only weathered the forces that killed off so many other groups, they seem to have prospered. The selection seems random; common denominators are not easily arrived at for either the winners or the losers. This is one of very many puzzles connected to the extinction.

Although animal and plant activists of our time wring their hands and hearts about extinctions, which they usually attribute to the depredations of the human species, it is a sad fact that evolutionary history reads like a series of extinctions. In spite of our singular egos, our kind cannot claim responsibility for the disappearance of 90 percent of all species ever to have inhabited the earth in the few billion years since life began. Even mass extinctions, defined as those

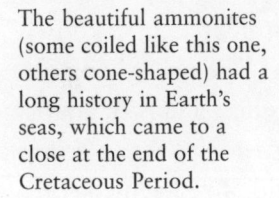

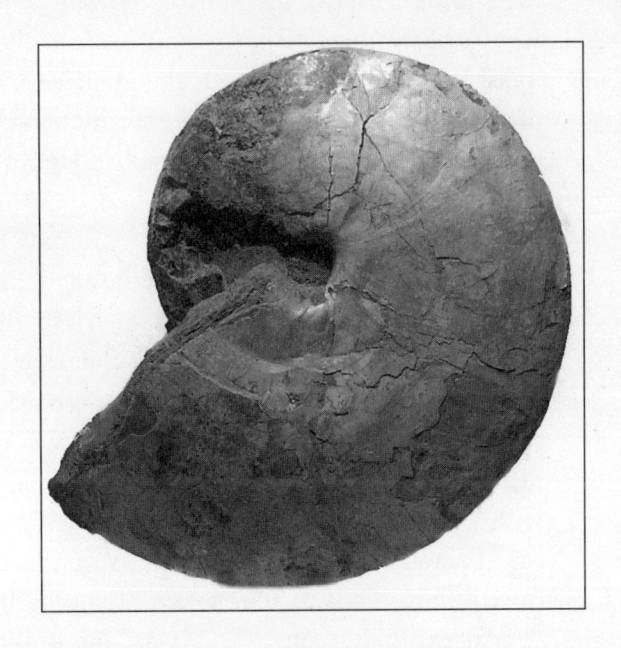

The beautiful ammonites (some coiled like this one, others cone-shaped) had a long history in Earth's seas, which came to a close at the end of the Cretaceous Period.

that in a relatively short period kill half of all species known to be alive at the time of their occurrence, are not that rare. At least five mass extinctions have taken place. The real blockbuster occurred at the end of the Permian, 250 million years ago, and destroyed far more life forms than the extinction that marks the end of the Mesozoic Era. One would think the very magnitude of the Permian destruction would make it the most interesting of all extinctions but this is not so. Undoubtedly, the death of the dinosaurs gives an edge to the more recent one.

Looking for the cause has persistently both attracted and bedevilled scientists. They are no more immune from dinosaur fever than the rest of us and one of the problems with some of the theories that have been advanced is that they ignore the widespread disappearance of other life to focus on the favourites. Racial senility making them incompetent to compete with mammals, poisoning or allergies caused by flowering plants and loss of their eggs to devouring mammals are among the many notions, now pretty much discounted, of why dinosaurs died out. It does seem incontrovertible that the mammals were waiting in the wings for their turn in the spotlight. Near the end of the Late Cretaceous Period, they were proliferating and new species were evolving. Some of the mammals' success in waiting out the great extinction has been attributed to the frequency of their reproduction cycles. Succeeding generations were perhaps able to make adaptations relatively quickly. Dinosaurs are thought to have had long life spans and perhaps they mated less frequently than mammals. This would have put them at a distinct disadvantage in the changing environment known to have characterized the end of the Mesozoic. The underlying objection to all of these suggestions is that they reflect a lack of adaptability on the part of dinosaurs and it is hard to accept that a group of animals with such a successful history could have been so completely wiped out. Earthbound solutions seemed unsatisfactory and, with penetration into space and a growing awareness of the delicate balance of the disparate units of the universe, scientists allowed their minds to soar outward in search of culprits.

An exploding supernova was one outer space suspect to be named. It was postulated that fallout from such a cataclysmic happening could have destroyed the ozone layer and irradiated much of the planet. To date, astronomers have found no evidence in space of an event of such magnitude.

Almost 20 years ago now, a team of scientists from the University of California at Berkeley, headed by the famous Luis Alvarez, brought to the attention of the world the fact that there were inordinate levels of the trace element iridium in sediments marking the transition from Cretaceous to Tertiary times, the K-T boundary as

Extinction

Just below the dark band of coal, clearly visible in this photo, lies a thin clay layer that marks the division between deposits of the Cretaceous and those of the Tertiary. This division marks the K-T boundary in the Scollard Formation. No dinosaur skeletons have ever been found above the K-T boundary.

it is called. They hypothesized that a huge asteroid or meteor, bodies known to have high iridium content, must have struck the Earth 65 million years ago, vaporized on impact and thrown up immense quantities of iridium-rich dust. The very large Chicxulub crater discovered later on the Yucatan Peninsula of Mexico has been pointed to by other scientists as proof of the event. The crater has since been the subject of ongoing study by teams of international earth scientists. It is probably safe to say that most are now persuaded of its extraterrestrial origin.

Corroborating evidence for the asteroid-impact theory comes from analysis of rock samples taken from K-T boundary exposures around the world. As you might expect, the best exposures in Canada are found not far from the Royal Tyrrell Museum of Palaeontology. Here, the boundary appears as a very thin stratum of clay, just two to three centimetres of rock, but it has captured the attention of geologists from around the world. Narrow as it is, it subdivides into two distinct layers. The lower tannish one contains impressions of glass beads that are thought to have formed when

133

rock at the site of impact was melted, thrown into the air and then cooled before drifting back to Earth. In the mahogany upper layer, grains of shocked quartz are found with fracture lines that could only be the result of a shattering collision. Rich in iridium and other minerals more plentiful in space than on Earth, this top layer indicates deposits of ashy fallout that might be expected from an extraterrestrial body exploding on impact.

Research into the subject of the K-T extinction extends well beyond the interest of earth scientists to include climatologists, astrophysicists, astronomers and other space explorers. The result of all these inquiring minds being focused on the subject is that related data is amassing, but as its interpretation varies from expert to expert, rather than bringing about harmonious clarity, it has created spirited, and often rather mean-spirited, controversy. While very few now dispute the evidence of the asteroid's impact with Earth, many, especially palaeontologists, question whether it was the agent of the Cretaceous extinction or whether the two events occurred coincidentally about the same time. If the latter assumption is made, it follows that reasons for the extinction must be sought elsewhere. Essentially, opinion divides into two camps: one group labelled "catastrophists," the other "gradualists."

The catastrophists present us with apocalyptic scenarios of a global holocaust: a cold, dark winter brought on by cosmic dust being thrown up from the impact of the asteroid to block the sun's rays. Earth was robbed of heat and light for a period of months or years, long enough to kill off much of its life. Wholesale climatic disturbances such as huge tidal waves and accompanying hurricanes or raging fires followed by acid rain are mentioned as possible players in the destruction. As horrendous as these forces seem, Earth did not return to a lifeless state such as it knew in Precambrian times. Some ecosystems were exempt, perhaps because of their position with reference to the angle of impact or for any of a number of possible reasons not yet understood or even thought of.

The gradualists take a more conservative approach in attempting to explain the K-T extinction. They say many forms of life on

Extinction

Some of the Survivors

Fossil remains show that all of these animals lived in the Red Deer River valley during the Late Cretaceous. Unlike the dinosaurs, they endured the extinction and carried on into the Tertiary Period. *Right:* the smaller skull belonged to an alligator, the larger to a crocodile. The other three fossils are representatives of a number of different turtles known to have lived here 75 million years ago. Although marine reptiles and many other ocean organisms became extinct along with the dinosaurs, relatives of the bony fish, *bottom*, survived.

Pterosaurs, "winged reptiles," first appear in the fossil record of the Late Triassic Period. They ranged from the size of a sparrow to a model with a 12-metre wing span. The latter was called *Quetzlcoatlus* for the winged god of the Aztecs. Remains of *Quetzlcoatlus* have been found in Dinosaur Park. Pterosaurs became extinct at the same time as the dinosaurs.

Earth did not meet a sudden end but were dwindling in numbers and diversity several million years before the close of the Cretaceous Period. If an extraterrestrial force played any role in the prolonged extinction, then it was but the final blow to already doomed hangers-on.

Theories favouring a gradual dying hinge on global changes effected by the spreading of the sea floor, and continental drift. Further drifting apart of the continents, a retreat of the warm, shallow seas, volcanic activity, and rising mountain ranges are factors thought to have brought about profound climatic changes over a long period of time. A cooling trend set in, bringing with it a markedly variable global climate. The result was a reduction of habitat, causing breaks in the food chain and, eventually, the decline of the various organisms that made up the links.

One bit of evidence used by both sides in the debate about whether death came with a "bang" or with a "whimper" is the count of fossils. It is reasoned that, if the end came suddenly you should expect to find consistent fossil populations right up to the K-T boundary. Otherwise, you should anticipate a diminishing of their numbers in the uppermost Cretaceous beds. Researchers in the Red Deer River valley have an important contribution to make to the amassing of fossil data because they are working in exposures that have a relatively continuous fossil record spanning the

12 million years of time leading up to the extinction. Comparisons between the numbers and diversity of dinosaurs in the different strata of the valley seem to support the gradualists' claims. Many more fossils representing a larger diversity of species are found in the 76-million-year-old Dinosaur Park Formation than in the 71s-million-year-old Horseshoe Canyon Formation, and the decline is even more marked in the 65-million-year-old Scollard Formation. This suggests that dinosaurs were under pressure for several million years before they reached extinction.

Once again, however, the limitations of fossil counts should not be forgotten. In the Red Deer River valley, the discrepancy in the fossil count may be a graphic reflection of one of the major biases in the fossil record; that is, an area such as the Cretaceous landscape of Dinosaur Provincial Park encouraged quick and relatively permanent burial in its deep mud-bottomed rivers. The upriver area described by the strata of the Scollard Formation was much drier and rockier. This means that burial was less likely. Much faunal evidence may have been destroyed by scavengers or the elements. In addition to this consideration, there are some specific biases in the history of Red Deer River valley collections. One is that, in the hunt for exhibition quality specimens, much material was overlooked. Once the Dinosaur Provincial Park badlands were discovered, those upstream commanded less attention, so there is a certain inherent inequality of emphasis on what was prospected and collected. And, although a pretty comprehensive fossil inventory has been kept for many years in Dinosaur Provincial Park, the ones for the Horseshoe Canyon and Scollard Formations have been less complete. To remedy these historical inaccuracies as far as is possible, a bone census of the stored collections was carried out at the Royal Tyrrell during the last decade. Upgraded procedures will assure that future fossil records are accurately compiled and, in time, contribute to a more definitive picture of dinosaur evolution in this area.

Dr. Dennis Braman, the curator of Palaeobotany at the Royal Tyrrell Museum of Palaeontology, has a particular interest in the K-T extinction. He has been collecting and analysing specimens from the boundary area since his arrival at the museum in 1993. The museum has participated in the Canadian Continental Drilling Program, funded equally by the federal government and Amoco Canada, which aims to locate the exact position of the K-T boundary in Alberta, Saskatchewan and Manitoba and to study its character at different sites. This is done by drilling through strata representing and including the 12 million years leading up to the extinction and then analysing the cores using a variety of approaches: lithography, geochemistry, etc. The museum's contribution is to look for indicators of plant and animal life in the core samples.

This program is one small part of the worldwide search by scientists for information that will shed revealing light on the K-T mass extinction. It is a bit like being on a scavenger hunt. Every new piece of information seems to engender another question and send researchers on in pursuit of the next partial answer. What fascinating questions and answers they are. Will the complete solution ever be reached? Perhaps not, but the quest itself leads to philosophical awe and respect for the cosmic complexities of all life and death.

For this badlands area, the thin clay line is definitive. Below it, there are dinosaur skeletons; above it, none. However it happened, the giant beasts died out and all evidence of their existence sank beneath the sands of time. There they waited for tens of millions of years until Nature put the forces in motion to resurrect their skeletons from rocky graves. In the region of the Red Deer, their disentombment was brought about by the geological events that created the badlands.

14

Creation of the Badlands

The initial shaping of the badlands was a cataclysmic feat of Nature. To get a perspective on it, it is necessary to return once again to that most awe-inspiring and renowned feature of the Alberta landscape, the Rocky Mountains. Since the time of their rising, they have determined the shape and character of the southern half of the province. Our winds, rains, and temperatures are influenced most dominantly by the high mountains that wall us off from the Pacific coast.

The episodes of their rising were many. As discussed earlier, mountains were pushed up out of the Pacific Ocean, dragging part of what is now British Columbia with them, as a result of tectonic activity near the end of the Jurassic period. There were intermittent restless recurrences of islands of oceanic rock thrusting up against the western edge of the continent throughout the Cretaceous period. This brought about the rising of the Coast Mountains and caused Vancouver Island to surface.

Near the end of the Age of Dinosaurs, the huge Pacific plate began to move in such a frenzied way that it split in two. Part of it sank below the western margin of the United States. The other part crashed and bumped northeastward. The tectonic pressures were such that the same rock that had earlier formed the sea floor at the continent's edge was now folded and shoved up inland to form the craggy peaks of the Canadian Rockies, part of the great mountain system being thrust up along the length of the North American continent. The general rising lowered the sea level and brought about the cooler, drier climate that accompanied the Cretaceous/Tertiary extinction and the end of the Mesozoic Era.

There was a reversal in the early Cenozoic when Alberta once again experienced a warm, wet environment. Several million years of this time are registered in the strata north of Drumheller. The top of the Scollard Formation, which occurs 40 metres above the K-T boundary, has been dated at 63.5 million years old. Its coal seams and meandering river channel deposits are indicative of the existence of swampy marshlands, populated by an amazing spread of ferns. Palaeobotanists refer to this vegetation phenomenon as a 'fern spike.' Heavy year-round rainfall and warm temperatures combined with localized rising of the water tables, were the major factors in creating a lush green world. These conditions predominated for approximately 10 million years into the Tertiary, as mammals

At the end of the Cretaceous Period, mammals, which had been around as long as the dinosaurs, were still very small. They are known mainly from teeth. It was in the Tertiary Period that they began a program of rapid diversification and established the Age of Mammals.

were diversifying and radiating out to lay claim to vacant niches left by the extinctions.

The fossils of marsupials are found in the Scollard Formation but they are less common than those of placental mammals. This is a reversal of the situation in the older strata of Dinosaur Provincial Park. Perhaps over millions of years, marsupials had been gradually losing out to a group of more advanced placental mammals, the insectivores. The eventual supremacy of the latter may be explained by the rapid propagation of insects, their food source, which accompanied the ubiquitous spread of flowering plants, all developments of the Late Cretaceous. The cooling climate was probably also a factor that brought about the southward emigration of the marsupials by the middle of the Tertiary. They succeeded in establishing themselves in Central and South America, and the only representatives of marsupials now in North America are members of the opossum family. Ferocious little shrews, hedgehogs and moles are a few of the varied and widely-distributed modern day survivors of the insectivores, which are first known from the Late Cretaceous.

The most abundant and successful mammals of the Early Tertiary were the multituberculates, which had been around in North America and Eurasia since near the end of the Jurassic Period. Although most were small, the size of mice, some were as large as beavers. They were, in fact, very rodent-like but had already become extinct before true rodents appeared about 57 million years ago.

Into the Cenozoic Era, spasmodic upheavals of the Rockies continued. The new mountains were laden with debris from all this tumultuous activity, and young, rushing rivers carried tonnes of deposits in both directions from the watershed. During millions of years, the deposits pouring eastward were dropped, eroded, and moved about until, finally, they coalesced into an unbroken plain. So enormous were the pressures, that folding and squeezing occurred in the foothills and extended to the plain, causing the gentle eastward downwarp of the Alberta syncline.

For the first half of the Tertiary Period, the entire planet was experiencing a boom in mountain building. The sea level was dropping and a general climatic cooling was taking place. As the Rocky

Creation of the Badlands

Mountains continued to strive towards the ultimate heights they reached finally about 45 million years ago, the face of present-day Alberta was shaped. The last drops of the Bearpaw Sea drained away, the wetlands dried up, and the two halves of the continent were reunited. The climate became steadily cooler and drier and, in this area, grasses and sedges gradually supplanted the hardwood forests that had begun to establish themselves while the dinosaurs were still around and become more dominant during the first half of the Tertiary Period. Ancestors of modern primates and hoofed species, along with rodent-like creatures and medium-sized flesh-eaters—early dogs, bears and cats—were all part of the faunal scene.

From the forty-million-year-old Cypress Hills, just east of Medicine Hat, come fossils of at least 100 different species of mammals, running the gamut from mouse to rhinoceros, along with evidence of many fish, reptiles, amphibians and birds. Grass itself does not fossilize well, but its spread is recorded in the animal skeletons found in the Hand Hills Formation near Drumheller, which dates from some 30 million years later than that in the Cypress Hills. Here, horses, which had evolved to become quintessential grazers, predominate. The presence of other grass-eaters—camels, primitive pronghorns and bison—is also registered in the fossil story.

The last major formative geological phenomenon leading to the sculpting of the badlands began two to three million years ago, and many scientists believe it continues into the present. Although there were several ice ages earlier in Earth's long history, it is customary to capitalize the most recent one. The reasons for the onslaught of the Ice Age are still not completely understood but many attribute profound changes in the climate to the tectonic activity that brought about the uplifting of mountains and the drift of continents to higher latitudes. Once glaciers begin to form, they are thought to make their own contribution to increased cooling by reflecting the sun's warmth away from the Earth. Alteration in the Earth's orbit that caused a reduction in the amount of sunlight reaching the planet's surface may have played a major role in the advance of glaciation.

The Ice Age has seen several glaciations, relieved by interglacials when warming caused the ice sheets to retreat.Some scientists believe that we are currently experiencing the most recent of these interglacial periods. The most recent glacial stage, the Wisconsinan, began about 80,000 years ago. Like armies massing for a forced march, ice caps formed in the north and east and consolidated into the Laurentide ice sheet to begin a slow but inexorable outward conquest. Simultaneously, the Cordilleran ice sheet was spreading out of the western mountains. Save for small areas of the Arctic coast, a few mountain peaks and high hills, such as Alberta's Cypress Hills, all of Canada was overpowered and locked in the frigid grip of ice. There is more glaciated terrain in this country than anywhere else in the world.

Nothing in the path of the ice flow was exempt from its destructive power. Its grinding action bore down upon the soft rocks and pulverized them to powder; the more resistant were yanked up and carried along in its run. Large areas of land were stripped to bedrock. The grip of the ice was not constant. Subject to prevailing climate, it advanced and retreated.

The last major advance of ice is known as the Late Wisconsinan. It reached its maximum extent over Alberta about 22,000 years ago. It is a moot point whether or not Alberta was directly attacked by any save this very last phase of glaciation. If it was subjected to earlier ones, all evidence has been erased, possibly because of the ferocity of the most recent one.

At glacial maximum, and for a time during its early retreat before the melting ice caused sea level to rise again, access between Siberia and North America opened across the Bering Land Bridge. Some archaeologists believe that the first humans made their way into North America by this route and then moved down the eastern slope of the Rocky Mountains and down into Montana as the ice withdrew. No irrefutable evidence of this has been found but there is fossil proof of other animals that weathered the Ice Age freeze. Near Medicine Hat, skeletons of mammoths, horses, reindeer, camels, and other animals have been found that both pre-date and post-date the last advance of ice.

The reasons for the climatic changes that produced the interglacials are as elusive to pin down as the ones that brought the

Creation of the Badlands

freeze. Break-up of the Late Wisconsinan ice sheets began about 20,000 years ago. The retreat of the ice, and the subsequent dispersal of its meltwaters, was rapid and not entirely orderly. In geologi-

This isolated knife-edge marks a division of flowing meltwaters at the end of the Ice Age. The small channels, or rills, on the face of the rock are a feature of most steep slopes in the badlands. They are caused mainly by fast-running rainwater.

cal terms, it happened in the blink of an eye, in less than 10,000 years. For some of this time, lakes covered much of the surface of the land. They were formed when large amounts of melting water were dammed by remnant glaciers. Glacial Lake Bassano and Glacial Lake Drumheller were two of these large bodies of water. When warming spells caused breaches in their ice walls, enormous volumes of water were liberated.

Flowing water takes the path of least resistance. In some cases, preglacial stream beds were reoccupied; in others, the water was compelled to carve out a new channel. In preglacial times, the headwaters of the Battle River were located near the city of Red Deer. As the waters of Glacial Lake Bassano began to look for an escape route, they were prevented by an ice block from using the ancestral river bed. Their natural tendency to flow east thwarted, the waters were diverted southward and the spillway they created became the Red Deer River valley. Glacial Lake Drumheller added its burden of water to the flow which carried on in a southeasterly direction to Dinosaur Provincial Park. Not until well east of the park does the river enter a wide preglacial channel, which carries it to its confluence with the South Saskatchewan.

Old age has mellowed the Red Deer. In the turbulence of its youth, it carried rushing volumes of meltwaters that cut easily through the thin protective layer of glacial rubble to expose a cross section of prairie bedrock dating from very ancient times. Slashing down 150 metres, it created the deep canyons of the Drumheller badlands. By the time the waters reached the Dinosaur Park area, they formed a gargantuan flood that carved out a valley five times as wide as today's river. Channels carrying the rapid runoff merged in many places, then veered off in new directions to link up with other streams. This branched network of watercourses can be discerned in the many discontinuous and isolated landforms characteristic of badlands terrain.

As the ice retreated, the debris that was entrapped in it was left behind. These deposits of debris are called glacial till, or drift. The thickness of the till and the resultant soil conditions of Alberta are proportionate to the rate of melting of the ice. The process was most rapid in southern Alberta where thin sandy soils are characteristic. Voluminous glacial waters met little resistance as they began the sculpting of the badlands. Once the soft bedrock was bared, it was easy prey to the more moderate forces of erosion.

This is a land of climatic extremes. The lowest annual precipitation of the Red Deer River badlands is registered in the Dinosaur Provincial Park area. It averages about thirty-three centimetres, most of which is concentrated in flash floods of summer, when rain races down the faces of the hills, washing away loose surface materials. Aside from these sporadic rainfalls, the prevailing conditions of summer are hot and dry. Temperatures soar to the mid-thirty-degree-Celsius range, or occasionally higher.

By contrast, the deep cold of winter frequently sends the mercury down to minus forty degrees Celsius. The winters would be harsh, indeed, were it not for a west wind beloved of prairie dwellers. Long ago, the Plains aboriginals christened this westerly after

Creation of the Badlands

This 1921 photograph shows
George Sternberg bridging
a narrow chasm.

a tribe living in the Columbia River basin of British Columbia. It is called "Chinook." It gusts down from the Rocky Mountains, at rates up to sixty kilometres per hour, raising temperatures as much as fifteen degrees Celsius within minutes. The Chinook is not an end to winter; it is merely a break, and freezing conditions inevitably return. Ice crystals form, like wedges, in the crevices of the badlands rock. Thawing and freezing, by turns, intensify a prying action that eventually splits the rock asunder.

Many people believe that the term "badlands" is synonymous with "desert" but although the micro-environment in the depths of the badlands approaches desert conditions—even boasting the occasional scorpion—badlands are a true prairie phenomenon. Average annual precipitation is thirty to forty centimetres in the badlands compared with less than half that amount in most desert areas. Some plant families, such as cactus, are common to both, but the distinctive prairie growth is grass.

The name "badlands," which has become generic for this type of erose landscape, derives from a description used by early French fur traders to denote similar areas in the Dakotas of the United States. The portion of that description in general use sounds categorically negative. In fact, the full phrase was *"mauvaises terres a traverser."*

Anyone who has approached the badlands with the assumption that the shortest distance between two points is a straight line would surely agree with the early trappers. Indeed, these are "bad lands to cross." Climb a hill to get to the other side and, where you might expect a gentle descent, you may well find yourself on the edge of a sharp drop into a canyon below. Steep ravines, undergoing ceaseless erosion, force lengthy detours for anyone not possessed of a mountain goat's ability to defy gravity.

The sandstones, siltstones, shales and clays that make up the badlands are similar to one another in that they are all soft and can offer little resistance to the onslaughts of the elements. But, within the broad scope of similarity, there are subtle differences at the root of the endless variations of shape and form.

Bentonite clay influences unique variations in the landforms. Its distinguishing component is volcanic ash that arrived here, borne on the west winds more than sixty million years ago. The clay containing a high proportion of this decayed ash is greenish gray in colour and has a crumbly texture when it is dry. In this state, it is as safe as any surface in the badlands. But it is possessed of a Dr. Jekyll/Mr. Hyde quirk. Wet, it changes character and appearance. Its particles swell to twice their dry size and take on a dark leaden tone, symbolic of the danger they hold for an unwary walker.

Mounds with the look of old-fashioned haystacks are common badlands forms. They are composed largely of bentonite clay, which has been worked upon by a process familiarly known as "popcorn erosion." Following saturation, the clay dries unevenly. The outer layer shrinks and cracks into kernels. These are vulnerable to quick removal by wind and rain. Vegetation is scarce on these hills, so they erode at a consistent rate, which results in their gently rounded contours.

Sandstone hills with a high bentonite content are distinctive for their decorative surface patterns. Once the covering layer of bentonite clay is soaked, excess water runs off it, as off an umbrella. It courses along the face of the soft foundation rock and, on its way to the coulees below, carves intricate top-to-bottom rills.

Other interesting characteristics of badlands topography are the sinkholes. These are the hollows in slopes, caused by runoff water eating through the surface to pursue a subterranean route. They hold the allure of caves and some of them go deep into the sides of the hills. There is no apparent connection between the point where the channel vanishes into the hill and its re-emergence. Lower down in the formation, it mysteriously re-appears as though from the depths of the earth. Often, the 'roof' of an underground channel caves in and only the remnants of land bridges remain to distinguish it from an ordinary surface stream.

Probably the most fascinating of all badlands forms are the curiously anthropomorphic hoodoos. These are the pillars of stone topped by flat horizontal cap rocks. The cap material may consist of consolidated sandstone, hardened by the action of minerals present in the ground water. It is commonly rich in iron which lends it a rusty tone. Many of the smaller hoodoos are capped by glacial erratics, rocks imported to the area by glaciers. The harder caprock of the hoodoos protects the more delicate one beneath it but gradually the pillar is worn thinner and finally it cracks. The cap topples and in the fullness of time may grace a new pillar of sandstone.

Hoodoos may be tall or short, they may stand singly, be arrayed in rows of military precision or form irregular groups. However they appear, they are the stuff of imagination—mysteriously assuming the guise of first one figment of fantasy, and then of another, according to the light and the angle from which they are viewed.

Rocks in foreground once formed
caps for some of the pillars in
this hoodoo complex. Erosion brought
them tumbling down.

In the badlands, the truism "change is the only constant" is visibly reinforced. Erosion alters the landscape with unremitting regularity. However, as is the case with most of Earth's processes, its progress is cyclical. Wherever conditions are at all conducive, vegetation will settle in to check its advances. The battle wages to and fro, but the essentially yielding nature of badlands rock predicates that, in the end, the elements will win. For several years, geomorphologists, those scientists engaged in the study of the features of Earth's crust, have conducted quantitative analyses of erosion in Dinosaur Provincial Park. These studies have measured the retreat of the barren scarps to be proceeding at the rapid rate of almost a centimetre per year. If weathering continues at this pace, and if the climate remains relatively unchanged, they predict that, within ten thousand years, the same forces that model the badlands forms will have battered them into oblivion.

For those of us who cherish the spirit and drama of the landscape, such a prospect seems lamentable. But, for the scientific world, this situation, brought about by Nature in the role of destroyer, is a positive development. It presents an unequalled opportunity to learn of a world that thrived millions of years before our time.

Undercut during spring runoff, these hoodoos will eventually collapse. Erosion eats at the soft rock causing its surface to crumble and be washed away.

15

Badlands Treasure

The meltwaters of the Ice Age thaw carried out a great rout of destruction through the ancient dinosaur graveyard. It is intriguing to wonder how long it was before the giant bones began to inch their way up to the surface. Did they lie exposed eleven or twelve thousand years ago when a small tribe of foot nomads pursued a herd of mammoths across the plains? In what long ago springtime did a young aboriginal boy, running to join the braves of his band for his first buffalo hunt, trip on a massive bone protruding from the ground in his path? Sadly, these are questions to which there can never be answers.

What little is known of aboriginal involvement with dinosaur fossils comes from an unpublished document written by Jean L'Heureux, a renegade priest who lived among the Blackfoot. In 1887, L'Heureux was present, as an interpreter for the great Chief Crowfoot, when the leaders of the Blackfoot tribes signed Treaty Number Seven with the Canadian government, accepting the limitations placed upon them by the advance of white civilization.

L'Heureux's manuscript, written in French, was translated into English by the Glenbow Museum in Calgary. The manuscript outlines several geographic features of southern Alberta, giving the aboriginal names by which they were then known. Since the map that must have accompanied the text is missing, the exact sites are difficult to pinpoint in many cases. All that may be said for certain of the following, taken from the translated manuscript, is that it describes a spot in the Red Deer River badlands:

> in a large coulee whose sides to the west are cut almost perpendicularly to a height of more than three hundred feet, among the debris of erratic blocks are found many fossils of dorsal vertebrae of a powerful animal. These enormous vertebrae measure up to twenty inches in circumference. The natives say that the grand-father of the buffalo is buried here. They honour these remains by offering presents as a means of making the spirit which gave them life to help them in their hunt.

Back row: Jean L'Heureux,
Red Crow (Blood), Sergeant W. Piercy (NWMP),
Front row: Crowfoot (Blackfoot), Sitting on Eagle
Trail (North Peigan), Three Bulls (Blackfoot).

The badlands country of the Red Deer lies at the heart of what was once the immense hunting preserve of the Blackfoot nation. In the eighteenth century, as fur traders ventured westward from Hudson Bay and Montreal, they reported that the Blackfoot were in control of a vast extent of land, stretching from the North Saskatchewan River south to the Upper Missouri, from the Rocky Mountains in the west to what is now the Alberta/Saskatchewan border. Three tribes made up the Blackfoot nation—the Peigan, the Blackfoot (Siksika), and the Blood. The small Sarcee tribe was allied to the Blackfoot and lived within their territory. So, too, did the Gros Ventres until they ran afoul of the more powerful Blackfoot and were forced out of the area sometime after 1800.

Few written records remain of the native presence in the badlands. Of these, a tragic account, contained in <u>David Thompson's Narrative,</u> tells of a smallpox epidemic believed to have terminated for many in the Dead Lodge Canyon of Dinosaur Provincial Park. Almost every evening for four months during which Thompson travelled with the Peigan, he listened to the stories of a very old Cree man, Saukamappee. One of these concerned a time, about 1730, when the Peigans gained ascendancy over other plains tribes because they had guns. Thompson paraphrases, "We thus continued to advance through the fine plains to the Stag [Red Deer] River when death came over us all, and swept away more than half of us by the Small pox,..." The fever drove "those that were near the river into which they rushed and died."

Peter Fidler, a fur trader like Thompson, is the first white man on record to have entered the badlands of the Red Deer River. Like Thompson, Fidler was dispatched to winter with the Peigan, learn their language and thereby improve the opportunities of the Hudson Bay Company to barter with them for furs. He left a journal of his five-month stay with the Peigan, full of detailed accounts of their way of life and of the country through which he and his fellow trader, a man named Ward, travelled with them on their wanderings over the plains.

Badlands Treasure

Slabs were arranged to create this 'dream bed' high on a hill in the heart of the badlands. In isolation from the others of his tribe, a brave went to such a vision quest site hoping, through fasting and prayer, to be blessed with a visit from a sacred power, in the form of an animal, to guide him through life.

On their way south from Buckingham House on the North Saskatchewan River, they camped in December of 1792 in the area of the Rosebud River below Drumheller. They were again in the badlands on their return journey in February of 1793, this time on Kneehills Creek. It was in this vicinity that the first discovery would be made of Red Deer River dinosaur remains, but although Fidler left us the first description of a cactus and the first record of the presence of coal strata, he makes no mention of bones.

He does report that, while in the badlands, the women occupied themselves collecting ochre, the red pigment used for, among other things, the symbolic adornment of the body before the hunt. All prehistoric cultures accorded spiritual power to red ochre, the colour of blood, of life itself. The plains aboriginals were no exception as evidenced by a couple of stories collected from their descendants in the 1920s by the ethnographer Marius Barbeau. His informant George McLean, a Stony, said, "The old people thought that mud, red paint, was a medicine. We still use it as a medicine." The power of the paint was extended to the place where it was found. From this, and from the presence here of the 'grandfather buffalo' bones they honoured, it is not too fanciful to assume that the Peigan and other plains tribes held the badlands to be a place of reverence. Fidler reported that his companions were shocked when he started a fire with some of the coal they found on Kneehills Creek. This may have been because of the sacred nature of its location rather than with the idea of using coal as fuel.

With these few exceptions, the prehistory of humans in this area is written in stone—not in fossils but in teepee rings, medicine wheels, cairns, and effigy figures. Each of these tells a part of the larger story of a bygone culture.

Located on a high, grassy, windswept hill in the depths of the badlands of Dinosaur Provincial Park, lies what is known as the 'dream bed.' Built of sandstone slabs, the rectangular bed measures one metre in width by two metres in length. A Blackfoot in search of spiritual strength would have gone to this site. There he prayed for four days during which he was exposed to the elements and without food or drink. Through prayer and fasting, he hoped to be blessed with a visit from a sacred helper, perhaps in the form of an animal, to direct him in his life. A vision-quest site similar to the one in Dinosaur Provincial Park was still in use in Montana at the beginning of the 1900s.

The meanings of a stone effigy, also in the area of the Park, are more elusive. The crude figure of a man, measuring about seven metres from top to toe, is outlined in boulders on a rise of land overlooking the badlands. He is firmly earthbound, yet the prostrate attitude of the figure seems to dispose it heavenward. Neither tree nor shrub intrudes between the figure and the distant dome of the sky. It is emphatically male, with a distinct connecting line running between the head and the heart. The arms reach out in supplication, the hands curved upward as though in anticipation of gifts from on high. No one knows how long this miraculously intact figure has lain here, nor from what creative impulse he sprang.

Stone effigies of this type have not been commonly found. Of those known, some have been in association with cairns, specially constructed rock piles, the significance of which is a matter for conjecture. Barnum Brown, one of the first palaeontologists to come into the Red Deer country, made a note in his field book of a boulder figure near Tolman Bridge. He said the figure was laid with its head to the east and measured approximately six metres from head to buttock. It was situated near a stone pile which was, originally, about one-and-a-half metres high and eight metres in diametre.

There is a sense of power and magic in the effigy of this stone man, although the purpose intended by his aboriginal maker is unknown.

In 1911, when Brown made a journey by boat with H. F. Osborn, the president of the American Museum of Natural History, Osborn's field notes mention that the stone pile was "partly destroyed by curiosity seekers." He says, also, that the complex included a presentation of a horse and that the stone pile had been made of "30 carloads of stone."

Medicine wheels, complex structures often incorporating cairns such as the one described above, are found on private land in the environs of Dinosaur Provincial Park. Some archaeologists have likened these to Stonehenge and believe they may have served as observatories to predict the auspicious day on which to hold the most important yearly gathering of the clans for the Sun Dance.

Jumps were features of the buffalo hunt for many thousands of years. These are naturally-occurring sharp drops over which the animals were driven to their death. The best-known one in Alberta is Head-Smashed-In which is now on the UNESCO World Heritage

List, with all the protection afforded such internationally recognized cultural sites. Unfortunately, the jump for which Dry Island Buffalo Jump Provincial Park, in the northern badlands of the Red Deer, is named had no such protection. By the time it was made a park, souvenir seekers had taken away so many artifacts that the site held little value for archaeological study. However, staff at Midland Provincial Park in Drumheller are available to interpret the site for visitors, who would find it difficult to understand without some guidance. This is largely because natural slumping has destroyed the original slope over which the buffalo were run. The drop was about 45 metres high, one of the highest in Alberta. It was the second most northerly jump in the province.

Competition for furs was the impetus for European penetration into the Northwest. As the raw materials of the fur trading industry were depleted by indiscriminate over-trapping in the eastern woodlands, those who served the trade pushed ever westwards in search of new stocks—chief among these were beaver pelts.

The main artery of the western fur trade was established along the North Saskatchewan River, which runs through pond-dotted, aspen woods favoured by the coveted little beaver. Trading posts were strung along the North Saskatchewan, like a few beads with long, empty gaps of chain between them; they stretched all the way to the foothills where Rocky Mountain House was built.

To the south of this lay the prairie, the territory claimed by the Blackfoot nation. It was partly fear of involvement in the continual warring of the Blackfoot with their enemies, and partly the poor potential for furs, that limited traders forays onto the plains. Trading posts operated, during the winters of 1801-2 and again for a time in 1822, at Chesterfield House, near the confluence of the Red Deer and South Saskatchewan Rivers. Aside from these short lived experiments at setting up shop on the southeastern prairie, trading between the Blackfoot and the fur companies was concentrated at the more northern forts. Another factor influenced the association between the trading interests and the Blackfoot nation: the fact that, try as they might, the traders were never able to persuade the Blackfoot to take up trapping in a serious way. The buffalo hunt was the traditional occupation of the plains tribes, not one they were prepared to abandon. Buffalo meat and pemmican were the main trading commodities offered by the Blackfoot in their treks to the trading posts on the North Saskatchewan. And so, for many years after the fur trade moved westward, the southern prairie remained Blackfoot hunting grounds and the European presence was very occasional.

After Peter Fidler's visit in 1792, almost seventy years were to pass before the next recorded exploration of the badlands country. It was in 1857 that the British North American Exploring Expedition set out from London under the command of Captain John Palliser. This expedition signalled a change in the way in which Britain regarded the Northwest. It had been exploited profitably for its furs. Now, the Palliser expedition was dispatched to determine its agricultural and mineral potential, with an eye to the possibilities it offered for settlement. Exploration of the vast wilderness by the Palliser expedition lasted for three years. The team of men who undertook this monumental task crossed and recrossed the plains, travelling by horse in summer and by foot, on snowshoes, in winter. It was during their last season's work in 1859, that they began the portion of their trip that took them along the lower Red Deer River to its confluence with the South Saskatchewan.

The reputation of the Blackfoot as both dangerous and hostile created problems for the expedition, which was slated to travel through the heart of their territory. There were difficulties with guides, first in engaging their services, and later with their desertion because they were afraid of the Blackfoot. Although nothing untoward actually happened, the expedition was harassed all along the way by small bands of young braves. Because of the propensity of these adventurers to make off with untended horses, the expedition was forced to mount a twenty-four hour guard over their saddle and pack horses.

One member of the expedition was a young Scottish geologist, Dr. James Hector. His detailed observations of the country he travelled through are highly spoken of by geologists who have succeeded him. Perhaps because of the administrative problems

Captain John Palliser (left) and Dr. James Hector (right) in 1860, following their historic exploration of the Canadian west.

encountered by the expedition during its explorations along the lower Red Deer River, Hector did not make as extensive an analysis of the strata of the valley as he could have done under more relaxed circumstances. He did collect marine fossil shells from the area below Drumheller; however, he did not come upon any dinosaur remains.

Although Fidler was the first to mention coal in the area of Drumheller, it was Hector's more extensive reports on the large coal deposits present that stimulated intensive exploration of this region by the Geological Survey of Canada.

As part of its plan for settling the Northwest, the Dominion of Canada negotiated the building of the Canadian Pacific Railway. Prior to the advent of immigration, which the railway would facilitate, the government fielded exploration parties to map large areas of the country and to assess its mineral wealth. Construction of the railway got under way in 1881. That same year, under the direction of George M. Dawson, the Geological Survey of Canada began work in what is now Alberta.

When he began the investigations that were to culminate with his "Report on the Region in the Vicinity of the Bow and Belly Rivers, North-West Territory," Dawson was already an old hand in the West. Almost a decade earlier, he had been a geologist with Her Majesty's North American Boundary Commission, the Canadian contingent of a joint American-Canadian expedition to survey and map the international boundary between the two countries, from Lake of the Woods to the Rocky Mountains. It was while on the boundary commission that Dawson made the first discovery of dinosaur fossils in western Canada. His find was made in 1874 in the Frenchman Formation at Wood Mountain, near what is today the village of Killdeer in Saskatchewan. His second discovery of dinosaur remains was made later that same year on the Milk River in southern Alberta.

During 1881, the first season of his work in Alberta with the Geological Survey of Canada, Dawson, with his assistant, R. G. McConnell, explored the Oldman (Belly) River. Here they found more evidence of the great beasts that had roamed the region in prehistoric times. The following year, in the area known as Scabby Butte, northeast of Fort Macleod, McConnell collected a large number of fossilized bones, which were later identified as belonging to dinosaurs.

Dawson's assistant in 1883 was a young geologist by the name of Joseph Burr Tyrrell. After only one year in the field in this capacity, Tyrrell was entrusted with an independent survey, stretching over a forty-five-thousand-acre area between the Bow and North Saskatchewan Rivers. The future site of Drumheller lay approximately in the centre of this large area; and it was there, in June of

George Mercer Dawson (3rd from left) with a Geological Survey Party in British Columbia in 1879.

During his career with the Geological Survey of Canada, Joseph Burr Tyrrell served as an officer with the Governor General's Foot Guards.

1884, that Tyrrell decided to begin the work that was to take him three years to complete.

Given the nature of the broken terrain and the steep descent from the prairie to the river, Tyrrell determined that the best approach for exploring the river walls was from their base upwards. In accordance with this decision, he abandoned his horse in favour of a canoe. It was to prove an excellent choice for his purposes and river travel was a mode of transportation that later explorers of the Red Deer would refine to suit their own needs.

The season began with a great burst of good fortune. In the course of one short week, Tyrrell discovered a wealth of dinosaur remains and one of the largest deposits of coal on the continent. He was aware that his discovery of dinosaur bones was not the first to be made in western Canada. But, as he examined these beds stretching along the river, his excitement mounted. He gradually realized that nothing previously uncovered could compare—in extent or richness—to this dinosaur graveyard on the banks of the Red Deer. About a month later, in the Kneehills Creek area where Fidler had camped with the Peigan almost a century earlier, Tyrrell encountered the first dinosaur skull to be found in the valley.

Sixty-nine years later, at the age of ninety-five, after a long and exciting career during which Tyrrell made numerous important mineral discoveries and was recognized for his contributions to the growing knowledge of Canada's geology, the old man could still recall vividly the discovery of the dinosaur skull in the badlands of Alberta. In a speech to the Geological Society of America, in Toronto, he described the experience. "I was climbing up a steep face about 400 feet high. I stuck my head around a point and there was this skull leering at me, sticking right out of the ground. It gave me a fright."

He had few tools suited to the job of excavating the skull and no proper packing materials but he took it carefully from its resting place. He also dug up several other specimens. Two months elapsed, in which he pursued other work, and it was fall when he returned to pick up his collection. Getting the fossils up to prairie level was an ordeal that might have discouraged a less persistent person. The face of the hills was wet with a cold drizzling rain. The horses could barely manage to pull an empty wagon up the steep incline leading out of the valley. But the precious fossils could not be abandoned. Packing them, a few at a time, on the backs of the horses, Tyrrell and his assistant made repeated trips, gingerly leading their ponies up from the valley to the plain and back down again for the next load. The trip to Calgary, from where the fossils were shipped to Ottawa, stretched into a week of very slow going. In an effort to lessen the jarring of the fossils in the wagon, they were hauled at a walking pace over the rough, roadless prairie.

At that time, there was no one at the Geological Survey, or anywhere in Canada for that matter, who was versed in the specifics of dinosaur anatomy. The skull was sent for study to Professor Cope at the Philadelphia Academy of Science. He identified it as belonging to a large flesh eater of the Cretaceous, later to be christened *Albertosaurus*.

Tyrrell's excitement about his fossil discoveries in the Red Deer was shared by his colleagues at the Geological Survey. The director decided that Thomas Weston, the official fossil collector for the department, should extend the investigation of the fossil-yielding strata of the prairie river. Weston came west in 1888 and began a trip along the Red Deer. Unfortunately, the trip had to be aborted eight miles downstream of its starting point at the town of Red Deer because of low water and a boat that was not riverworthy.

Thomas C. Weston in the 1880s, the decade of his expeditions into the Red Deer for the Geological Survey of Canada.

The following year, Weston returned to the Red Deer and this time, with better preparation, he succeeded in his objective. With two able assistants and two boats to carry provisions and fossils, he took up from the point where he had left off the previous summer.

It was to be a trip of short duration, but one of historic importance to the future of palaeontology. Between the 17th of June and the end of the month, Weston explored the formations from above Big Valley to the mouth of the Rosebud River, going over much of the ground covered earlier by Tyrrell. In early July, however, he drifted into new territory. His field diary records his location on the 1st of July, 1889, as Range 16, Township 25, between the Drumheller badlands and those of Dinosaur Provincial Park.

> left vicinity of Rosebud and continued downstream making about 30 miles. We are now quite out of bone locality, in fact only a few weathered bits of fossil bone have been seen for the last 50 miles. . . Hoisted flag for Dominion Day on a high butte below Rosebud.

This entry has a discouraged tone, but his mood was soon to alter. By July 5th, the party reached the Dead Lodge Canyon. As soon as he began to examine the fossil beds here, he realized that he had reached the richest fossil lode of the Red Deer River valley. His collecting attempts yielded disappointing results. Hours of work were lost when most of the fossils he excavated crumbled. But he was able to assess the potential of the beds; and, although he spent only a few days exploring the area, he was highly optimistic about it. "This is a grand field for collecting—much the best seen so far on this river," he wrote. Even this enthusiastic endorsement now seems pale, in the light of the proven wealth of the oldest dinosaur beds in the valley. However, several more years were to pass before experienced bone hunters would realize how incomparably important Weston's trip had been in pointing the way to one of the great dinosaur repositories of the world.

Lawrence Lambe was the next member of the Geological Survey to explore the badlands for dinosaur fossils. He made, in all, three collecting trips to the Red Deer. In 1897, Lambe began, as those who preceded him had done, at the town of Red Deer. From this point, between 31 July and 31 August, he and his party explored the valley all the way to the mouth of the Red Deer.

When he came out in 1898, Lambe took what may have seemed a more direct route to the fields he was interested in exploring further—the Dead Lodge Canyon badlands. He came from Ottawa by rail to Medicine Hat. From here, on 19 July, he and his party set out for the Red Deer River. Heavy rains had turned the prairie sod to mud. The horses were sorely taxed by having to pull the wagons loaded with provisions and a four-metre spruce boat through the soggy plain. It was

Lawrence Lambe directed preparation of dinosaur exhibits for study and display in the GSC's Victoria Museum.

the 23rd of July before the party finally caught sight of the cutbanks of the river, but every time they attempted to move directly toward them, they would strike a precipitous coulee and be forced to detour. It was late in the day on 24 July before they finally reached the mouth of Berry Creek, where they set up camp. A month later Lambe's field notes summarize his activities. He and his assistants had packed up twelve boxes of fossils which Lambe estimated to weigh about a tonne and a half.

Lambe returned to the Red Deer one more time. In 1901 he worked for two months at the heart of Dead Lodge Canyon, obtaining the best yield of fossil materials to that time. Unfortunately, he had only a rudimentary knowledge of collecting methods and, as a result, much of the material he amassed was fragmentary.

Lambe's first job with the Geological Survey of Canada was as an illustrator. When an excavation job was beyond his ability, he often made detailed drawings of it *in situ*, carefully noting its dimensions. In his field notes, accounts of the day's activities are interspersed with fine line drawings. Most of these are of bones, but there is an occasional elegant little sketch of a badlands scene.

Lambe was the first Canadian palaeontologist to attempt scientific descriptions of the dinosaur fossils of the Red Deer. With the assistance and encouragement of H. F. Osborn of the American Museum of Natural History in New York, Lambe undertook to write a monograph describing the fauna collected from the Judith River Formation (now known as the Dinosaur Park Formation). It was published in 1902. Later palaeontologists have criticized Lambe for his tendency to name genera and species of dinosaurs on the basis of insufficient material. Only hindsight, however, could have told of the many intact skulls and skeletons lying in wait for the expert bone hunters soon to come upon the scene.

16

The Great Canadian Dinosaur Rush

It was the summer of 1914. The ominous clatter of European nations making ready for a war that was to drag the world headlong into its vortex made only the faintest rumble in the remote badlands of the Red Deer River. Here, the preoccupation was with a race of peaceful proportions, one in which there were no losers. Minor irritations occasioned by territorial disputes among the contestants faded in the face of the rich treasure of dinosaur remains in the valley. As autumn drew on, vying parties from the American Museum of Natural History and the Geological Survey of Canada departed triumphant from the field, each with a fair share of the booty.

In this fifth season of a period that has been called the "Great Canadian Dinosaur Rush," efforts were concentrated in what is now Dinosaur Provincial Park. In those days the area was known as the Steveville - Dead Lodge Canyon badlands. Steveville was a village north of the ferry crossing which was a short way downriver of the present-day Steveville Bridge on Secondary Highway 876. Dead Lodge Canyon is a stretch of the river closely flanked by badlands in Dinosaur Provincial Park.

A party from the American Museum of Natural History, under the direction of Barnum Brown, was situated on Little Sandhill Creek near where today's park visitors camp. On the opposite bank

Early bonehunters prospected from a floating camp. Here the scow of the Sternberg party is towed to a new campsite in the northern badlands.

of the river, eight kilometres downstream in the heart of Dead Lodge Canyon, Charles H. Sternberg and his three sons, George, Charles M., and Levi, located a base camp and set to work on behalf of the Geological Survey of Canada.

Impetus for the rush for dinosaurs was set in motion in 1909 when Barnum Brown made a reconnaissance trip into the Drumheller badlands. Ironically, it was not the meticulous drawings of Lawrence Lambe's 1902 monograph that ignited Brown's interest, but a chance remark made by a rancher from the Red Deer on a visit to the American Museum. In a 1938 Calgary Herald interview, Brown related this story. He said, "Wagner [sic] ...passing the door of the dinosaur hall remarked that he had tons of bones like that at the Drumheller Ranch." Brown was hooked. He wound up his work in Montana that summer and then, in September, paid a visit to the ranch of J.L. Wegener on Michichi Creek.

He returned to New York charged with excitement about the rich virgin fields crying out for exploitation. His enthusiasm quickly infected his superiors and, at the beginning of the following summer, the American Museum's first expedition into the Red Deer was underway.

In the seasons of 1910 and 1911, with Peter Kaisen who would act as his assistant until the end of 1914, and a Mr. Davenport from Montana who doubled as cook and teamster, Brown worked the stretch of the river from Big Valley down to Willow Creek. The usual procedure for fossil hunting was to set up a camp at a central location and fan out from there to explore the surrounding country. It was apparent to Brown from his first view of the steep narrow badlands lining either side of the winding river in the Drumheller area that this system, which worked well in the Montana badlands, would be inadequate here. To locate a base camp on either bank would risk being cut off by the river's flow from a rich field directly opposite and less than a mile distant. Easy accessibility to both sides of the river was what was wanted.

River transport had been used by earlier explorers and Brown now adapted it to better serve the needs of bone hunters. At a sawmill in Red Deer, he had a five-by-twelve-metre flat boat built, large enough to transport a wagon and team plus all their supplies, equipment and camping gear. When it was ready to launch, a small curious crowd gathered to see them off. A man called Charles Bremner was hired to navigate the big scow through 100 kilometres of boulder-scattered rapids below the city.

Once into calm waters, they used their vantage point at midstream to scan the cliffs on either side as they passed through the deep canyon of exposures. When they spied a promising area, they poled their way to shore with the long oars attached to either end of the scow, tied up and made camp. Their first collecting stop was at Big Valley.

They remained in one place long enough for the party to thoroughly prospect a given area and to collect any specimens they uncovered. They then loaded the specimens aboard and shoved off again downstream. The boat had a carrying capacity of eight tonnes. By the end of the season it rode low in the water, every available space jammed with box upon box of fossil cargo.

They finished their excavations in 1910 near where Tolman Bridge is located, arranged with local ranchers for winter storage of their possessions, and made the 65-kilometre haul to the railroad at Stettler. Brown's early estimate of the rewards awaiting him in these beds proved to be conservative. Each season crates of fossil material, much of it new to science, were recovered to enrich the already impressive dinosaur collection of the American Museum of Natural History.

The association between the American Museum and the Geological Survey of Canada had always been cordial and cooperative.

Hauling fossil collection from Barnum Brown's camp at the mouth of Little Sandhill Creek to the railway siding, 1914.

When Barnum Brown undertook his first foray into the Red Deer, the Survey supplied him with maps and various geological data to forward his efforts. Canadian geologists who had explored the Red Deer country for the Survey in the late 1800s were well aware of its fossil wealth. Now, Brown's successes confirmed that the valley was teeming with the remains of the ancient Cretaceous world.

Dinosaur collecting by the Survey had been sporadic, partly because there was no one on the staff acquainted with the special techniques for excavating large specimens so early efforts had been less than successful, and partly because the cramped quarters occupied by the Survey precluded storage and exhibition of the giant fossil animals. A significant change in the tradition of the Survey occurred when it moved to the newly built Victoria Museum in 1911. The luxury of space allowed for expansion of the collections and an accelerated rate of acquisition.

Obviously, the time was ripe for the Canadians to enter the lists as serious dinosaur hunters. But who was to undertake the job? There was no one in Canada qualified. Naturally, eyes were cast southward to where bone hunters had been perfecting their trade for several decades. The Survey had bought some specimens from Charles H. Sternberg, who was a freelancer. He was highly respected in his profession. When he was offered the post of chief collector and preparator for the new vertebrate palaeontology section of the Geological Survey, he accepted. So, in July 1912, he and two of his sons journeyed to Drumheller to begin what was to be a romance of long standing between the Sternberg family and the fossil-yielding valley of the Red Deer River.

This was Brown's third field season in the valley. He seems to have been a gregarious man. Or perhaps a lonely one — his wife had died suddenly in the spring of 1910. At any rate, his notes for the month of June 1913 read like a social calendar — birthday celebration with the Hands on June 16, supper with the same family June 20, overnight visit to Postels June 22, ten visitors to his quarry "A lovely day" on June 23. Then came July and the arrival of George Sternberg, whose services he had engaged for the season. George brought with him the "disquieting news" that the arrival of his father and brothers on the Red Deer was imminent.

Brown and the elder Sternberg shared a reputation for unerring success in sniffing out fine dinosaur specimens. The famous hall of dinosaurs in the American Museum of Natural History is largely the result of Brown's prowess in the field and many museums in North America and Europe enjoy the benefits of Sternberg's instincts.

Brown was born in Kansas. Following graduation from university, where a freshman course in palaeontology determined his future path, he joined the staff of the American Museum of Natural History and was associated with that institution throughout his long working life. For nine seasons preceding his first expedition to the Red Deer, he collected in the dinosaur beds of northern Montana.

More than twenty years Brown's senior, Sternberg was a seasoned veteran of the dinosaur hunt. He was sixty-two years old when he came to the Red Deer and had spent his entire adult life in pursuit of fossils in the richest fields of the United States. Born in New York state, he moved westward to Kansas in his youth. All of his children were born and raised there. His oldest son, George, had been his assistant from the time the boy was twelve years of age. Charlie joined the family concern in 1908. Levi's introduction to the business of bone hunting was in 1912 when he joined his father and brothers on the Red Deer.

Although the Sternbergs and Brown came from the same part of Kansas and were employed in a young and sparsely populated profession, it seems their paths had not crossed prior to their meeting on the banks of the Red Deer. Of course, each knew the other by reputation and their mutual respect was sincere enough to sometimes be rather grudging. Brown was the first palaeontologist of international calibre on the scene and, perhaps understandably, he had a proprietary feeling toward the valley in which he had pioneered and been so richly rewarded. From 1910 to 1912 his party had the two-hundred-kilometre stretch of river erupting with fossils virtually to themselves. The Sternbergs' arrival disturbed this

In 1913, the Sternbergs followed Brown into the Steveville – Dead Lodge Canyon badlands. The Sternberg crew is paying a friendly visit to the scow camp of the American Museum of Natural History.

pleasant arrangement, and the race to be the first to the best the valley had to offer heated up.

Brown had made a scouting trip by canoe in 1911 in the company of some senior staff of the American Museum of Natural History. He assessed from this reconnaissance that even richer fossil finds awaited downriver. Acting on impulse, he moved quickly to be first into the Judith River beds (now the Dinosaur Park Formation). In 1913, the Ottawa party followed his lead. Both Brown's party and the Sternbergs spent the next three seasons between what is now the western boundary of Dinosaur Provincial Park and the Red Deer's easternmost badlands.

Relations between the two parties were quite friendly until 1914. They were camped near one another, and sometimes one group joined the other for a meal and conversation. One incident with a pleasant international flavour took place when the American Museum party relocated camp, moving flat boat, motor boat, and row boat a short distance downstream, and passing the Sternbergs' similar outfit of crafts en route. A photograph recorded the respective 'fleets,' one flying the United States Stars and Stripes, the other with the Union Jack, Canada's flag at that time, waving on high.

Unfortunately, resentment lay beneath this outward camaraderie. Brown wrote to his superiors in New York in 1913 that he was "really provoked that they [the Sternbergs] should follow our footsteps so closely." George Sternberg worked for the American Museum in 1912 and was engaged for the 1913 season; but shortly after his arrival that year, he moved to join the Geological Survey group headed by his father. Brown confessed in a letter to the American Museum president that George's departure, though an inconvenience in that it left him a man short, was a relief because now the Sternbergs would not be informed of his every move. He neglected to mention that George had been equally candid with him about the activities of the Ottawa party. Cool heads back in New York cautioned that the American expedition relied upon the good will of the Canadian government and that Ottawa, in view of Brown's accomplishments in the Red Deer fields, would continue to look favourably upon his presence there only if those in its own party were having comparable success in their search for dinosaurs.

When the bone hunters arrived in the Steveville - Dead Lodge Canyon badlands, the surrounding area was fifty times as populous as it is today. These were the heady high-hopes years of homesteading. One young man who had taken a quarter-section in The Bend near Steveville was hired by Brown in 1913 to replace George Sternberg. Taking the job was to essentially alter the pattern of A.T. Johnson's life. He quickly advanced from cook to excavator and Brown was so impressed by his aptitude for the work that he hired him for the 1914/15 winter as a technician at the American Museum. Johnson returned in the spring to sow his crop but was back at work in the badlands by the middle of May. When the 1915 field season wound up, Johnson left the tilling of the soil behind and moved to New York to join the staff of the American Museum. In his future lay Roy Chapman Andrews, dinosaur eggs, and the Flaming Cliffs of the Gobi Desert.

Before joining Brown's team, Johnson had done some work for a freelance bone hunter, William Cutler. According to an account left by W.G.Hodgson of Dorothy (a dabbler in the fossil business who, in later years, gained some fame for wood carvings made from juniper root), Cutler was a well-educated Englishman who had earlier ranched up on Three Hills Creek. Other writers have given him a homestead in the Steveville environs. Wherever his career in Alberta began, he had left it behind at this point to hunt for bones. He had spent the spring prospecting and, before either Brown or the Sternbergs arrived, was camped below the Circle Ranch, about 30 kilometres downriver from the Steveville settlement.

Under what seems to have been a very loose arrangement, Cutler was bone hunting for the Calgary Natural History Society which had been formed in 1910 with the intent of creating a museum for the city. Financing for Cutler was to be provided by a group of the Society's members who set up the Calgary Syndicate for Prehistoric Research. This was a rather pretentious title for an organization that seemed unable to rustle up sufficient funds for plaster. From his camp below the Circle Ranch came a series of complaining

The Great Canadian Dinosaur Rush

Specimens are packed to be moved by horse and sled to where they can be loaded onto a wagon.

letters addressed to Dr. Sisley, the president, about the impossible situation Cutler found himself in with two beautiful skeletons and no money to hire someone to help him lift them nor materials to attempt the job himself. A.T. Johnson was the "kind man" who helped him move camp and one of the letters asks that Johnson be paid the small amount of money owing him. Cutler goes on to complain that he has no team or wagon, not even a saddle horse to take him the 20 miles to Steveville to see if lumber and plaster have been sent him from his Calgary patrons.

Cutler had invited both Kaisen and "a Sternberg son" to look at his finds *in situ* and been assured by them that he was right in thinking they were important specimens. When Brown arrived in July he confirmed these opinions. He saw right away that one of the skeletons held promise of being a very important discovery; it was what he thought might be an as-yet-unknown duck-billed dinosaur but what was even more noteworthy was that it had left skin impressions in the rock. He coveted the specimen for the American Museum and, as each man had something the other wanted, they struck a bargain. In exchange for teaching him the techniques for getting large skeletons out of the rock with the bones intact, Cutler would turn his specimen over to Brown. The only proviso was that if it turned out that the animal was indeed new to science, it would be named for Cutler. Both men, in separate communications, informed Dr. Sisley and the Calgary Natural History Society of the arrangement, Brown offering to prepare a specimen for them free of charge in exchange for the one Cutler had found. True to his word, when he wrote the scientific paper describing what turned out to be, not a duck-bill, but a new horned dinosaur, Brown called it *Monoclonius cutlerii*.

The season with Brown's team paid off for Cutler. It seems that, like Brown and Sternberg, he had a good nose for where dinosaurs were hiding and he now had the necessary skills to rout them out. In 1914, he found an excellent skeleton of an armoured dinosaur which he sold to the British Museum. This began an association

A block and tackle was used to load this one-tonne section of a duck-billed dinosaur excavated in 1921 by George Sternberg for the Field Museum of Chicago.

that would continue until his death. After army service in France, he came back to the badlands and continued his solitary search for fossils. Much of what he found he sold to the British Museum. In 1924, when that institution was looking for someone to lead an expedition into the fossil fields of Tendagaru in what is now Tanzania, Cutler was contacted. He headed up the British Museum East African Expedition with the assistance of a young man who was to become the world's best known palaeoanthropologist, Louis Leaky. Sadly, Cutler contracted malaria and died in Lindi in 1925.

In 1913 Brown's party worked the large pocket of badlands on the south bank of the river stretching back from Little Sandhill Creek. Time did not permit the excavation of all the specimens they located that season so Brown's intent was that they should complete the unfinished work in 1914. He viewed this portion of the badlands as exclusively his for the season. Prior to Brown's arrival in late July of that year, Peter Kaisen, his assistant who had been encamped since early June, visited the Sternbergs at their camp down river and, according to his diary, they agreed with the boundaries Brown had designated as defining the American Museum preserve. Apparently, the agreement was not so clear as he supposed. His temper flared when he discovered the rival party was working not far from his camp. He recounts how he attempted to come upon them unawares as they were prospecting the area and how, to his annoyance, he lost sight of them in the steep gorges that cut through the rough terrain. He did, however, go to their camp to confront them with the charge that the word of a Sternberg counted for very little.

Brown, upon his arrival, complained once again in a letter to the museum in New York denouncing the Sternbergs for a lack of ethics, an accusation he later repeated in his annual report for that year. The question of bone-digging ethics was clearly open to interpretation. Following the confrontation with Kaisen, it seems Sternberg wrote to his employers in Ottawa requesting clarification of their ground rules in this regard. The reply came back that while it would clearly be a breach of collecting ethics to take up a specimen marked for excavation by the rival party, there was no transgression involved in prospecting any area of the badlands and no one group could legitimately lay claim to such a large area.

Perhaps the nub of the disagreement was a bit of chagrin on Brown's part which erupted over George Sternberg's discovery of a very fine skull and partial skeleton of a new type of horned dinosaur. It was the most complete skull of a ceratopsian found up to that time and it was retrieved from an area where Brown had prospected earlier. Footprints assumed by the Sternbergs to be his were noted a short distance from where the skull was eroding from the earth. There is nothing surprising in Brown's having missed this specimen. Prospecting is an unpredictable business and a few feet one way or another can mean a find or, alternatively, a miss. All bone hunters know this, but most have great difficulty maintaining their equanimity when capricious luck deserts them to play into the hands of a rival.

Barnum Brown, (left) and H.F. Osborn, (right) from the American Museum of Natural History. They are shown developing a Diplodocus prospect in Wyoming in 1897.

A mild sort of avarice is characteristic of a collector of any stripe. Although he may manage to acquire fine samples of whatever he is amassing, he will still eye the collection of another enviously, suspicious that it may be better than his. This minor vice has enriched the holdings of the world's great museums and, by extension, the cultural life of all who visit them. Fossil hunters are not exempt from it; and, in the case of Brown and the Sternbergs, the result was a lively competition from which the world of science benefited immeasurably, as each was driven to beat the other to the finest representatives of the ancient dinosaur world of the Red Deer.

The Great Canadian Dinosaur Rush

The senior Sternberg looks pleased with the horned
dinosaur skull emerging from the rock, 1913.

The dispute over territory had the potential to turn nasty and might have done so had there been a scarcity of specimens. As it was, the Dinosaur Park area was a bone hunter's El Dorado. Each party had more than enough fine skeletons to engage its complete attention. It was fortunate, too, that the 1914 field season was most propitious for bone hunting. Recently arrived settlers to the Red Deer country watched with heavy hearts as the near-drought conditions burned their crops crisp. But, to paraphrase an old adage, it's an ill sun that warms nobody. The long, hot, cloudless days were a boon to the fossil hunters. Through June into early October, only three days of work were lost because of rain. There was little time to sit in camp and brood about what those in the other party were up to. Once specimens were selected for excavation, there was much to be done to lift them from the ground before the frosts came. The nature and intensity of the work guaranteed physical exhaustion at the day's end, a powerful antidote to petty concerns.

The days were growing short and the valley was tinged with the golds of early autumn before the final phase of the season's work was done. At the end of September, the long haul of wagons packed to the brim with crates of fossils began the journey from the badlands edge to the nearest loading points on the newly built Canadian Pacific Railway branch line running between Bassano and Swift Current.

By Barnum Brown's assessment, 1914 was the most prosperous of all the years he worked in the Red Deer badlands. He carried away no less than eight important skeletons, all of which he judged to be of exhibition quality.

The Sternbergs, too, had reason to feel pleased with their efforts. It took a party of five men a full day to haul and load their specimens. An entire box car was required to transport the fruits of their season. In <u>Dinosaur Hunting in the Badlands of the Red Deer River, Alberta, Canada</u>, C. H. Sternberg gives us this description:

> On the 28th of September, 1914, we hauled in our last load of fossils and loaded our car at Denhart. This point was a switch on the open prairie; the store building was deserted. It was a miserable day, with the wind blowing a gale from the north. I built an oven of some loose bricks that were lying and cooked a meal as best I could on the wind-swept plain. It was four o'clock in the afternoon before we started on our thirty-mile drive to Brooks, where we were to take our train homeward bound.

Wearily, they climbed into the wagon and moved off through a cold, clear night across a prairie lit by a crescent moon and millions of stars. And then, to continue in Sternberg's words:

> Suddenly, as if to relieve our tiresome journey, God's moving pictures, the Northern Lights, burst upon us in all their glory. It seemed as if a heavy map was suddenly unwrapped in the sky, the folds taking a fan-like perpendicular, radiate shape, then another and another unrolled, until the whole northern arc of the heavens was vibrating with light in white bands, edged in colours of many delicate and exquisite tints.

The elder Sternberg was a man with a mystical reverence for Nature who saw the hand of God in all its workings. To him, the ethereal display must have seemed a splendid end to a season divinely blessed.

If working conditions in 1914 were a bone hunter's dream, those of 1915 were his nightmare. Heavy rains kept the river running out of its banks for much of the summer. Water inundated coulees that had for many years lain dry, save for spring runoff. The soaked, soft clays of the hills were slimy and treacherous underfoot. As a result, prospecting was curtailed and there were days when simply negotiating from camp to quarry was an ordeal. With the rains came a plague of mosquitoes. Brown wrote that they were "fearless of smoke, ferocious and in numbers equal to the Kaiser's army."

By way of compensation for the physical discomforts endured, the fossil harvest was, as always, bountiful. The Geological Survey fielded two parties in 1915. One, led by George Sternberg, worked for five months over a sixty-five-kilometre stretch from above Big Valley down to the village of Rowley. The other, with C. H. Sternberg in charge, was once again in the Steveville - Dead Lodge Canyon badlands. They extended their efforts east as far as Jenner.

American Museum of Natural History camp on Berry Creek below Steveville in 1913.

Netted against mosquitos, the crew from the American Museum of Natural History is prepared for work.

Brown was back in the seemingly inexhaustible Little Sandhill Creek area. He worked this season with Johnson as his only full-time assistant, thoroughly covering the ground he had only skimmed in previous seasons. This second look paid off. Several times in Brown's field notes and correspondence, he says how dearly he wishes to find the "much desired *Palaeoscincus*," a name used at this time for an armoured dinosaur that is now called *Panoplosaurus*. Its discovery was a fitting finale to the 1915 expedition which was to be the last the American Museum would make into the Red Deer. At the end of the season, it was estimated that it would take five technicians, working two full years, to prepare the specimens collected in these fields. It was assessed a fine representa-

Dr. W.A. Parks (right), Director of the Royal Ontario Museum, paying a visit to his crew camped on Little Sandhill Creek in 1921. They are (left to right): 2 local assistants, the cook (seated), G.E. Lindblad and Levi Sternberg.

tive collection of the major varieties of dinosaurs to be found in the valley. Sounds were beginning to be heard from Alberta residents about the wisdom of allowing this wholesale export of the valley's fossils to foreign countries. All in all, it seemed the time had come to move on to other fields.

The year brought another major change to the configuration of the groups at work in the badlands. It was the last year the Sternbergs worked as a family unit. The war was having its effects on government budgets and, with Brown out of the picture and the compulsion to compete for fossils relaxed somewhat, the Geological Survey decided that the only field work for the 1916 season would be George Sternberg's completion of what he had undertaken the previous year in the Drumheller badlands.

Denied the fossil hunt, the very soul of his existence, the elder Sternberg resigned his post with the Survey and, taking Levi with him, went back into the Steveville badlands as a freelance operator. He suffered a blow at the hands of the German navy in 1916 when two very fine skeletons of duck-billed dinosaurs bound for the British Museum went to the bottom of the Atlantic aboard the torpedoed SS *Mount Temple*. He wound up his sojourn in the fossil fields of the Red Deer with the highly productive season of 1917. Among several excellent discoveries were a number purchased by the American Museum of Natural History to round out its holdings. This transaction was made on the recommendation of Barnum Brown, a fine tribute to the skill of his old bone-hunting adversary.

The Great Canadian Dinosaur Rush had slowed to a steady pace. In the years that followed, the name of Sternberg became inextricably linked with the Red Deer badlands. Charles M. Sternberg spent his life studying, describing, and adding to the fossils he, with his father and brothers, had gathered for the Geological Survey of Canada. When the collection was transferred to the control of the National Museum in 1920, Charlie went with it.

Much of the outstanding dinosaur collection in the Royal Ontario Museum is the result of the field work of Levi Sternberg. He joined the staff of the Toronto museum in 1919 and remained in

Charles M. Sternberg (Charlie) came to Canada in 1912 as a bone hunter, but gradually assumed responsibility for scientific descriptions of his discoveries. He published almost 50 papers, most of them on dinosaurs, during his career with the Geological Survey of Canada and, later, the National Museum of Canada. He died in Ottawa in 1981 at the age of 96.

its employ until his retirement forty-three years later. Over the years he led numerous expeditions into the Red Deer.

George Sternberg left the Geological Survey in 1918 for much the same reason his father had two years before. He worked independently around the Little Sandhill Creek in 1920, sold his season's collection to the University of Alberta, and then worked that winter preparing the specimens for the geology department of that university. The 1921-22 season he spent collecting for the Field Museum of Natural History in Chicago, after which he returned home to the United States.

With so many Sternbergs in the valley, it is not surprising that the local people often confused one with another, sometimes with unexpected results. In 1921 all three brothers, under the auspices of their respective employers, had parties in the Steveville - Dead Lodge Canyon badlands. The National Museum had arranged for a film to be made to inform its public of the work of the palaeontologist in field and laboratory. Charlie Sternberg made every attempt to coordinate his summer's work so that when the film crew arrived, they would be able to record each stage of its development. The weeks passed with no sign of cameramen nor any message that they were on their way. The season neared its end and, as he crated his specimens for shipment, Charlie assumed plans for the film had fallen through. He went to call at his brother George's camp before departing for the East and only then did he learn that the film crew had, in fact, been in the badlands that summer. From the discussion between the brothers, it became clear what had happened. When the strangers asked at the nearby village of Patricia for directions to Sternberg's camp, they were sent to George rather than to Charlie. George, knowing nothing of the background, did his best to provide the camera crew with suitable subjects to photograph. The end result was a hybrid recording of George's work in the field for the University of Alberta and Charlie's in the laboratory of the National Museum of Canada in Ottawa.

Although the Royal Ontario Museum got a little later start in dinosaur collecting, it made up for lost time and now houses one of the outstanding exhibits of Red Deer River dinosaurs. Actually, to be strictly accurate, Alexander McLean was sent out from this museum in 1912, the same year that the Sternberg family began bone hunting in the valley. McLean was completely inexperienced in the collecting of such large specimens and the results he achieved were negligible. W. G. Hodgson was the local rancher engaged to assist McLean. On a tape filed at the Glenbow Museum in Calgary, he left this recollection: "I guided the first dinosaur expedition on the river for the Royal Ontario Museum. The leader of the expedition was Dr. John [sic] McLean.... When I went out with McLean, he didn't know anything about it, so we learned together."

In 1918 William Arthur Parks, director of the palaeontology department at the ROM, made a collecting trip and Hodgson was again hired: "Then, I went out with Dr. Parks from Toronto University. We got a *Kritosaurus*. We got a pretty good specimen and got them mounted." The problems encountered in getting this specimen prepared moved the staff of the Royal Ontario Museum to go in search of an experienced practitioner of the art. It was at this time that Levi Sternberg was hired.

Every history of human endeavour marks out a special place for its pioneers. In the annals of palaeontology in the Red Deer, the names of Barnum Brown and the Sternberg family share that hallowed position. It should be remembered, however, that many others contributed to their successes—their assistants who left the comforts of city life behind to moil for bones in the heat and dust of a badlands summer, and the local workers who bent their backs to their labours with no thought of fame. Photographs of expedition crews sometimes included the latter, but only very rarely were their names given in the captions.

After those early years, when one new find after another spurred the competing parties on, the race for dinosaurs was never again as intense. Widespread interest in the beasts waned as the century wore on. Parties from the Royal Ontario Museum and the National Museum of Canada in Ottawa continued to send expeditions into the field for some years, but after the mid-1950s, the hunt abated. Then, with the rebirth of enthusiasm for dinosaurs in the 1960s and 1970s, it was taken up with new vigour.

With the passing of time, the complexion of the dinosaur hunt in the country of the Red Deer has altered. No longer is it quite the freewheeling adventure it once was. It is now conducted under the direction of the Royal Tyrrell Museum of Palaeontology. There are strict controls over the removal of fossils from the valley, especially from the fossil preserve of Dinosaur Provincial Park where much of the attention of today's bone hunters is concentrated.

17

The Fossil Hunt Continues

The methods used to collect specimens have altered little over the years. The craft of successful location and excavation of the friable, ancient bones of the dinosaurs and their fellow creatures remains labour-intensive and painstaking.

Palaeontologists begin their field work each year in late spring. Throughout the season, prospecting teams comb the hills and coulees for evidence of recently exposed fossils. Nature is a cooperative partner in the search; erosion eats away at the soft sediments and brings new exposures of bone to the surface with each new season.

Not so many years ago, when the science of palaeontology was in its infancy, the discovery of fossils was rather a hit and miss affair. Through experience and improved methods of dating sediments, earth scientists have learned which horizons of strata yield which particular assemblage of fossils. A bone fragment found in the grassy bed of an ancient stream or halfway up the steep face of a cliff is a clue for the prospector to scramble up to the level where the rest of the skeleton may be. Of course, not every isolated tooth or piece of bone leads to a complete skeleton; but, considering the odds against fossilization, the number of intact dinosaur skeletons found in the Red Deer River badlands is astounding.

Once the prospector, slogging his way through the rough terrain of the badlands, comes upon an exposure of bone that holds the

Levi Sternberg and crew from the Royal Ontario Museum work on a narrow ledge preparing a skeleton for removal from the quarry, 1930.

promise of more skeleton to come, he records all relevant information about location, geographic alignment, and surrounding sediments, for future assessment. Based upon data collected by prospecting teams, sites are chosen each season for excavation.

Bone hunters refer to excavation sites as quarries. A typical quarry is the shape of a hollow bowl, cut into the side of a steep hill. As the quarry is unapproachable except on foot, and a sure foot at that, supplies and equipment are carried in by the crew. Various stages of the work may entail lugging jackhammers and the gasoline to fuel them, or twenty-five-kilogram bags of plaster and the water to mix with it, over roughly cut paths for over a kilometre.

For fear of damaging the fossils, dynamite is no longer used to remove the tonnes of rock that may lie on top of them. Now, the heaviest mass of the rock is shattered by a jackhammer; picks and shovels complete the rough work.

The working area carved out by this method is limited and the noise and dust created in the constricted space is far from pleasant, even when protective gear is worn. Once the rough work is finished, dust continues to be a problem as hot, dry winds are an ever-present summer feature of the badlands. So, too, are the invisible insects, which attack without mercy. And the bowl of the quarry

The Fossil Hunt Continues

Overburden of rock is loosened with a jackhammer and shovelled out of the quarry to expose the skeleton

acts like a heat trap, offering little protection from the burning rays of the sun. When relief does come, it is usually in the form of flash rain storms that hinder progress with the work and make footing in the badlands treacherous.

All in all, these are not conditions designed to attract enthusiastic workers. Yet, palaeontologists love their chosen vocation and volunteers return year after year, often on holiday from their regular jobs, to help in the search for fossils. The obvious question is: "Why?

Part of the answer surely rests upon the fact that each quarry is like an unsolved mystery. A few exposed bones are the tantalizing clues. Not until all of the scattered pieces are uncovered and the collected evidence examined will the crew know what secrets lie hidden in the rocks. An air of expectancy hovers over the quarry as the work begins. Will they find an entire skeleton? Will it be one of the finest specimens of its kind known to science? Will it represent a species rarely found? Or, most exciting of all, will it be a dinosaur never before discovered?

This horned dinosaur skull is being coated with a glue preservative as soon as it emerges from the rock

The answer to any one of these questions might well be positive. On the other hand, after the labour of jackhammering and shovelling rock to get to them, the bones may simply peter out a meter into the hill. In that case, what the crew is left with is some isolated bones and a knowledge that the rest of the carcass was scattered by scavengers or by rapidly moving water shortly after the animal met its death. The information scientists are able to glean from such materials is worthwhile, so the time cannot be said to have been wasted. Nevertheless, a slight feeling of deflation accompanies the closing of a quarry.

When the find proves more extensive, the bones continue to emerge as the heavy overburden of rock is removed. Once most of the rock is gone, the crew switches to finer tools, such as geologists' hammers, chisels, awls and soft brushes, to remove the last of the covering matrix. Great care is required to remove the matrix without damaging the fragile bones. Immediately upon exposure, the bones are coated with a glue mixture to seal up fractures and to halt deterioration from the elements.

Most skeletons uncovered in Alberta are destined for removal to the Royal Tyrrell Museum of Palaeontology. Because the season is short, it is impractical to remove each bone of a large skeleton individually. Instead, a trench is dug around a group of closely positioned bones, deep enough to allow for the inclusion of any bones that may lie under those the crew has exposed. Several layers of burlap soaked in plaster are wrapped around the block, encasing the bones and some of the rock in which they rest. This

The Fossil Hunt Continues

Royal Tyrrell Museum crew has plastered the top of the specimen and undercut the rock beneath it.

acts to protect the bones just as a cast does a broken limb. After the plaster has set, the block is undercut with hammers and chisels until it resembles a mushroom in shape. It is then toppled to expose its underside. All excess matrix is removed from this face to reduce weight, and the plastering procedure is repeated. The plaster jackets are left to harden; and, then, the skeleton is ready to ride forth from the tomb where it has lodged for millions of years.

While methods for collecting these large specimens have remained similar over the years of bone-hunting history, what has changed considerably is the focus of the fossil hunt. No longer are exhibition-quality specimens the major preoccupation of palaeontologists. They have turned their interest to the behaviour of the dinosaurs; the question of how the animals looked has given way to how they, and their fellow creatures, lived. The science of ancient ecologies has grown to be a multi-disciplinary study, with vertebrate and invertebrate specialists working in conjunction with palaeobotanists, palynologists, sedimentologists and taphonomists to decipher the complexities of the Late Cretaceous world from the many and diverse clues left for them in the rock.

The result of the application of all this diverse expertise is that knowledge about the area is frequently enhanced and/or refined. As an example, studies of the Dinosaur Park strata by Royal Tyrrell Museum sedimentologist, Dr. David Eberth, and a colleague, Dr. Anthony Hamblin of the Calgary branch of the Geological Survey of Canada, led to the recognition of distinctions within the Oldman Formation. Above a marker occurring consistently at a low level in the park, the character of the rock alters sufficiently to indicate a difference in the conditions under which the deposits were laid down. These strata are now known as the Dinosaur Park Formation. Studies such as these shed new light on the adaptability, or lack thereof, of living organisms to changing environments.

It is only in recent years that the study of bone beds has been elevated to become a priority of the research program at the Royal Tyrrell Museum. Palaeontologists had been aware of the existence of bone beds since the early days of prospecting in the badlands but had more or less ignored them in preference for the complete skeletons which they so frequently found. The *Edmontosaurus* bed incorporated into the Day Dig program at the museum is an example of this. The very fine skull of the horned dinosaur *Pachyrhinosaurus* in the Drumheller Dinosaur and Fossil Museum

Plaster coats are made today almost exactly as they were in 1916. Here, George Sternberg has flipped his specimen over and is applying the final plaster-soaked burlap strips to it.

The Fossil Hunt Continues

Bringing order to the jumbled scattering of fossils in a bone bed is done by a combination of collecting and mapping

was recovered from this bed in 1960 but no further attention was paid to the other material deposited there until almost thirty years later.

Bone beds appear as a carpet of weathered fragments over the surface of the ground. For many enquiries, they are more likely to hold answers than are beautifully articulated single skeletons. From such a jumble, patterns are suggested of herding behaviour, migration, parental care, growth rates within groups and vulnerability to natural disasters or disease. Scars on bones and the presence of teeth give hints about predation.

Working a bone bed demands care and patience. Only a thin layer of rock covers the bones. Crew members work with fine tools—tiny awls, dental picks, and artists' brushes—and extreme care, since the excavation of one bone might well damage another in close proximity. A grid system, based upon a metre square, is superimposed over the bone bed. Coordinates are established and the location of each specimen is transferred to a map, using the appropriate grid coordinates. Specimens to be collected are treated with a glue mixture, catalogued, and removed for laboratory study.

After many seasons of work in the football-field-sized *Centrosaurus* Quarry 143 wrapped up, excavations were initiated in other *Centrosaurus* bone beds in Dinosaur Provincial Park. In the Drumheller Horseshoe Canyon Formation, work continues on the *Edmontosaurus* bed and plans are afoot to begin digging in 1998 in a recently rediscovered mass grave site of the flesh-eating *Albertosaurus*. Further north in the Grande Prairie area, a *Pachyrhinosaurus* bone bed is being excavated.

All fossilized remains that are not skeletal body parts are known as trace fossils. Footprints and trackways are examples of these. They yield important information about foot anatomy, gait and body posture. The animal that made a print can often be identified by comparing the print with preserved foot bones. Trackways may speak of migration routes or, more simply, of watering holes or shorelines. The trackways most studied by staff now at the Royal Tyrrell were submerged beneath the waters of the Peace Canyon in 1979. Before that happened, large sections of the trail were cut out, casts made of other parts, and extensive photography and mapping done. The trackways are over 100 million years old and record the earliest evidence in the province of hadrosaurs, certatopsians and birds. Some of the Tyrrell staff are now working in the Grand

A large specimen excavated in an area inaccessible to trucks may be lifted from the quarry by helicopter.

The Fossil Hunt Continues

Technicians attaching the skull of the Allosaurus *that is now on display in the Dinosaur Hall at the Royal Tyrrell Museum*

Cache area of Alberta investigating recently discovered trails of footprints and other fossilized dinosaur remains.

Skin and feather impressions offer hints of outward appearances and inner metabolism. Questions of parental care, reproduction cycles and group behaviour find some possible answers in the fossils of eggs, especially those with embryos, and in nests and rookeries. Stomach stones and fossilized faeces are clues to diet and digestive systems. All of these fall into the category of trace fossils and are a part of the body of data left behind by the dinosaurs.

If techniques in the field, of necessity, remain relatively primitive, those in the laboratory are beginning to take advantage of such technological advances as electron microscopy, 3-D computerized imaging, and computer tomography (CT scans). Computer programs are used extensively to diagnose relationships for taxonomic classifications. Data storage is vastly improved by good computer programs. Some institutions store their database on-line, accessible within minutes to scientists around the world.

The internet has exploded with information on dinosaurs, for the general public as well as for experts in the subject. It opens up formerly unimaginable possibilities for carrying out the educational function of museums. Many institutions, including the Royal Tyrrell Museum of Palaeontology, operate world wide websites that feature on-line tours of their collections and frequently updated information on their programs. Virtual reality may be just around the corner with the simulated sights, sounds and smells of life with the dinosaurs.

Now, back to the bare bones. It was commonly said, in the years following the Great Canadian Dinosaur Rush, that the fields of the Red Deer were almost exhausted, but the resurgence of fossil-hunting activity has shown this to be far from true. Staff of the Royal Tyrrell and their colleagues from other institutions, assisted by volunteers in the Field Experience program, have enjoyed great success from the re-examination of ground covered many times before, as is shown by the following recent discoveries from Dinosur Provincial Park alone. In 1995, while jackhammering at a fossil plant locality, workers chanced upon an ornithomimid skeleton. Many partial skeletons of these fragile fine-boned creatures have been collected in the past but this one turned out to have one of the best skulls ever found in North America. The following season, excavation of a large tyrannosaur, *Gorgosaurus libratus,* revealed it had an intact wishbone, a skeletal feature of particular interest to current discussions of dinosaur/bird evolution. Disarticulated skeletal remains of fish are not uncommon in the Park, but because of the delicacy of their bones, they are usually splintered and smashed. Prospectors were, therefore, very pleased in the field season of 1996 to discover a well-preserved metre-long sturgeon. That same year, during work in the hadrosaur Bonebed 47, a skull of a crocodile was found in excellent condition.

Every few years still sees the uncovering in this valley of a dinosaur new to science. Recently discovered and named is a small theropod, *Ricardoestesia,* of which evidence has been found in both the Dinosaur Park and Horseshoe Canyon Formations. There was a surprising discovery in Dinosaur Provincial Park in 1995 of the

The Fossil Hunt Continues

jaw of a protoceratopsid. These animals were known previously only from much later deposits in the Scollard Formation upriver. Such a find brings up short many of the theories about the group and forces a reappraisal of all of the evidence pertaining to it. It is clear from these few examples that there is much still to be learned from the database of raw materials stored in the rock of the Red Deer River badlands.

18

Dinosaur Graveyard: A World Heritage Site

On a pleasant June morning in 1980, a large group of government representatives and members of the public gathered on the rim of the prairie overlooking the badlands to celebrate the inclusion of Dinosaur Provincial Park on the World Heritage List. This prestigious list is the result of an international agreement, known as the World Heritage Convention, adopted in 1972 by the United Nations Educational, Scientific and Cultural Organization (UNESCO). The Convention recognizes that cultural and natural heritage transcends national boundaries and should be preserved for future generations. Its purpose is to identify sites of outstanding importance to all humankind and to foster concern among the member states of UNESCO for their protection. Only those countries that are signatories to the World Heritage Convention, some 145 at this time, are eligible to nominate properties within their borders for inscription on the World Heritage List. In Canada, Parks Canada is the federal agency responsible for implementation of the World Heritage Convention.

Nominations undergo rigorous scrutiny. In the case of a natural site, technical evaluations are carried out by specialists from the World Conservation Union, a non-governmental, international organization headquartered in Switzerland. Careful consideration

Dinosaur Graveyard: A World Heritage Site

is given to the management policies applied at the site to determine whether conservation is accorded priority. Every effort is made to maintain the integrity of the World Heritage List. One safeguard is provided by the World Conservation Union through ongoing reports on the state of natural heritage properties. Signatories to the World Heritage Convention pledge, first and foremost, to protect their sites and, second, to raise public awareness and respect for them. Should a country fail to fulfil these obligations, and the site become threatened because of neglect or industrial development or civil strife, it may be transferred from the World Heritage List to the List of World Heritage in Danger. This latter mechanism is designed to mobilize international efforts to preserve properties of universal value. A World Heritage Fund exists to provide financial aid to member states in emergency situations.

In the twenty-five years since the World Heritage List was established, the names of more than 500 sites have been inscribed on it. Most of these are of cultural importance. Just over 100 of the total are natural heritage sites and Dinosaur Provincial Park is one of these. It was chosen for several reasons in addition to the chief one, that being the enormous fossil wealth that makes it an outstanding example of the Cretaceous period in Earth's history. It also contains within its borders the largest and most spectacular

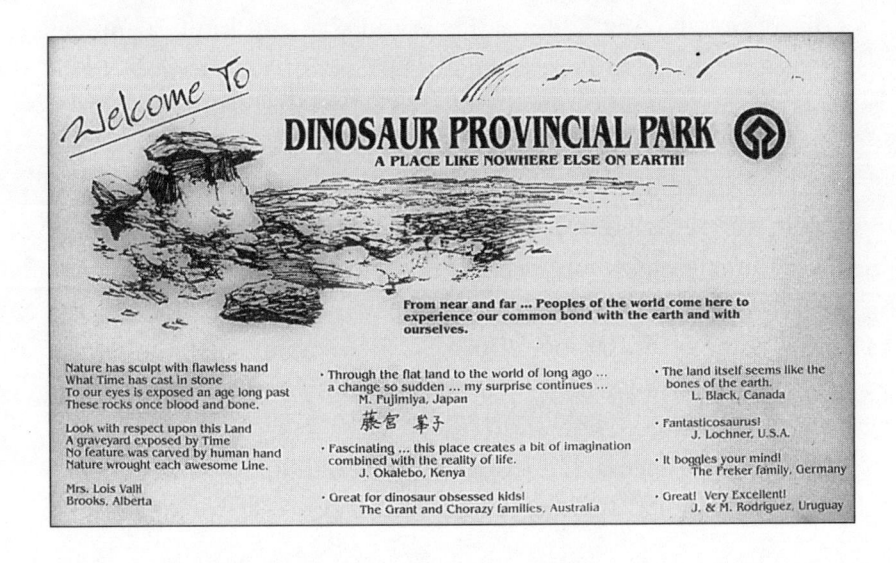

Welcome To DINOSAUR PROVINCIAL PARK
A PLACE LIKE NOWHERE ELSE ON EARTH!

From near and far ... Peoples of the world come here to experience our common bond with the earth and with ourselves.

- Nature has sculpt with flawless hand
  What Time has cast in stone
  To our eyes is exposed an age long past
  These rocks once blood and bone.

  Look with respect upon this Land
  A graveyard exposed by Time
  No feature was carved by human hand
  Nature wrought each awesome Line.
  Mrs. Lois Vahl
  Brooks, Alberta

- Through the flat land to the world of long ago ...
  a change so sudden ... my surprise continues ...
  M. Fujimiya, Japan
  藤宮 早子

- Fascinating ... this place creates a bit of imagination combined with the reality of life.
  J. Okalebo, Kenya

- Great for dinosaur obsessed kids!
  The Grant and Chorazy families, Australia

- The land itself seems like the bones of the earth.
  L. Black, Canada

- Fantasticosaurus!
  J. Lochner, U.S.A.

- It boggles your mind!
  The Freker family, Germany

- Great! Very Excellent!
  J. & M. Rodriguez, Uruguay

Edith Hall, wife of Steve Hall for whom the hamlet of Steveville was named. In 1910, the Halls homesteaded on the north side of the Red Deer River just below today's Steveville Bridge. They built a stopping place and a ferry to serve the landseekers pouring into the country.

---

badlands scenery in Canada which, in addition to its aesthetic appeal, affords a laboratory for the study of erosion and other geological current events. Finally, its endangered riverside environment, in which groves of plains cottonwoods provide critical habitat for a diversity of bird and animal life, is added justification to number Dinosaur Provincial Park among the ranks of such famous landmarks as the Grand Canyon and the Galapagos Islands.

When the news about the park reached home from the World Heritage Committee meeting held in 1979 in Egypt, many local people were amazed to learn that a sophisticated scientific jury of international experts considered the old bones and familiar badlands to be a universal treasure. Others greeted world recognition as the culmination of grassroots efforts initiated many years earlier to persuade governments of their responsibility to preserve the rich resource for future generations.

When the Great Dinosaur Rush floated downriver from Drumheller in 1912, Alberta had been a province for only seven

Dinosaur Graveyard: A World Heritage Site

years, and the area around the Steveville - Dead Lodge Canyon badlands was in the throes of homesteading. One of the few diversions from the demands of trying (and in most cases, failing) to wrest a living from the resistant prairie was an occasional Sunday afternoon horse-and-buggy outing to the badlands. Fossil excavation sites were points of interest on these tours. It is somewhat surprising, given all the preoccupations of an emerging society, that there were some few among the settlers who recognized the significance of the fossil lode of the valley. One of the most vocal of these was a doctor-homesteader, W.G. Anderson.

Born and raised in Stratford, Ontario, and educated at the University of Western Ontario in London, Doctor Anderson came to Alberta immediately upon graduation, first to Granum in 1905 and then to his homestead east of Wardlow in 1911. He had hoped for a break from the demands of practising medicine but in a country filling up with landseekers, the need was such that Doc, as he was known, soon found himself carrying on a country practice typical of the time, travelling many miles to minister to the needs of patients and caring for others in his own home. After telephones arrived, when the Wardlow exchange closed for the night, the community was hooked directly into his line.

Early bone hunters rented horses from the homesteaders. George Sternberg is about to move downstream with horse and sled to transport fossils from a quarry, 1916

Dinosaur Country

Almost no trace is left today of Steveville but in the 1920s, when this photo was taken, it was a bustling little centre for the homesteaders. During field seasons the bone hunters came to Steveville for mail and supplies. The buildings in this picture are from left to right: barber shop and pool hall run by Gus Grove; Al Henley's blacksmith shop; Steve Hall's meat market; Bert Coultis's general store and post office.

Once while attending a woman in an airless homesteader shack in the heat of summer, he arrived carrying a salvaged window. After shoving a plug of Piper Heidsik tobacco into his cheek, he set to work to install it. In this case, he thought the patient's welfare demanded more than just doctoring. Doc was loved by his patients for this sort of unpretentious generosity. Years later, he told the reporter John Schmidt, "If the patients couldn't pay, well, all right. I lost no money, only my time and that didn't amount to much."

He also ran a sheep farm and helped his wife to raise their three children. This sounds like enough activity to fill the waking hours of most people. Anderson, however, had the unusual good fortune of being able to function well with little sleep so he found the time to pursue interests other than professional ones, often reading far into the night on whatever subject his lively intelligence lit upon.

An interest in dinosaurs was stimulated by the arrival of the bone hunters in the badlands. He gained first-hand knowledge through visits with Barnum Brown and the Sternbergs. He followed each summer's field work with keen interest but it was not too many seasons before an uneasy feeling crept over him that

Dinosaur Graveyard: A World Heritage Site

something was amiss. As he watched carload after carload of specimens depart for faraway places, he began to worry that he might be witnessing the depletion of an irreplaceable resource. He was bothered by the presence of the American Museum of Natural History and, even more, by the fact that freelance bone hunters had *carte blanche* to dispose of the Red Deer River dinosaurs to the highest foreign bidder.

Backed by a group of local people who shared his concerns, Anderson began to agitate for the imposition of tighter controls over the removal of fossils and especially over their indiscriminate export. He pressed government officials in Ottawa to ensure the area's protection by declaring it a national park but, with its Rocky Mountain parks already in existence, Alberta was deemed to be getting more than its share of the funds allocated for federal parks.

Jurisdiction for Alberta's natural resources was transferred from the federal to the provincial government in 1930. The Legislature passed a Provincial Parks and Protected Areas Act but no one in Alberta had a heart for park development during the Great Depression that now set in. This was a particularly cruel

George Sternberg's assistants, Mr. Cryder (left) and Mr. Kelly (with folded arms) pause from the work of excavating a *Gorgosaurus* for a welcome visit with the Gayfer family, 1921. Mr. Gayfer was a construction engineer with the CNR.

Following his retirement to Medicine Hat, Doc Anderson took up "whittling" juniper root.

decade for prairie farmers in general and especially for those who had taken up homesteads in the Palliser Triangle, the large area encompassing much of southern Alberta and Saskatchewan. These families watched while their crops withered in the unrelenting drought that exacerbated the collapse of agricultural economies. It was so dry that they could not grow enough even to feed themselves. When the topsoil drifted off, most of the homesteaders followed it, taking with them the hard-won knowledge that they were leaving land that should never have come under a plough. Titles reverted to the government, gradually the grasses came back and the 160-acre homesteads were leased and absorbed into much larger holdings suitable for the livestock operations that became the livelihood of those who remained.

World War II followed hard on the heels of the Great Depression and the resultant lack of money in government coffers meant that the fossil hunt slowed to a crawl in the 1930s and '40s. This took much of the pressure to legislate controls off the authorities for a time. However, Doctor Anderson was constant to the cause. He continued to talk with politicians and others about the importance of the badlands resource to science and about the responsibility the province had to protect it. He had the ear of many influential Albertans who listened and agreed and, perhaps, brought the matter to the attention of those in power. He was widely known and respected: in agricultural circles through his service on the board of the Wool Growers' Association; and in the medical profession through his tenure—in 1920, 1935 and again in 1943—as president of the Alberta College of Physicians and Surgeons. He also represented Alberta on the council of the Canadian Medical Association from 1937-40.

Over the years, he had maintained his friendship with the Sternbergs who, as might be expected, felt as he did about the preservation of dinosaur fossils. With the authority behind them of their respective employers, the National Museum and the Royal Ontario Museum, Charlie and Levi both leant their support to his efforts. Finally, in the 1950s, persistence paid off. The Alberta government took steps to establish a badlands park.

Lobby groups from Drumheller, too, had been asking for a park for some years. In 1939 they succeeded in having the area on the river north of Drumheller, between Munson and Morrin, declared a protected area. When it was learned that the Alberta government was at last planning to establish a badlands park, both the Drumheller citizens and those in the Steveville area considered their portion of the badlands as the ideal spot. Before making a choice between the two, the government wisely sought the advice of Charles M. Sternberg, who knew the badlands of both areas like the proverbial back of his hand. On his recommendation, the Steveville - Dead Lodge Canyon site was selected, both for its extensive badlands terrain and for its fossil wealth. As part of the 1955 celebrations marking Alberta's 50th "Jubilee Year" birthday, the Steveville Dinosaur Provincial Park was established.

It had taken 40 years of battling to bring the park into being; and when the fanfare died down, it seemed only an empty victory had been won. Although Doc Anderson was by now in his mid-70s, he continued to lobby vigorously for action. Most of his efforts were behind the scenes, as he had a well-earned reputation for being a vociferous critic of Social Credit, the party that governed Alberta, with a huge majority, from 1935 to 1971. Politicians, in general, did not rank high in his regard, although he himself had run in 1926 on the Liberal ticket and been defeated. He referred to that period as his "degeneration into politics."

Charlie Sternberg was Anderson's close ally in the effort to bestir the government to proceed with development. In a 1955 private letter to his friend Dr. George Johnson of the Calgary Zoological Society, Anderson, after carping about the untrustworthiness of Social Crediters, says that some time ago Charlie had told

Charlie Sternberg (centre) and Roy Fowler
(right) in conversation with local
rancher, Ernest Pierson, about 1960.

Anderson that, in order to get the park going, he would come out and work for two years for one dollar a year plus expenses. Anderson goes on to say that he had not mentioned this in "the salons of Edmonton" because he felt the government could well afford to pay Sternberg. Now, Doc says, he has had a letter from Charlie stating that he has personally made the offer to the minister responsible for Alberta parks.

On the face of it, this seems an opportunity the parks department should have jumped at. But enlightened management by the various government departments involved was not to be a feature of the park's history. Bureaucrats churned on for the next couple of years holding sporadic meetings with the Brooks Board of Trade that resulted in no apparent resolution to take the first baby-step on the road to creating what most of us imagine when we hear the term 'park.'

Roy Fowler was present at one of these meetings and offered his services if no one more qualified could be found. He was a

Dinosaur Graveyard: A World Heritage Site

farmer with an enthusiastic interest in palaeontology. For some years, he had been an active member of the Calgary Zoological Society. In the field, he had worked with Dr. Loris Russell of the Royal Ontario Museum and with Dr. William Bell of the National Museum of Canada. Finally, in 1958, the minister of parks offered Fowler the job of warden. Given only 30 days to dispose of his cattle and farm machinery and make the move , he accepted.

That summer, Charlie Sternberg came to the park, as promised, to prospect for a suitable dinosaur within walking distance of the proposed site of the new park office. He had his usual success. He found a nice specimen of a duck-billed dinosaur and stayed on to prepare it, with Fowler's help, for public viewing *in situ*. Three additional skeletons were located and prepared by the two men in the following summers. Protected by a little glass house, one of the original four skeletons is still on display and a popular attraction for visitors to the park.

The announcement of the intent to create Steveville Dinosaur Provincial Park received rather a lot of media attention locally, which brought visitors to the area. It was not long before this unprecedented traffic pointed up a glitch that no one involved with the project had anticipated. The problem was in the name. People

Packing the summer's work at the railroad station, Patricia.
1930 ROM Expedition under Levi Sternberg.

in search of the park naturally journeyed to the only place on the map marked Steveville. By this time, the hamlet had disappeared and the only sign of civilization was the ferryman's house. It became his unpleasant task to tell motorists who had already come many miles over very bad roads that the park was another hour's drive away. Those who journeyed on were pretty disgruntled by the time they reached the park, and Mr. Fowler often got an earful. The Brooks Board of Trade received its share of complaints. There was concern also about people who did not continue on to the official park entrance but decided to explore the badlands from the ferry site. Since there was no staff to provide adequate supervision of this part of the park, the fear developed that fossils would be carted off by souvenir seekers. It soon became clear that a new name would be required to direct visitors to the designated entrance.

Many here thought of Charlie and Levi Sternberg as old friends. Chat among neighbours over the kitchen table might easily include the suggestion, "I hear Charlie's in Dead Lodge Canyon this summer. Want to take a run over after haying and see what he's digging up?" The Sternbergs were intimately identified with the badlands and the dinosaurs. Incorporating the family name into that of the park was seen as a chance to give a nod of recognition for all they had contributed to this area, and to their adopted country, over the many years since 1912 when they first came to the Red Deer. Unfortunately, the opportunity was lost when narrow local controversy arose. The innocuous title the park now bears was the result. It became Dinosaur Provincial Park in 1962 and the Sternberg name has yet to be fittingly commemorated.

For the following two decades, modest efforts were made to upgrade the facilities, but progress was slow. There was no groundswell of popular demand for change because, in those years, most grassland dwellers, living in the shadow of the breathtaking Rockies, could not imagine being included in a list of must-sees for tourists. Also, where farming, ranching and petroleum underpin the economy, many people are, if not averse, at the very least, indifferent to the potential of tourism. The park's location in an area

Dinosaur Graveyard: A World Heritage Site

The Field Station at Dinosaur Provincial Park was opened in 1987. An addition is planned in the near future to allow for larger display, research and office space.

of sparse population accessible only over rutted, frequently impassable gravel roads made it easy for successive parks ministers to ignore it and apply funds available to them where it would make a difference politically. The occasional flurry of demands from the town council or Chamber of Commerce in Brooks could always be smoothed down by commissioning yet one more study to put on the shelf with all the others. Should the question of the park's status be raised elsewhere, whichever government minister was then responsible stated euphemistically that it was "in development."

Fourteen years after the province celebrated its 50th birthday by promising its people a new park, Dinosaur Provincial Park was declared officially open to visitors in 1969. Gradually, improvements took place. Funds were made available to purchase some land from private owners and, following somewhat protracted negotiations, boundaries were rationalized to enclose 73 square kilometres. The big change to the park's profile came with its elevation to the World Heritage List. This prodded the government to upgrade and enlarge facilities to a level befitting this new international stature and to cater to the increasing numbers of people attracted by it. Dinosaur Park remains a semi-wilderness park, however, in that a campground offers the only onsite accommodation and the nearest cluster of hotels, motels and restaurants is in the town of Brooks, about 50 kilometres away.

It was in the early 1960s, some years prior to the park's opening, that the international scientific community again focused on the treasures lying in Alberta's badlands. Out of fashion for several decades, dinosaurs had begun to re-exert their magnetism and to pull vertebrate palaeontologists towards their burial grounds. When inquiries from foreign scientists about working in the park area began to reach Alberta, the government moved decisively to accord due regard to the unequalled fossil resources of Dinosaur Provincial Park and to bring the province into the mainstream of dinosaur palaeontology. A department for fossil study was set up at the University of Alberta and, in 1966, the first collecting expedition from the new Provincial Museum of Alberta in Edmonton took to the field. Legislation was enacted to give the province control over the acquisition of fossils by institutions outside the province. All palaeontological work in the province is now regulated by the Royal Tyrrell Museum of Palaeontology. The opening of the museum at Drumheller in 1985 was an event of great significance to the province. At last, Alberta's dinosaurs are accorded the recognition on their home turf that they have enjoyed for so many years in museums far away.

Each summer, field crews from the Royal Tyrrell are to be found in the park. Working alongside them will be professional colleagues and volunteers from around the world, all intent upon gathering the fossils that will add to the sum of knowledge about the Late Cretaceous world. Much of the initial preparatory work on the excavated specimens is done in the laboratory of the Field Station in Dinosaur Provincial Park. This multi-purpose building, opened in 1987, is a satellite of the Royal Tyrrell Museum. In addition to supporting the museum's summer collecting activities, it functions as a visitor centre. From here, interpreters conduct bus and hiking tours designed to give participants an enriched experience of Park life, both ancient and modern. Public access to about 30% of the park, the Natural Preserve, is permitted only on guided tours. This is done to regulate the amount of traffic over the fragile badlands. In unrestricted areas, several self-guided trails have been marked out to introduce the varied terrains in badlands country. In the Field Station, there are engaging displays in the exhibit hall, some of which are permanent, others which change to reflect growing knowledge about what life was like here 75 million years ago.

With the number of visitors to the park increasing annually, there is a growing emphasis on fulfilling the second part of the obligation accepted along with being named to the World Heritage List: to strengthen appreciation and respect for the site through educational programs. This means we can expect programs to be enhanced, perhaps suggesting longer stays than the one and one-half to two days the Park staff now advises should be adequate time to partake fully of current programs. Visitors should be warned, too, that they may share Doctor Anderson's experience and find that a lifetime is insufficient to absorb what the badlands has to offer! He often joked that if he were to build a summer house, it would be in the heart of the badlands. As it is, his connection with the place is year-round. When he died in 1966, at the age of 85, his ashes were scattered over the ragged hills he loved.

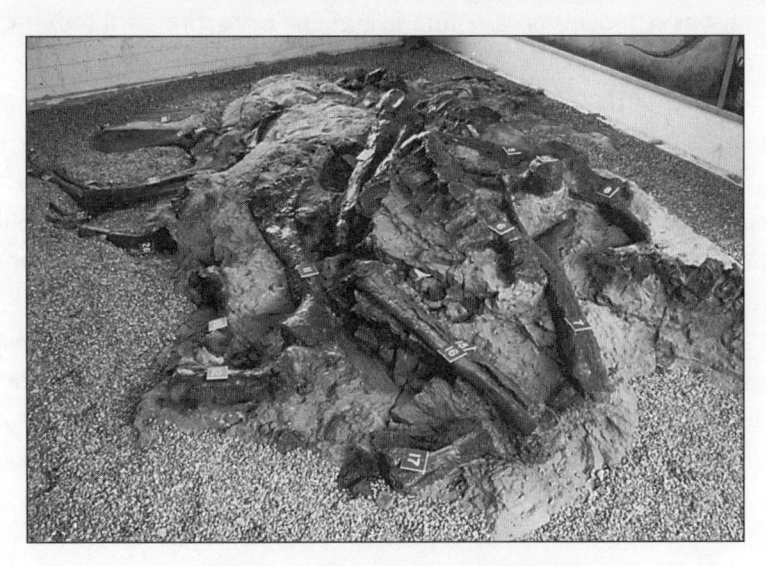

This hadrosaur is displayed where it was found by Charles M. Sternberg about 1960.

19

Present–Day Life in Dinosaur Park

The living plants and animals in Dinosaur Provincial Park form a unique modern ecological picture that is as interesting in its way as is the prehistoric one. Because of its size and remote location, the park functions as a haven for a specialized range of species, some of which are threatened in other less protected places. Its ability to conserve the endangered riverside environment within its boundaries was a second compelling argument in favour of naming the park to the World Heritage List.

Flanking the river along its twenty-six-kilometre run through the park, the green belt has a softening effect in contrast with the austere, sculptural beauty of the badlands hills. Its cool microclimate is enticing to humans and animals alike when summer scorches the badlands country. And, in winter, it offers protection for wildlife from cold and bitter winds.

Although always limited in breadth, these wooded expanses were once common to rivers flowing through the semi-arid southern prairies. Now, only a few areas of indigenous growth remain. During the early days of settlement, trees and shrubs were appropriated for lumber and firewood or cleared to make way for hayfields that could be irrigated from the river. The latter practice continues even now. This sort of human predation is, obviously, not a concern within the confines of the park. However, ordinary conservation measures are no solution to a recent problem brought about by the construction upriver of the Dixon dam. Its purpose of regulating river flow and eliminating major flooding may, in the main, be desirable, but it has one serious negative side-effect for this scarce riparian plant complex; it threatens the dominant riverside tree, the Plains (or Western) cottonwood. Propagation for these seed-bearers is hit and miss. Regeneration of the cottonwoods depends upon their catkins bursting at the same time as mud beds created by river floods are receptive to their seeds.

Historically, massive flooding took place every 30 to 50 years, depositing voluminous quantities of mud over the floodplain. Now, the dam will prevent this and the fear is that, without periodic replenishment, the soil will compact so much that seed falling on its hard surface will lie ungerminated. Minor flooding will still occur and regeneration of cottonwoods on a small scale can be expected near the river's edge but naturalists believe that back from the river there will be few young saplings spring up to replace the aging groves. Left to fend for themselves, the cottonwoods face a very uncertain future. Park staff and volunteers are doing what they can to come to the rescue. To extend the lives of mature trees, they ring their bases with wire to discourage predation from beaver and porcupine. Of more long-term significance, they are conducting a regeneration study in hopes of finding effective techniques to artificially nurture replacement stock. Established, a cottonwood tree may grow to 20 metres and live for as long as 200 years. It is well adapted for survival in badlands conditions, with waxy leaves and thick bark designed to conserve water.

The layout of the river terraces is changed with astonishing frequency by the meandering channel movements of the river back and forth across its broad floodplain. The fast-flowing outward bend of the current may undercut one portion of the bank until it slides in chunks into the water's flow, its soft sediments to be carried along and deposited at a spot somewhere downstream where the river slows for an inward bend. On the sand bars and on islands created in the stream by the deposits of the channels, willows seed and establish roots. They stabilize the soil against the river's quixotic attacks until, eventually, it can once again support a range of plant life. Geese and ducks home in on these spits of land, which they share with a variety of shore birds such as dainty sandpipers, long-billed curlews, and marbled godwits.

Runoff waters and underground springs in the coulees leading down from the prairie support growth similar to that of the river flat. Saskatoon, chokecherry and buffaloberry bushes are common to both. They were an important food source for the nomadic plains tribes and continue to be valued for the jellies, syrups and pies that can be made from their fruit. Wild roses and sea buckthorn often share space with the berry bushes but true aficionados in pursuit of the distinctive-tasting fruits accept a few pricks and scratches as a small price to pay.

Brambly patches, wherever they occur in the park, offer shelter for the little Nuttall's cottontail, known locally as a bush bunny. One threat to it in the coulees and on the river flat is the great horned owl that often nests in the hollow trunk of an old cottonwood. Its main predator, however, is the coyote. Coyotes are among the most adaptable of animals, able to adjust to a wide variety of habitat. They often den in the coulees and in the riverside thickets but may also make their home up on the prairie in an enlarged badger hole or in a patch of shrubs. A lone hunter is occasionally to be seen moving across a field, on the search for voles or hare to bring back to its mate and pups. The reputation of coyotes falls into bad odour from time to time because of their opportunistic tendency to snatch unwary farm chickens or baby lambs but badlands country is cattle country and, since coyotes kill calves only rarely, most ranchers here let them live in peace and are grateful to them for keeping the rodent population under control. The chief charm of coyotes for many badlands dwellers is their evening concert. It begins with one high-pitched voice emanating from a thicket; that voice is soon joined by one from a coulee upriver; then another chimes in, and then another until the woeful, eerie, discordant sound echoes and re-echoes from wall to wall up and down the river valley.

A sweeter sound of the riverine environment is that of its many songbirds. Time spent near the river is richly rewarding for bird watchers who commonly report sightings of cedar waxwings, brown thrashers, eastern kingbirds, goldfinches, yellow warblers, rufous-sided towhees, downy woodpeckers and common flickers, to name but a few of over 65 species of resident and migrant birds for which the cottonwood groves provide critical habitat. Colourful butterflies are attracted by the flowering shrubs and meadows of wild flowers where early blue beardstongue and Canada anemone are followed throughout the summer by common yarrow, flax, bergamot, harebells, dotted blazing stars, gaillardia, prairie asters and goldenrod.

Away from the river in the older parts of the floodplain, where there is less moisture and the soil is overlaid with clay from badlands' erosion, vegetation is correspondingly sparser. It is in this area that extensive sage brush flats occur to guide the eye in transition from the rich warm green of the river terraces over the dull, soft hues of the sage to the earth tones where the badlands hills begin. A walk through the sage brush engages the nose as well as the eye. At the slightest touch, the silvery green leaves release a crisp spicy scent.

Should you chance to visit when the tiny yellow blossoms of the wolf willow appear or when the spiny wild rose is fleetingly adorned with masses of pale pink flowers, you will truly understand the efficacy of aroma therapy.

Deep in the heart of the badlands, ferruginous hawks, golden eagles, and prairie falcons nest on the rocky ledges of the bluffs. Raptor populations are particularly vulnerable to man's alteration of the environment and, because of diminishing habitat and pesticide use, have suffered radical reductions to their numbers. Even with sincere efforts to rectify the damage done to their populations, recovery is slow. Naturalists have counted between twenty and thirty pairs of breeding raptors in the park in recent years, which makes it one of North America's most important protective habitats for birds of prey. Birds of another ilk add a distinctive touch to the sculpture of the hills. Colonies of cliff swallows attach their mud-jug nests to the faces of steep scarps.

In recent years, management of the prairie environment within the boundaries of Dinosaur Provincial Park reflects a heightened awareness of the intrinsic worth of prairie as prairie, rather than as just flat space to be easily converted to ploughed fields. Native grasslands are threatened worldwide. The situation in Alberta is that only 14 percent of the province's

American cowboys came into Canada with stock from the south. One of these, the colourful Happy Jack Jackson, was foreman of the Mexico Ranch. When his boss was killed in 1907, Jackson stayed on in the sod-roofed, hand-hewn log cabin and adapted to the 'nesters.' By the time of his own death in 1942, he had seen the homesteading experiment fail and the land return to grass and ranching.

Present–Day Life in Dinosaur Park

Near the end of the 19th Century, ranching spread from the foothills of the Rockies following the river courses eastward. The romance of the open range is symbolized in the Dinosaur Park area by the Mexico Ranch. Established in 1902 by a son of the British nobility (some say a remittance man) Delaval James de la Poer Beresford, the Alberta Mexico was an extension of his holdings in Mexico and New Mexico.

---

prairie region has been retained in a state similar to the one that welcomed the first settlers just over one hundred years ago. Grasses are still the dominant vegetation, but they are now mostly in the form of tilled grains and cultivated tame pastures made up of introduced varieties.

Oldtimers spoke of riding horseback through waving grasses so high they caught in the rowels of their spurs. That was in the early days of this century when ranches were being established up and down the river valley. The grasses they encountered were the result of a long rest from big grazing animals, a span of time that began when the last buffalo were wiped out in the early 1870s and lasted until cattle and horses were introduced almost a quarter of a century later. Classified as dry mixed prairie, a picture of what those early ranchers found can still be seen in areas where grazing of cattle is limited to fall and winter and only the deer and pronghorn have unrestricted access. There, communities of tall stature wheat grasses, medium spear grasses and short blue grama, June grass and low sedges grow out of a ground cover of mat muhly. Even in the most barren of badlands environments, sand grass and foxtail barley establish themselves in the sandy deposits of ancient stream beds, or in moisture-catching chinks on the rounded bare pediments. Dry slough bottoms with a water source near the surface sprout taller sedges and tufted hair grass.

In the plant world, grasses are a fairly recent development, having appeared first in the Tertiary Period. They seem simple modest plants, but their modes of existence are quite sophisticated. One of the most important adaptations of the grasses that survive and thrive in the inhospitable badlands environs is their development of a shallow, matted root system that absorbs and husbands moisture. Native grasses, in particular, devote about two-thirds of their energy intake to establishing and promoting their roots, which account for about 90 percent of the weight of an individual plant. In the case of the introduced pasture grasses, such as crested wheat or Russian wild rye, most energy goes toward developing leaves and seed.

The unobtrusive flowers produced by most grasses are not for the purpose of attracting insects; rather, they bend to the wind's

Work–sharing is a ranching tradition still observed at branding time. In this 1968 photo, (L to R on horseback) Marvel Eide, Ike Zeer and Warren Fulton rope yearlings while(L to R on foot) Eric Rowan, Ian Zeer and Terrill Pierson move to "rassle" them down and apply LaValley's brand.

Present–Day Life in Dinosaur Park

John Ware came to the Alberta foothills in 1881, on a cattle drive from Texas. He was much admired in ranching circles for his knowledge of stock and skill with horses. Mr. and Mrs. Ware and family moved to the Red Deer River about 1900. Both died in 1905, she from pneumonia, he when his horse tripped and fell on him. In 1954, their cabin was moved to Dinosaur Park through efforts of the Brooks Kinsmen. It is currently being rejuvenated as a museum of ranching history.

will and rely upon it to carry their seed. Cool weather grasses such as the spear, or needle, grasses go to seed by late June most summers. By producing seed early in the season, a plant allows itself time to grow up again from the base of the stem and make new seed for a second try at propagation should an animal crop it and foil the first attempt. Western wheat grass hedges its bets for success through a three-way root system: shallow roots about 10 cm below the topsoil; very long roots that reach down to deep underground aquifers; and, in maturity, it establishes its territory with a dense complex of spreading rhizomes. Recent tests on blue grama suggest that it protects its turf by manufacturing a chemical substance in its roots that acts like a herbicide to other plants.

Prairie grasses cure on the stem for winter feed and have a high energy count. While it may be true that in the short term fewer cattle can be finished for market on native pasture than on tame pasture where indigenous grasses have been ripped up to make

Dinosaur Country

Life After Dinosaurs

Clockwise from left: mule deer visits the campground; porcupine poses as a tree cactus; prairie rattle snake; burrowing owls are daytime insect-eaters; prairie hare at rest.

Present–Day Life in Dinosaur Park

Counter clockwise from right: tours include information on present-day life in the park; greasewood roots in the most arid terrain; cottonwood in spring; pincushion cactus in bloom.

way for crested wheat, Russian wild rye and alfalfa, good ranchers are very cognizant of the long-term benefits of native grassland. It requires only prudent management of grazing practices to ensure yearly renewal of pastures by resilient, tenacious plants, perfectly adapted to survive rain or drought in summer, deep snow cover or ground laid bare by the Chinook wind in winter.

Three varieties of hoofed animals are found in the Park. Whitetail deer are at home on the river terrace, favouring the protection of the brambly bush. The best way to identify this animal is by its tail, which is raised when it runs to display a white underside. This habit gives it the name by which it is sometimes called, flagtail. By whatever name, these deer are less often seen than the more confident mule deer. Intelligent creatures these, they recognize the protection offered them by the park and seem to relax their vigilance within its boundaries. Visitors are regularly treated to the charming sight of a doe and her large-eyed, spotted fawns nibbling at rose hips and berries growing near the campground.

A dweller on the high, wide prairie is the handsome tan and white pronghorn, usually called an antelope. Inquisitive by nature, this animal seems to find humans as interesting as they do it. At the first sign of danger, however, the white hairs on its rump flash erect in warning to its mates, and it sprints away on strong legs at speeds that have been clocked at 80 kilometres per hour.

Not quite so fast but still no slouch as a racer is the frequently seen jackrabbit, or white-tailed prairie hare. Unlike the bush bunny which relies upon cover for protection, the jackrabbit lives its life in the open. While the bush bunny stays brown year round, the jackrabbit camouflages itself with a brown coat in summer and a white one in winter.

Luck may grant you the sight of a little owl sitting on the prairie beside a badger hole that it has appropriated for its summer sojourn in Alberta. Disturbance of native grasslands has brought burrowing owls onto the endangered species list and Operation Grassland Community, aimed at protecting their nesting sites, has been undertaken by the Alberta government with the aid of grassland ranchers. These small insect eaters are active

Present–Day Life in Dinosaur Park

during the day. Another daytime hunter, this one on the winter prairie, is the snowy owl which may sometimes be seen perched on a fence post.

The animal of the prairie most familiar to summer visitors is the little yellowish-brown rodent that makes its home in burrows beneath the prairie. Its name is Richardson's ground squirrel, but it is commonly called a gopher. Unlike the true gopher, which is a solitary, molelike creature, this little animal is bright-eyed and perky. It survives on almost no water, getting what little it needs from the insects, fruits and leaves that it eats. The underground colonial life-style of 'gophers' is similar to that of prairie dogs. Prolific breeders, these little animals form an important link in the prairie food chain, supplying a summer diet for coyotes, badgers, hawks, owls and snakes.

Should you chance upon a large snake during your walks, it will likely be a harmless bullsnake. This is the largest snake found in Alberta. The poisonous prairie rattlesnakes can grow to be almost as large, but most are reported to be much smaller, measuring

Dinosaur Park in winter

little more than a metre. They are less commonly seen than the bullsnake. To better understand the movement patterns and monitor the numbers in the snake population, park staff (in cooperation with the Operation Grasslands Community of Alberta Fish and Game Association and with some aid from The Canadian Wildlife Service) has implanted radio tracking devices in several snakes and bar-coded all those captured at one of several known hibernation places in the park. It is expected that the results of this study will help in future management of the snakes, whose importance to the ecological balance is their contribution to rodent control.

The snake study is classified as a resource management study. In addition to work carried out by park staff, research in a variety of fields is conducted by scientists from other institutions. Facilitating scientific research that will add to the knowledge about the park is one of the management aims for a World Heritage Site. Studies done recently have included collection of fungi and observation of habitat selection by small mammals. Moths and bats common to the badlands have also come under the scrutiny of scholars. There are ongoing investigations of the badlands themselves that fall within the broad classifications of geology and geography.

The Committee responsible cited the aesthetic quality of the largest badlands area in Canada as a third reason for inscribing Dinosaur Provincial Park to the World Heritage List. This may surprise first time visitors. Unlike gentler landscapes, this one is not quickly understood. The lofty nobility of mountains, sun glinting on ocean waves, a rolling grassy meadow dotted with stands of leafy trees—all of these are possessed of immediate and comprehensible beauty. Only in the badlands does the imagination play such an integral role in the experience of Nature. This is a landscape that enters the mind of the beholder, is sifted and refined, and exits in processed form. Confronted with a wilderness of strange and haunting shapes, juxtaposed one to another with no ostensible logic, one's instinct is to impose a human dimension where the traces of civilization are few. One person will distinguish the ornate domes and minarets of an Islamic city; another sees the ramparts and battlements of a feudal lord's stronghold; still another will single out a barren table enclosed on three sides by sheer drops of rock as the setting for <u>Star Wars</u> or <u>King Lear</u>. Even those very familiar with the surroundings, the Dinosaur Park naturalists, refer to the camel, the citadel, the valley of the castles, the valley of the moon.

The strange beauty of the badlands has much to do with light, colour, and shape. The warm grays, ochres, siennas, browns, and blacks carry the eye from shape to shape over the sweeping panorama. The effect is of a huge gallery of modern sculpture where every piece is calculated, through its colour and shape, to echo and enhance every other piece. Like sculpture in the round, intended for viewing from every angle, the hills have many aspects and dimensions. Seen from a certain angle, a form evokes one feeling; change viewpoint, and the mood alters.

Prairie light has an exceptional atmospheric power, which plays upon the mind of the beholder. A group of life-size hoodoos seen in the searing sun of midday may be reminiscent of Victorian ladies at a garden party, each bedecked with a hat slightly different from those of her companions. An imperceptible change takes place when the sun drops behind a high spire of nearby rock, backlighting its jagged upward thrust; deepening shadows blue the surrounding hills. Nighthawks out for their evening feed of plump insects swoop and cavort overhead and the air fills with the primitive wails of their hollow, echoing whoom, whoom, whoom. Glance now at the little grouping of hoodoos and they have exchanged their former innocuous guise for one of darker hue. Hooded priestesses, they ring round to intone the chants of some primeval pagan rite.

It is a landscape of inexhaustible raw material to amuse the mind and of infinite variety to stimulate the senses. Ike Zeer is a local rancher with an abiding love and deep understanding for the country where he has lived all his life. As a very young man, he rode for the Circle Ranch which was then headquartered east of Dinosaur Provincial Park. He captured perfectly the essence of the badlands in these few words, "When I cowboyed in that country, we rode through them hills every day. And you know," this with a bemused shake of his head, "I never seen the same thing twice."

Alberta Dinosaurs on Display

> Alberta dinosaurs are on display in some of the best known museums around the world. Listed below are some of the places where they can be seen.

Academy of Natural Sciences, Philadelphia

Corythosaurus

American Museum of Natural History, New York

Anatosaurus, Anchiceratops, Ankylosaurus, Centrosaurus, Chasmosaurus, Corythosaurus, Lambeosaurus, Montanoceratops, Ornithomimus, Pachycephalosaurus, Panoplosaurus, Saurolophus, Struthiomimus, Styracosaurus, Triceratops, Tyrannosaurus rex

British Museum of Natural History, London

Euplocephalus

Canadian Museum of Nature, Ottawa

Albertosaurus, Anchiceratops, Brachylophosaurus, Chasmosaurus, Daspletosaurus, Dromiceiomimus, Gryposaurus, Hypacrosaurus, Leptoceratops, Panoplosaurus, Styracosaurus, Thescelosaurus, Triceratops, Troodon

Carnegie Museum of Natural History, Pittsburgh

Tyrannosaurus rex

Denver Museum of Natural History, Denver

Anatosaurus

Drumheller and District Fossil Museum, Drumheller, Alberta

Edmontosaurus, Pachyrhinosaurus

Field Museum of Natural History, Chicago

Albertosaurus, Anchiceratops, Lambeosaurus

Los Angeles County Museum, Los Angeles

Tyrannosaurus rex

Museum of La Plata, La Plata, Argentina

Centrosaurus

Museum of the Rockies, Bozeman, Montana

Maiasaura, Triceratops

Pratt Museum, Amherst, Massachusetts

Kritosaurus

Provincial Museum of Alberta, Edmonton, Alberta

Ankylosaurus, Corythosaurus, Lambeosaurus, Struthiomimus

Royal Ontario Museum, Toronto

Albertosaurus, Arrhinoceratops, Edmontosaurus, Kritosaurus, Lambeosaurus, Ornithomimus, Parasaurolophus,

Parksosaurus, Prosaurolophus,

Royall Tyrrell Museum, Drumheller, Alberta

Albertosaurus, Brachylophosaurus, Centrosaurus, Chasmosaurus, Corythosaurus, Dromaeosaurus, Edmontonia, Edmontosaurus, Gryposaurus, Hypacrosaurus, Kritosaurus, Lambeosaurus, Montanoceratops, Parasaurolophus, Stegoceras, Triceratops, Tyrannosaurus rex

Senckenburg Natural History Museum, Frankfurt, Germany

Anatosaurus, Edmontosaurus

Smithsonian, Washington

Albertosaurus, Prosaurolophus

University of Alberta, Edmonton, Alberta

Albertosaurus, Prosaurolophus

University of Michigan Museum of Paleontology, Michigan

Anatosaurus

University of Wyoming Geology Museum, Wyoming

Anatosaurus, Anchiceratops

Sources

Archival materials in the Brooks Public Library and the Glenbow Archives in Calgary (newspaper and magazine clippings, promotional brochures and correspondence files), and personal interviews were the sources for the history of the development of Drumheller Fossil Museum (Chapter 2)and Dinosaur Provincial Park (Chapter 18). For settlement history, I referred to:

Gross, Renie and Lea Nicoll-Kramer. 1985. *Tapping the Bow*. Brooks: Eastern Irrigation District.
The Hills of Home.1973.Drumheller Valley History Association.
Howe, Helen. 1971.*Seventy-five Years along the Red Deer*. self-published.
Jones, David. 1987.*Empire of Dust*.Edmonton:University of Alberta Press.
Roen,Hazel.1971.*The Grass Roots of Dorothy*.self-published

For Chapter 3, I used:
Alberta: Studies in the Arts and Sciences 1/1. 1988. Issue devoted to the (Royal) Tyrrell Museum of Palaeontology.

To update the chapters on dinosaurs, their world and their extinction—4 through 13—I used the following books extensively:

Currie, Philip J. and Kevin Padian, eds. 1997. *Encyclopedia of Dinosaurs*. San Diego: Academic Press.
The Land Before Us: the Making of Ancient Alberta. 1994. Red Deer:

Red Deer College Press.
Reid, Monty. 1990. *The Last Great Dinosaurs*. Red Deer: Red Deer College Press.
Timescapes: the Geology of Dinosaur Provincial Park. Brooks: Dinosaur Natural History Association.
Weishampel, David B., Peter Dodson and Halszka Osmolska, eds. 1990. *The Dinosauria*.Berkely:University of California Press.

A major change, between the time of researching for the first edition of this book and now, came about because of an explosion of information on the Internet. Some of the sites I found helpful are:

American Museum of Natural History. http://www.amnh.org
Dino Russ's Lair(Jacobsen, Russ). http://denr1.igis.uiuc.edu/isgsroot
Dinosauria On-Line(Poling, Jeff). http://www.dinosauria.com
Dinosaur Pages(Keesey, T.Mike). http://www.gl.umbc.edu/~tkeese1/dinosaur
Dinosaur Trace Fossils(Martin, Anthony). http://www.emory.edu/GEO SCIENCE/HTML/Dinotraces.htm
Field Museum of Natural History,Chicago. http://www.fmnh.org
Gateway Country Fossil Page(Leuck, Shane). http://www.tst-medhat.com/~sleuck. Articles by Hope Johnson.
National Museum of Natural History,Smithsonian,Washington,D.C. http://www.nmnh.si.edu/paleo.
Natural History Museum,London. http://www.nhm.ac.uk/museum
Nova On-Line. http://www.pbs.org/wgbh/nova
Royal Tyrrell Museum of Palaeontology. http://tyrrellmuseum.com
University of California Museum of Palaeontology. http://www.ucmp.berkeley.edu/exhibit/exhibits.html

Some of the current discussion about glaciation and the Ice Age (Chapter 14) is available on the Internet at:

Illinois State Museum(Richard S.Toomey III, Project Director). http://www.museum.state.il.us
Laboratory for Environmental Biology, University of Texas at El Paso. http://www.utep.edu/leb/pleist
Provincial Museum of Alberta. http://www.pma.edmonton.ab.ca/

Much of the material on plants and animals (Chapter 19) is based upon my own observations and those of my badlands neighbours. I did, however, find fresh insights from the following:

Sources

Dinosaur Provincial Park. http://www.gov.ab.ca/~env/nrs/dinosaur
Reid,Gordon.1986.*Dinosaur Provincial Park*.Oakville:Mosaic Press.
Romuld, Maggie. 1996. *The Ecology of Dinosaur Provincial Park*.self-published.
Willock,Thomas.1990. *A Prairie Coulee*.Edmonton:Lone Pine Press.

I added only a small amount of new information to Chapters 15 and 16, which deal with early exploration and bone hunting in the Red Deer valley. I did, however, review the field notes of geologists and palaeontologists and the annual reports of their institutions. To the suggested reading about the Great Canadian Dinosaur Rush published in the first edition, I would now add:

Spalding, David.1993.*Dinosaur Hunters:150 Years of Extraordinary Discoveries*.Toronto:Key Porter Books Limited.

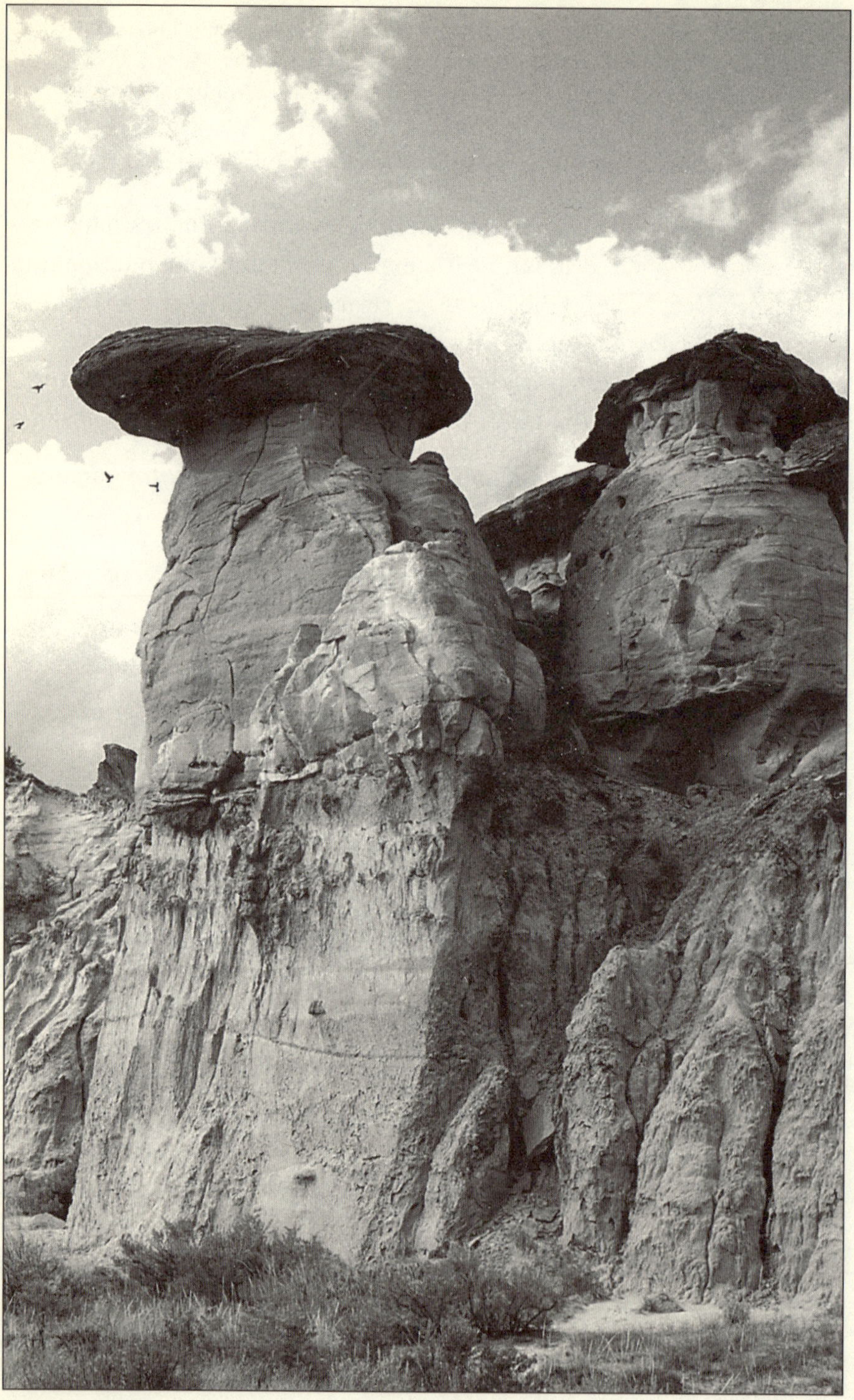

Illustration Credits

x-xi,	Drawing by S.Haeseker	33,	Maps, Royal Tyrrell Museum
xii,	John Mitchell/Figment Films	34,	Robert Gross
2-3,	Map, Trish Bohan	35,	Robert Gross
6,	Renie Gross	36,	Top & bottom, Robert Gross
7,	Canadian Museum of Nature, 37875	37,	Canadian Museum of Nature, C. Douglas
8,	Glenbow Archives, NA 3250-6	39,	Robert Gross
10,	Robert Gross	43,	Top, Robert Gross
14,	Glenbow Archives, NA 2389-20	43,	Bottom, Map, Royal Tyrrell Museum
15,	Glenbow Archives, NA 4965-64	44,	Chart, Trish Bohan
		46,	Robert Gross
16,	Glenbow Archives, NA 4965-67	47,	Dinosaur Provincial Park
		48,	Right, Royal Tyrrell Museum
17,	Glenbow Archives, NA 4965-40	48,	Left, Robert Gross
		49,	Robert Gross
18,	Drumheller Museum	51,	Map, Royal Tyrrell Museum
21,	Royal Tyrrell Museum	53,	All photos, Robert Gross
22,	Glenbow Archives, NA 1311-3	56,	Royal Tyrrell Museum
		57,	Royal Tyrrell Museum
23,	Robert Gross	62,	Canadian Museum of Nature, C. Douglas
24,	Left & right, Robert Gross	63,	Canadian Museum of Nature, C. Douglas
25,	Royal Tyrrell Museum		
27,	Royal Tyrrell Museum, Allan Bibby	72,	Canadian Museum of Nature, 97183
28,	Royal Tyrrell Museum, Philip Currie	73,	Earth Sciences Information Centre, Earth Sciences Sector, 83381
29,	Robert Gross		
31,	Chart, Trish Bohan	74,	Left & right, Royal Tyrrell Museum
32,	Canadian Museum of Nature, C. Douglas		
		77,	Canadian Museum of

233

	Nature, J5779B1	151,	Dinosaur Provincial Park
78,	Canadian Museum of Nature, 81287	153,	Glenbow Archives, NA 13-1
80,	Canadian Museum of Nature, J10014	155,	Royal Tyrrell Museum
		157,	Dinosaur Provincial Park
80,	Bottom, Robert Gross	160,	Glenbow Archives, NA 588-1
81,	Canadian Museum of Nature, C. Douglas	161,	Glenbow Archives, NA 302-7
84,	Robert Gross		
85,	Robert Gross	162,	Earth Sciences Information Centre, Earth Sciences Sector, 201735
86,	Robert Gross		
90,	Robert Gross		
91,	Robert Gross	164,	Canadian Museum of Nature, 81450
92,	Canadian Museum of Nature, C. Douglas		
		165,	Earth Sciences Information Centre, Earth Sciences Sector, 109384
96,	Left & right, Canadian Museum of Nature, C. Douglas		
		168,	Canadian Museum of Nature, 33918
98,	Robert Gross		
100,	Royal Tyrrell Museum	170,	Neg No 19493, Brown 1914, Courtesy Library Services, American Museum of Natural History
102,	Robert Gross		
104,	Glenbow Archives, NA 3250-14		
		172,	Canadian Museum of Nature, 25422
106,	Robert Gross		
107,	Robert Gross	175,	Canadian Museum of Nature, 35151
109,	Glenbow Archives, NA 3250-13		
		176,	The Field Museum, Chicago, Il Neg No 44835
110,	Royal Tyrrell Museum		
113,	Canadian Museum of Nature, C. Douglas	178,	Neg No 17808 Photo Menke, Courtesy Dept of Library Services, American Museum of Natural History
115,	Irene Vanderloh		
120,	Robert Gross		
124,	Royal Tyrrell Museum		
127,	Robert Gross	179,	Canadian Museum of Nature, 25421
128,	Canadian Museum of Nature, C. Douglas		
		181,	Neg No10428 Photo B. Brown, Courtesy Dept of Library Services, American Museum of Natural History
129,	Dinosaur Provincial Park		
131,	Robert Gross		
133,	Robert Gross		
135,	Robert Gross	182,	Top: Neg No 18547 Photo Brown, Courtesy Dept of Library Services, American Museum of Natural History
136,	Canadian Museum of Nature, C. Douglas		
137,	Canadian Museum of Nature, C. Douglas		
		182,	Bottom: Canadian Museum of Nature, 46586
141,	Robert Gross		
145,	Renie Gross	184,	Robert Gross
147,	Glenbow Archives, NA 3250-9	188,	Walter Hutchinson
		189,	Robert Gross
150,	Renie Gross	190,	Robert Gross

Illustration Credits

191,	Royal Tyrrell Museum	207,	Walter Hutchinson
192,	Canadian Museum of Nature, 37862	209,	Royal Tyrrell Museum and Dinosaur Park
193,	Dinosaur Provincial Park	211,	Royal Tyrrell Museum
194,	Dinosaur Provincial Park	213,	Dinosaur Provincial Park
195,	Royal Tyrrell Museum	216,	Royal Tyrrell Museum
199,	Robert Gross	217,	Dinosaur Provincial Park
200,	Glenbow Archives, NA 48-2	218,	Ike Zeer
		219,	Dinosaur Provincial Park
201,	Canadian Museum of Nature, 37863	220,	All photos, except bottom left, Dinosaur Provincial Park
202,	Glenbow Archives, NA 48-1	220,	Bottom left, John Mitchell / Figment Films
203,	Glenbow Archives, NA 3250-12	221,	All photos, Dinosaur Provincial Park
204,	Irene Vanderloh	232,	Dan Aire
206,	Irene Vanderloh		

Index

Bold numbers refer to illustrations

Aboriginals. *See* Blackfoot
Age of Dinosaurs. *See* Mesozoic Era
Alberta: petroleum 5
Allosaurus **195**
American Museum of Natural History. *See also* Brown,Barnum; Kaisen,Peter; Osborn,H.F.; Johnson, A.T.; 27, 103, 166, 171 173-174, 203; field camps **170, 172, 181, 182**; Red Deer dinosaurs and 68, 108, **120**, 125
Anderson, W.G. 201–203, **204**, 204–205, 211; Social Credit and 205
Andrews, Roy Chapman 27, 81, 174
animals: of Cretaceous 38–39, 40; of Jurassic 36–38; of Triassic 35–36; present-day 214-216, 222-224, **220**
ankylosaurs 93–99, **94, 96** ankylosaurids 96–97; behaviour of 93–95; Canada-China Dino Project and 93–95; description of 95–99; distribution of 95, 99; *Euoplocephalus* **98**; evolution of 93; nodosaurids 95–96
Archaeopteryx 37, 126–128; **128**
Aulenback, Kevin 75

badlands: aesthetics of 224–225; bedrock of 148; birds in 216; creation of 1–4; definition of 148; erosion and 4, **145**, 146–147, **147**, 149–151, **150, 151**; European exploration of 159–166; in Drumheller area 7; landforms 148–151; northern 6; prairie and 147–148; psychological effects of 4, 224–225; shaping of 146; sites in Red Deer valley 6
Baird, David 20–21
Bakker, Robert 59
Barbeau, Marius 155
Bassano,Glacial Lake 145–146
Battle Formation: 45; fossils in 51; palaeoenvironments: **44**, 51
Battle River 145
Bearpaw Formation 45; age of 49; fossils in 49
Bearpaw Sea 49, 50–51; **43, 51**; life in **53**
Bell, William 207
Beresford, Delaval **217**
Berry Creek 73, 165
Big Valley 164, 168, 169, 181
Blackfoot: badlands and 152–157; buffalo and 12; buffalo jumps 157; chiefs **153**; dinosaurs and 153; dream bed **155**, 156; fur trade and 158–159; stone effigies **157** 156–157; tribes of 154
Bleriot Ferry 85, 86
bone beds: of *Centrosaurus* 193–194; of *Edmontosaurus* 192–193; of *Pachyrhinosaurus* 194; study of 192–194
Braman, Dennis 137–138
Bremner, Charles (boatman) 169

Index

Brooks 210
Brooks Board of Trade 206, 208
Brown, Barnum
  4, 68, 108, 125, 157, **178**, 202; competition with Sternbergs
  173, 177–180; dinosaur hunt and 167–173; in Drumheller area 1913 171; in Steveville 1912 173; in Steveville 1914 167, 177–180; in Steveville 1915 181–183

Calgary Natural History Society 174
Calgary Zoological Society 205, 207
Canada - China Dinosaur Project 27–29; ankylosaurs and 93-95; small theropods and 116–117
Canadian Museum of Nature. *See also* National Museum of Canada; 28, 66, 77, 114–115
Canadian Pacific Railway 13–14
ceratopsians 79–88. *See also* Dinosaur Park Formations; Horseshoe Canyon Formation; Scollard Formation; *Anchiceratops*: 85; behaviour of 87; centrosaurines 83–84; *Centrosaurus*: 85; *Centrosaurus* bone beds 87–88; chasmosaurines 84–85; *Chasmosaurus*: 84; eggs in Mongolia: 81; evolution of 80–83; frills of 85; *Leptoceratops* **80**, 79–83;   ; *Pachyrhinosaurus* **86** 192–193;   ; *Pachyrhinosaurus* bone bed 83; skin impressions 84–85; *Styracosaurus*: 87, 87–88; teeth of 85; *Triceratops* 79–83;   80; world distribution of 88
climate: badlands today 146–147; in Cretaceous 40; in Jurassic 36; in Late Cretaceous 59–60; in Tertiary Period 143; in Triassic 32
coal 52, 155, 160; forming of 50; mining of 14–17, **15, 16, 17, 22**
coelurosaurs: definition of 112
continental drift. *See* Plate tectonics

Cope, Edward D. 163
Cretaceous Period: duration of 30; geography of **33**, 34
Currie, Philip 20, 26–27, **27**, **28**, 75, 108. *See also* Canada - China Dinosaur Project
Cutler, William 174–176

Danis, Gilles 115
Dawson, George M. 160–162, **161**
Dead Lodge Canyon 164, 165, 166, 167, 168
Deinonychus. *See* dromaeosaurs
Devil's Coulee: Hypacrosaurus egg site 74–77; Hypacrosaurus eggs: 75
Dilophosaurus 36
Dimetrodon 34
Dinosaur Park Formation 44, 45; age of 47; fossils in 47–48; naming of 192; palaeoenvironments 47–48,
Dinosaur Park Formations: ankylosaurs in **94**, 95; ceratopsians in **82** 83, 84, 85, 87; dinosaurs in 8; dromaeosaurs in 125; hadrosaurs in: **70**; mammals in 142; ornithomimids in 120, 121; pachycephalosaurs in 90–91; small theropods in **114**; 123; tyrannosaurs in: **103**; **104**, 105, 106, 107–108
Dinosaur Provincial Park 6; Alberta government and 205; Canada-China Project and 116–117; development of 205–210; Field Station 10, **209**; grassland environment 216–222; natural preserve 210; protection of fossils 210; riverside environment 212–216; sagebrush flats 215–216; World Heritage site 9–10, 198–200, 209, 212, 224
dinosaurs. *See also* Red Deer valley dinosaurs; anatomy of 56, 59, 126; birds and

237

38, 61, 64–65, 110, 111–112, 116–117, 126–129; bone tissue of 60; classification of 61–65, 126; first discoveries 55; first discovery in West 161; first discovery of eggs 27; first shown in Canada: 77; in Crystal Palace exhibit 55; limbs of 58–59; metabolism of 57–62; new interest in 58; of Cretaceous 38–39; of Jurassic 35, 36–37; 127; of Late Cretaceous 59–60; of Triassic 35–36; predator/prey in Red Deer valley 61; predator/prey ratios 60–61; skin impressions of 48; trackways: (pic) 57; warm-blooded. *See herein* metabolism of
Diplodocus 37
Dong Zhiming: Institute of Paleontology and Paleoanthropology in Beijing 28–29
dromaeosaurs 39, 124; behavior of 122–127; birds and 126–129; *Deinonychus* 38, 39, 58, 111–129, 116; description of 122–127; distribution of 124–125
Drumheller 7; city of 4, *14*, 49;
Drumheller, Glacial Lake: 145–146; farming and *16–17*; formation of *16–17*
Drumheller Dinosaur and Fossil Museum 83, 86; founding of *17–19*
Drumheller, Sam *14*, *14–15*
Dry Island Buffalo Jump Provincial Park 6, 51

Eberth, David 48, 192
erosion. *See* badlands: erosion and
Ex Terra Foundation 28
extinction, Cretaceous-Tertiary (K-T): 6, 30, 130–131; ammonites **131**; asteroid impact and 132–133; Canadian Continental Drilling Program and 138; catastrophists vs gradualists 134–137; climate and 141; evidence in Red Deer valley 52–54; fossil counts and 136–137; K-T boundary 132–133, **133**; pterosaurs and **136**; study by Royal Tyrrell 136–138; survivors of **135**; theories re: 132–137;
extinction: mass 131; Permian 30, 42, 131; Triassic 42

Feathers 38
Fidler, Peter 154–155
Field Museum of Chicago **176**, 184
Foremost Formation 45; fossils in 45; palaeoenvironments 45
formations, geological. *See* geological formations
fossilization 40–41
fossils: biogeography and 32; count of in Red Deer valley 51, 52–54; excavation of 188–191; multidisciplinary studies and 191–192; prospecting for 187–188; trace 194–195
Fowler, Roy 206, 208
Fulton, William R. *17*

Gayfer family: visit Sternberg quarry **203**
geological formations. *See also* Battle Formation; Dinosaur Park Formation; Horseshoe Canyon Formation; Oldman Formation; Scollard Formation; Whitemud Formation; age of in Red Deer valley 1–4, 6, 7, **44**; definition of 45; in Dinosaur Provincial Park 8, **44**, 45–49; in Drumheller area 7, **44**, 50–51; in northern badlands **44**, 51–54; in Red Deer valley 45–52; marine 7
Geological History of Life on Earth: 31
Geological Survey of Canada

Index

12, 73, 90–91, 169–171; exploration of Red Deer valley 160–166, 167; field camps **168, 172, 175**
glaciation. *See* Ice Age
Gleichen 13
Gondwana **33**, 34, 38;
Greentree, Thomas **14**, 14–15

hadrosaurs 66–78. *See also* Dinosaur Park Formations; Horseshoe Canyon Formation; Scollard Formation; behaviour of 67–71, 72–74; *Brachylophosaurus* 71; *Corythosaurus* 68 *Corythosaurus* model: **72**; crests of 71–73; description of 67, 69–74; discovery of eggs and embryos of 74–77; *Edmontosaurus* 66–67; *Edmontosaurus* bone bed 107–108; eggs and embryos of 74–77; fossil sites in world 66; from Red Deer valley 70; *Gryposaurus* 71; *Hypacrosaurus* 67, 74; *Hypacrosaurus* eggs 75; *Kritosaurus* 69; *Lambeosaurus* 39 73; *Parasaurolophus* **76**; size of 66; skin impressions 68–69; teeth of 69
Hall, Edith **200**
Hamblin, Anthony 192
Hand Hills 16
Hector, James 159–160, **160**
Heterodontosaurus 35
Hodgson, W.G. 174, 185
homesteading: Drumheller area 13; Steveville area 201, 203–204
Horseshoe Canyon Formation 7, **44**, 45; age of 50; ankylosaurs in **94**, 96; ceratopsians in **82**, 83, 85; fossils in 50–51; hadrosaurs in 66, 70, 74, 77, 192–193; ornithomimids in 119–120; palaeoenvironments 44, 50–51; small theropods in: **123**; tyrannosaurs in 103, 107–109
Huxley, T.H.: birds-dinosaurs and 127

Ice Age 143–146; causes of 143; end of 144–146; Red Deer River and 1–4, 145–146; Wisconsinan glaciation 144
Iguanodon 55

Jackson Hansel 'Happy Jack' **216**
Jenner 181
Johnson, A.T. 174, 175
Johnson, George 205
Johnson, Hope 114
Jungling, C.F. 18
Jurassic Park 37, 101, 121, 124
Jurassic Period: Alberta in 42-43; duration of 30; geography of 32-34, **33**, 36

Kaisen, Peter (Brown's assistant) 168, 175, 177
Kneehills Creek 12, 155, 162

Lambe, Lawrence 73, 90–91, **165**, 165–166, 168
Late Cretaceous: landscapes in Red Deer valley 4–5, 45–54; sites in world 9
Laurasia **33**, 34, 38
L'Heureux, Jean 152, **153**
Linblad, G.E. **182**
Little Sandhill Creek 167, 177, 184

Mamenchisaurus 37
mammals 6, 54; in Jurassic 38; in Tertiary Period 141, 142, 143, 144
McConnell, R.G. 161
McLean, Alexander 185
McLean, George 155
McVeigh, Irene 19
Megalosaurus 55, 56

239

Mesozoic Era 4, 30–41, 59, 141. *See also* Cretaceous Period; Jurassic Period; Late Cretaceous Period; Triassic Period
Mexico Ranch **216, 217**
Michichi Creek 66, 77
Mongolia 27
Munson 83
museum. *See* American Museum of Natural History; Canadian Museum of Nature; Geological Survey of Canada; National Museum of Canada; Provincial Museum of Alberta; Royal Tyrrell Museum of Palaeontology

National Museum of Canada 185, 186. *See also* Canadian Museum of Nature
Noble, Brian. *See* Ex-Terra Foundation
Northwest Mounted Police: Sgt.W.Piercy **153**

Oldman Formation **44**, 45; age of 46–47; fossils in 46–47; palaeoenvironments 46–47;
ornithomimids 75, 119–121; **120**; 1995 find 196; behaviour of 120–121; description of 119–121; distribution of 119; *Dromiceiomimus* 62; troodontids and 113; tyrannosaurs and 63
Osborn, H.F. 157, 166, **178**
Ostrom, John 38, 111, 116
Owen, Richard 55

pachycephalosaurs 89–92, **92**; ceratopsians and 63, 90; description of 90–92; distribution of 89; flat-headed 92; in Red Deer valley 89; *Pachycephalosaur* **91**; skull caps of 89; *Stegoceras* **90**
palaeontology: technology and 195–196

Palliser,John **160**
Pangaea 32–34, **33**, 36
Parks, William A. **182**
plants: angiosperms (flowering) 38; gymnosperms 38; in Late Cretaceous 47; in Tertiary Period 143; of Cretaceous 38, **48**; of Jurassic 37; of Late Cretaceous 46, 50–51; of Triassic 34
plate tectonics: **33**; continental drift and 32–34; Ice Age and 143; in Cretaceous 39–40, 43, 140–141; in Jurassic 42–43, 140
Pluto, Leo J. 18
Provincial Museum of Alberta 20, 210

ranching 12–13, **216, 217, 218, 219**
Read, W.R. *19*
Red Deer: city of 5, 145, 163, 165, 169
Red Deer River: course of 5–8
Red Deer valley dinosaurs 1–4. *See also* ankylosaurs; ceratopsians; dromaeosaurs; hadrosaurs; ornithomimids; pachycephalosaurs; theropods, small; *Thescelosaurus*; troodontids; tyrannosaurs; at Field Museum of Natural History, Chicago 184; at University of Alberta 104, 109, **184**; discoveries of 12; fossilization of 46–47, 48; in American Museum of Natural History 68, **120**; in Canadian Museum of Nature 66, 77; in Royal Ontario Museum 69; in world's museums 10; rush for 1909-17 4, 167-186
reptiles: archosaurs 35; *Dimetrodon* **34**; earliest known **32**; marine 42, 43, **46, 49, 53**; synapsids 35
Rocky Mountains 5, 39, 140–141, 142–143, 147
Rosebud River 155, 164
Rowley 181
Royal Ontario Museum 59, 185, 186
Royal Tyrrell Museum of Palaeontology 10, **21, 24, 25,** 190; architec-

Index

ture of 21–24; building of 20–21; exhibits 24–25; field season in DPP 210; logo of **23**, 110; mascot of 21, **29**; new discoveries by 196–197; programs 26, 107; research 4; staff of 26
Russell, Dale 28, 108, 114–115, 118
Russell, Loris 59, 207

Scollard Formation 45; age of 51–52; ankylosaurs in
94; ceratopsians in 79–81, **82**; fossils in 51–52; hadrosaurs in 70; K-T boundary **44**, 52, 141; mammals in
142; palaeoenvironments **44** 52; small theropods in:
123; tyrannosaurs in: **103**
Sinosauropteryx 38
Sloboda, Wendy 75
Stegosaurus **36**
Sternberg, Charles H. 67, 171–172, **179**; freelance 1916-17 183; in Steveville 1915 181; on loading fossils 1914 180
Sternberg, Charles M.(Charlie) 7, 73, 172, 183, **184** 205, 207, **206**, 208
Sternberg family 202; in Drumheller area1912 171; in Steveville 1913 173; in Steveville 1914 168, 175, 177–180; in Steveville 1921 184–185
Sternberg, George
109, **147**, 171, 172, 173, **192**, **201**; in northern badlands 1915 181; in northern badlands 1916 183; in Steveville 1920,21,22 184
Sternberg, Levi 172, **182**, 183, 185, **188**, 205, 208
Sternberg ,R.M.(son of Charles M.) 122
Stettler 169
Steveville 68, 84, 167, **200**, **202**, 207

Tertiary Period: Alberta in 141–143
theropods, large. *See* tyrannosaurs
theropods, small 111–129. *See also* dromaeosaurs; ornithomimids; troodontids; classification of 112, 121–122; description of 112; fossilization of
112; *Ornitholestes*:
127; tyrannosaurs and 113
Thompson, David 154
Tolman Bridge 6, 7, 51, 157, 169
Triassic Period: Alberta in 42; climate of 32; duration of 30; fossils of Wapiti Lake 42; geography of 32, **33**
troodontids **113**, 115; birds and 116–117; description of 118–119; distribution of
116; ornithomimids and
113; *Psittacosaurus* and
117; search for 113–118
tyrannosaurs 101–110, **102**, **106**. 109; 1996 find
196; *Albertosaurus*
98; *Albertosaurus* bone bed 108; arms of: 104–105; behaviour of: 106–109; classification of 102–103, 110; description of 103–106, 109; footprint of **107**;
juvenile **105**; ornithomimids and 63; small theropods and 63; *T. rex* **100**; *T. rex* public image 101–102; *T.rex* skull **110**
Tyrrell, Joseph Burr 12, **21**, 161–163, **162**; Albertosaurus discovery 162–163

University of Alberta 185, 210

Vanderloh, Irene 114–116, 118, 125

Ware,John and family **219**

241

Waterhouse Hawkins, Benjamin 55
Wegener, J.L.(rancher) 168
Western Interior Seaway 5, 34, **43**, 51
Weston, Thomas 163–164, **164**
Whitemud Formation 45; fossils in 51; palaeoenvironments 44, 51
Willow Creek 7, 168; hoodoos 49–50
wind: Chinook 147
Wintering Hills *16*
World Heritage list. *See* Dinosaur Provincial Park: World Heritage site

About the Author

Renie Gross, her husband, Bob, and assorted other animals live within view of the Dinosaur Park badlands. <u>Dinosaur Country</u> (1985) is her first book. That year also saw the publication of <u>Tapping the Bow</u>, a history of the Eastern Irrigation District, which she co-authored with Lea Nicoll-Kramer. She is currently at work on a biography of Carl Anderson, a pioneer who helped build the infrastructure that supports Alberta's agriculture industry today.